PEPYS AND THE REVOLUTION

Pepys
and the
Revolution

ARTHUR BRYANT

COLLINS
ST JAMES'S PLACE, LONDON

William Collins Sons & Co Ltd
London · Glasgow · Sydney · Auckland
Toronto · Johannesburg

First published 1979
© Arthur Bryant 1979

ISBN 0 00 211635 9

Set in Bembo
Made and Printed in Great Britain by
William Collins Sons & Co Ltd Glasgow

Contents

Illustrations

Introduction

Except for the epilogue I wrote this story of Pepys and the Revolution of 1688 more than forty years ago, before the last War. It formed a part, and rather more than half, of *The Saviour of the Navy*, the third volume of my life of Samuel Pepys. Asked in 1931 by the Cambridge University Press to write his "definitive" biography, its research and writing, including that of the as yet only partly completed, and unpublished, fourth and final volume, it occupied most of my thirties and of the decade before Hitler temporarily brought an end to all peaceful human activities. These three volumes, each published as a separate self-contained book, were re-issued by Collins in successive years after the War. But both *The Saviour of the Navy*, and its predecessor, *The Years of Peril*, have since gone out of print and for some time have been virtually unobtainable.

The story contained in the former's last eight chapters, and now retold in this book, is of considerable importance, both for an understanding of Pepys's achievement—the creation of our permanent Naval administration and discipline and, with it, of our two and a half centuries' supremacy at sea —and as a first-hand narrative of England's only and bloodless political revolution. An admirably clear and scholarly study of the latter by Maurice Ashley— first published in 1966 and in Panther paperback two years later—has examined and set out the causes and

7

consequences, as well as the course, of the Revolution and the motives and character of its chief par-
ticipants. My book—a narrative reconstruction of
"the living past"—tells the story of what happened
at the time to a principal actor who lived through it,
being based on the day-to-day correspondence of
Samuel Pepys. And Pepys was Secretary of the
Admiralty, then by far the greatest spending
Department of State. As such, he was both the political and administrative head of the Service responsible for guarding the autumn seas which William of
Orange, the "Liberator", and his Dutch transports
had to cross to answer the appeal of the "Immortal
Seven" who had signed the secret daring, but, at the
time, treasonable invitation to James II's Dutch
nephew and son-in-law, to invade their country for
"the preservation of the Protestant religion and the
restoring of the laws and liberties of England".

In my pages are thus intertwined two themes—
one the culmination of Pepys's life's work of build-
ing and restoring England's battle-fleet and of re-
establishing, in an enduring form, the rules he had
laid down to prevent the corruption and indiscipline
which had hitherto vitiated all her attempts to
achieve permanent command at sea; the other, the
cumulative effect of King James's folly in trying to
coerce his people and, in doing so, outraging their
deepest instincts and prejudices. The dramatic—
and, for the Secretary of the Admiralty and his
work, at the time tragic, though for the nation's
future, ultimately fortunate—sequence of events set
in train by the obstinacy, stupidity and weakness of
his royal master, all but brought the country to the
point of social dissolution and anarchy. What then
happened is described in my pages. Faced by successful invasion, betrayed by most of his trusted
advisers, including his own daughter, and by a spon-

taneous rebellion of his people brought about by his incredible folly, the despairing King gave orders to disband the Army unpaid—there was no police force—threw the Great Seal into the Thames and fled the kingdom, thus depriving it of all rule and leaving it to revert to that "state of nature" desiderated in all ages by utopian radical theorists but which, in actual effect, is anarchy.

"It was this presumably that the King had intended —a just punishment on a stubborn, treacherous and stiff-necked people. They had denied the divine ordinance of kingly government: they should have a taste of the opposite—of anarchy or the war of all against all.

By his own withdrawal, his destruction of the writs, his removal of the Great Seal and his desperate orders to the heads of the armed forces, he had removed every recognised agency by which the business of government could be continued. And he had done it with dramatic and staggering suddenness.

It was an interesting situation, and of a kind to puzzle the ingenuity of learned political philosophers. But the English are not a race of abstract philosophers, and James never displayed a more remarkable incapacity to understand them and their institutions than in this fatal and final act. In logic and law alike the government of the kingdom had ceased. The leaders of the English proceeded to act as though it had not ceased at all.

Within a couple of hours, in the midst of a prodigious uproar and confusion, a provisional government had been set up. The King's brother-in-law ordered the Captain of the Guard to muster his disbanded troop and declare for the Prince of Orange. The leading officers of the Army resolved to do the same. The Lords Temporal and Spiritual, or such of them as were in London, assembled at the Guildhall under the presidency of the Archbishop of Canterbury, and constituted themselves a provisional Government."

History never repeats itself. But national character does. Whoever in England—King or corporation, monopolist or mob—tries to override the Law or the Parliament which throughout the English ages has given expression to the national insistence on "counsel and consent"—is liable to find the English people reacting as they did to James II's attempt to overturn the Law.

To simplify the text I have omitted a number of reference footnotes, which can be consulted in the original volume, but have retained the full appendix of references.

The Close
Salisbury
1979

Chapter I

The Great Secretary

"This High Dignity was lately executed by Commissioners . . . But their Commission being at length dissolved, the execution of their office was committed to the care of his then Royal Highness the Duke of York, now King of England, since when it has been executed by the indefatigable care and pains of that most ingenious and expert person, Samuel Pepys Esquire."
Dr Edward Chamberlayne, *Angliae Notitia* (16th ed. 1687).

In the spring of 1686 Samuel Pepys, then in his fifty-fourth year, seemed at the summit of earthly power and glory. He stood at the King's right hand, ruled the Royal Navy, and all his ventures prospered. He was Secretary of the Admiralty, Member of Parliament for Harwich, Master of Trinity House and President of the Royal Society. His former confidential clerk, Will Hewer, who, in his far-away secret diary days, had once slept in his attic and done his chaws, was now a man of vast wealth, a great financier and Master of the Clothworkers' Company; his poor brother-in-law, Balty, a Special Commissioner for the Navy. His private house was the Admiralty of England. By the measure of this world Pepys had arrived.

Yet across the bright course of his success there lay a shadow. Of his own fidelity to his master, James II, who had succeeded his brother, Charles II, two years earlier, there could be no question: he was bound to him by the ties of ancient service, common enthusiasm for a great work and the plain loyalty of an obedient subject. That James was a Catholic was to him no valid reason for his withholding the minutest part of his whole-hearted service. Duty, patriotism and love of his work all combined to make Pepys's path a straight one—unswerving obedience to the gracious master who trusted him and who loved his Navy almost as much as he did himself.

But to Englishmen who did not possess Pepys's passion for order and rule in secular affairs and his liking for tolerance in those of the spirit, allegiance to a Catholic King was no easy matter. Even the most loyal had been nursed in a faith whose very essence was a loathing for what was held idolatry and priestly despotism—the forms and ideals of the Roman Church. The Anglican Tories, who had rallied to the defence of the throne against Shaftesbury's triple assault by republican, non-conformist and atheist, had been ready to accept the royal supremacy in religion. But when that supremacy was seen to be a mere channel for the more ancient dominance of a foreign priesthood their loyalty was shaken to its foundations. For James's piety grew with the years, and the Closet, the Chapel and the Bedchamber were alike seen to be crowded with priests and confessors. In the great Cavalier revival of the early sixteen-eighties, Englishmen had shown their willingness to kneel to the throne. But when its sacred occupant was observed to be kneeling also, with his back to his subjects and his face to a painted altar set up by the Bishop of Rome, what then?

James himself had his own view of the situation, and one which he was always ready to expound. During his brother's reign, he explained, he had risked the loss of three crowns for the sake of his religion. Now that God had blessed his fidelity by giving him the regal power, he felt bound to use it for the maintenance and advancement of his religion, which stood in the greatest need of his aid. This was difficult to answer, for by the law of England Catholic priests were liable to a horrible death and even laymen were subject to penal taxation and deprived of all the most cherished rights of citizenship. The Roman rites and beliefs were ceaselessly held up to obloquy in the public pulpits and insulted by ignorant and brutal mobs. How, James asked, could he as an honest man be expected to stand by and not use his power to protect those of his subjects who were being persecuted merely because they shared his own Faith? And how as a King expect his authority to be observed when his Creed was branded and ridiculed by those who ate his bread and owed him allegiance?

Though to the defeated republicans and the ignorant and bigoted bulk of the population who loathed Popery for the joy of hating, all this meant nothing, to the better and more thoughtful Protestant English there was a great deal in the King's argument which it was impossible to answer. They had called him to the throne to save the realm from anarchy and their estates and Church from spoliation. They could not grumble because he used his power to protect the religion which he had openly professed in the days of exile and proscription. The dominant tory and Anglican interest had therefore begun the reign by accepting an illogical situation as best they could, swearing allegiance and even expounding a mystic philosophy of non-resistance to a King whose Faith their laws and religion condemned and trusting to his royal promise and good sense to preserve their own Church in its monopolistic integrity while he did what he could to mitigate the harsh lot of his own.

Had circumstances not been against them it is just conceivable that this tremendous compromise bet-

ween diametrically opposing ideals might have succeeded. After all the scene of the experiment was
England. But three circumstances were adverse.
These were the international situation, the state of
the succession and the royal temperament. The
former made itself felt from the first moment of the
reign. It was all very well for a Catholic King to
preach tolerance to Protestant England when across
the Channel his cousin and nearest ally, the Catholic
King of France, was subjecting his Protestant subjects to one of the most cruel religious persecutions
the world had seen. In the autumn of 1685 Louis
had revoked the Edict of Nantes, the charter by
which a former French sovereign had guaranteed the
immunity of the Huguenot community from persecution. Englishmen, whose jealous Protestantism
had been nursed on tales of the Massacre of St
Bartholomew and the woodcuts of grilling co-
religionists in Foxe's *Book of Martyrs*, were now
treated to the spectacle of thriving and respectable
French Protestants hunted from their homes by
dragoons, chained to galleys under the Mediterranean sun or flying penniless and homeless to England,★ while their children, torn from them, were
driven by priests to Mass. In the ensuing uproar the
royal sermons in favour of tolerance fell on somewhat deaf ears.

Whatever James's ultimate intentions, such a
moment was one that called for the greatest forbearance and tact. These were qualities he did not possess. Instead of accepting the *status quo* until the panic
caused by his ally's cruel display of zeal had died
away, he publicly pressed forward every measure
that could alleviate the lot and advance the influence

★ James, who was shocked at his cousin Louis's intolerance, gave
them £1500 out of his privy purse and ordered a collection to be made
for them throughout the kingdom. *Ailesbury Memoirs* 1, 103.

of his fellow Catholics. Had there been no ill-feeling towards the Roman Church, the stream of promotions that now came the way of its adherents, the swarm of alien priests at Whitehall, and the conversions in high places, all of them loudly acclaimed by the triumphant proselytisers, would have aroused opposition. As it was, they produced a panic. The tory tide that had still been flowing strongly at the King's accession suddenly stopped. By the spring of 1686 the ebb had set in.

The King, blind though he was to public opinion, had some excuse for his precipitancy. He was already in his fifties, a far more advanced age then than it is accounted today. His eldest daughter, the heir presumptive, was married to a Protestant prince who had allied himself with all that James most hated. Unless he could firmly establish civic and religious freedom for his persecuted co-religionists in the few years of power God gave him, it would be taken from them again by the accession of the wife of William of Orange. Unhappily, spurred on by his priests, whose very circumstances deprived them of all knowledge of the Protestant English, and by his own arrogant and impatient temperament, he imagined that he could best accomplish this object by riding roughshod over the laws and prejudices of his subjects. In this the poor, gullible man was encouraged by the worst and most treacherous Minister any King ever had to advise him—the enigmatic Lord Sunderland who, from being his former enemy, exercised an ever-growing ascendancy over him, luring him on to blind and rash courses that alienated him from his best subjects and proved his ruin.[1]

★   ★   ★

So it came to pass that the good rules and strong and honest administration which Pepys was so industriously introducing into the English governmental system were in danger of appearing to his countrymen more in the nature of a tyranny than a boon. Though they created an executive instrument giving hitherto unguessed-at opportunities to England, they were associated with regal power which protected a hated religion and insolently dispensed with ancient laws to do so. They depended for their existence on the will of a sovereign who increasingly based his authority on the subservience of venal judges and the might of a professional army. English religion and liberty were alike ranging themselves in the forces gathering in the path of Pepys and his King.

But in the spring and summer of 1686 Pepys still paid little regard to the growing strength of the Opposition. He had his work to do, and that was enough. On April 22nd he marched the now thoroughly contrite members of the old Admiralty Commission into the King's presence to thank him for his continued favours and acquaint him that they had taken a house on Tower Hill in which to perform their business. Five days later he escorted his sovereign and the members of the Special Commission, which he had set up to restore the neglected battle-fleet, round the empty Stores and docks at Chatham. Here the great ships, which he had laid down during his first tenure of the Admiralty Secretaryship ten years before, lay rotting at their moorings, their planks patched with old boards and canvas, their buttocks blistered by the sun and their holds with toadstools growing in them as big as one's fist. All the time, while the Commissioners tramped round the derelict battleships and the King probed the mouldering timbers of England's defences with his own hand, Pepys kept up a running lecture on the causes which had brought them to this pass.

Afterwards there was a solemn conference in the house of Mr Gregory, the Clerk of the Cheque, attended by the King, Prince George of Denmark, the Duke of Grafton, Lord Dartmouth, Rear-Admiral Herbert and the Special Commissioners. Here his Majesty listened to a further speech from the Secretary of the Admiralty on "the universal supineness of his officers". This was followed, as Pepys in his record of the expedition described it, "with a proof of it the same evening beyond all expectation or imagination upon our seeing him aboard his yacht in the evening bound for London, and we back again from below Gillingham up the river in a violent storm of rain all that evening and night, without one port shut upon any one of the ships in our passage but what we had by hailing caused to be so, . . . neither shipwright nor assistant nor any other officer minding it . . . Nothing being more evident than the evil that this negligence has brought upon the Navy by ships being kept with their ports either always shut in dry weather or open in wet, to the occasioning that succession of heat and moisture that has ruined them. . . . This seems to give a perfect consummation of the late business of our Navy settlement by the King's becoming an ocular witness of the necessity of it from the state of his ships."★[2]

This trip to Chatham was followed by visits to the other Yards. At the end of May, Pepys accompanied the King and the Special Commissioners to Portsmouth; in June he was at Chatham again: and in August, when the King went on a progress in the West, back at Portsmouth. On these expeditions he seems to have travelled in some style, judging by his

★ Tuesday, April 27th, 1686. *Pepysian MS*. No. 1490, pp. 66–71.

subsequent claims for expenses. The two days' visit
to Chatham worked out at £31.12s., those to Portsmouth at £15.8s. and £20—no trifling sums in the
money values of the time. From the same accounts
we know that he was much that summer at Windsor
in attendance on the King; between June 6th and
September 26th he travelled there twenty times with
his young clerk, Josiah Burchett. In addition there
were occasional journeys to Hampton Court to
attend meetings of the Council which were held
there weekly during the King's summer sojourn at
Windsor. And, when at the Office, he was accus-
tomed to begin his day's routine before eight.★[3]

The wet summer of 1686 saw the Special Commission fairly launched on its work of restoration. It
witnessed also two other of Pepys's triumphs—his
vindication from the charge of having built the
thirty new ships of inferior foreign timber and his
famous "Establishment in lieu of Plate Carriage".
Almost the first official act of the Special Commission was to confer with a delegation of leading
Thames shipbuilders convened by Pepys. Their tes-
timony established it beyond question that for vessels of over 300 tons burthen Prussian and Bohemian
plank was cheaper, more reliable and more enduring
than English. This was officially confirmed by the
Privy Council on October 8th, when the King after
studying the evidence declared himself "convinced
of the safety, benefit and present necessity of making
use of plank of foreign growth". The onus for the
state of the 30 ships was thus officially laid where it
belonged—on the old Navy Board. What was more
important, the royal declaration left the Special

★ "It would be a particular favour to me if you could . . . give me an
opportunity of conferring with you here upon Monday morning next
about 8 of the clock, or as much earlier as you please." S. P. to Mr
Bowtell, May 22nd, 1686. *Pepysian MSS., Adm. Letters* XII, 105.

Commission free to purchase the larger timbers of the Baltic, which were so urgently needed for the work of reconstruction. In this, as in so much else, Pepys was a pioneer, applying the results of scientific investigation to the conduct of public administration. It is among the major achievements that constitute his claim to be regarded as the father of the modern Civil Service.[4]

Even more far reaching in its results was the issue on July 15th of "His Majesty's Regulation in the business of Plate Carriage, etc., with his Establishment of an Allowance for their tables and other Encouragements to his Sea-Commanders". This great measure was the direct fruit of Pepys's voyage to Tangier and Cadiz three years before and of what he had seen there of the system of private trading in the King's ships. It was twofold in its scope, depriving naval officers of the power of offending while providing them with regular allowances to place them above the reach of temptation. Henceforward no captain was to carry plate, bullion, jewels or any other species of merchandise without a written warrant under the royal hand, upon pain of being immediately discharged and rendered incapable of future employment. The same prohibition was extended to the carrying of passengers, saving only "our subjects redeemed from slavery, shipwrecked or taken at sea out of foreign ships". Any profits made in violation of these orders were to go to the Chatham Chest for maimed seamen.

As with all Pepys's administrative rules, provision was made to enforce them. On arrival at a foreign port every captain was to notify the Secretary of the Admiralty by the first post home, continuing to supply him with accounts of his proceedings and abstracts from the ship's journal by every post so long as he remained there. To safeguard against loss or pretended loss of correspondence, a copy of every letter and abstract was to be deposited with the English Consul. Other provisions were inserted for regular transmission to the Admiralty of copies of all orders given by Admirals and Commanders-in-Chief to their subordinates. At the end of every voyage, ships' journals were to be forwarded at once to York Buildings for inspection. In the rules which Pepys prepared for erring captains there were no loopholes.

While he discouraged and punished the bad, he encouraged the good. The King's Regulation established a system of rewards and allowances to compensate commanders for the loss of irregular perquisites and enable them to support their position with comfort and dignity. Over and above their pay and the existing victualling allowances,* every captain was to receive a table grant proportionate to the importance of his command. Thus the present pay of £273.15s. p.a. of the captain of a 1st rate of the line was to be supplemented by an additional £250, and the £136.10s. of the captain of a 4th rate or cruiser by another £124.5s. To appreciate how much more liberally Pepys and his sovereign interpreted the needs of serving officers than later administrators, it is necessary to multiply these sums in today's money twenty- or even thirty-fold and to recall that income-tax did not exist. The table grant was to commence on the day on which the ship was reported as fitted for sea and ready to execute her sailing orders.

Provision was also made for dividing the value of prizes between captains and crews. Insistence on rule and precedent was to be accompanied by special rewards for "signal instances of Industry, Courage, Conduct or Frugality". Pepys's impress was stamped

* £12. 3s. 4d. a year. *C.P. MSS.* 1, 212.

firmly and, as time was to prove, permanently on the discipline of the Navy. The profession which before 1686 could breed a Herbert as its shameful exemplar, purified and redeemed was in the next century to give Britain an Anson, a Hawke, a Jervis and a Nelson.[5]

This historical reform was explained to an assembly of naval captains by the King himself in its author's presence at Windsor in the summer of 1686. For many months after Pepys's correspondence was full of reminders of its existence. Before every voyage a formal notice was despatched to every captain together with a copy of the new Regulations:

> This serves to convey to you his Majesty's written orders pursuant to his resolutions lately opened to yourself (among other Gentlemen Commanders . . . then attending his Majesty at Windsor) touching the business of plate carriage and his Establishment of an Allowance for Tables and other encouragements.

> Whereof wishing both to his Majesty and you the satisfaction graciously intended by him therein, I remain, etc.

With this notice Pepys always enclosed the formal certificate of the ship's readiness for sea, which a commander had to complete, sign and return before his table allowance became payable.[6]

In this year all the birds that Pepys had roused during his Tangier voyage of 1683/4 came home to roost. In April his earlier Establishment of May 1676—now long neglected—for Volunteers and Midshipmen Extraordinary was revived as an encouragement "to families of better quality . . . to breed up their younger sons to the art and practice of navigation". The most careful rules were laid down to govern their service, both as to the number that could be carried in any ship and their own behaviour on board. Pepys believed in catching his future Admirals young. Volunteers were not to be admitted over the age of sixteen. They were to receive a small allowance in addition to their victuals as ordinary members of the ship's company, and were to be content "with what accommodation shall be afforded them". In return for these privileges they were to study and practise "the art and duty of a seaman" in a lively hope of further favours to come. Those who had formerly served as lieutenants or commanders, but for whom no present employment offered, might be admitted as Midshipmen Extraordinary on production of a certificate of good behaviour signed by their former captain. Midshipmen Extraordinary unlike Volunteers were to be granted an allowance for a servant according to their quality. But no Midshipman was to receive any pay before he had delivered to the Secretary of the Admiralty "a perfect journal, fairly written, kept and signed by himself, expressing in distinct columns the place where the said ship shall have been each day at noon, the daily change of the wind, and all extraordinary accidents happening in the voyage". Pepys's passion for naval education had not grown less with the years.[7]

Another Establishment of the same kind was promulgated in the autumn for Boatswains' and Carpenters' Sea Stores. Till now such stores had been issued in a haphazard and, as well may be imagined, exceedingly expensive way "at the pleasure and discretion of inferior officers in the yards". This, Pepys and the Special Commission resolved, could continue no longer. Henceforward elaborate regulations were laid down governing "the qualities, quantities and proportions of each distinct species of stores" to be supplied to every rate of ship according to the length and nature of its voyage. In the same way the old rule about the use of the King's flag was reissued and strictly enforced, and all breaches of it sternly punished. An instance of this occurred in the autumn, when news reached the Admiralty that the private packet boats plying between Holland and England were taking the outrageous liberty of hoisting the King's Jack as soon as they got out of the Thames. Having caused Mr Skelton, the royal Envoy Extraordinary at the Hague, to investigate the matter, Pepys did not rest till he had brought the offenders to a reckoning.[8]

The summer of 1686 produced the usual minor incidents between Great Britain and the rival naval powers of France and Holland, the long drag of the frigate war against the Sallee pirates, and the alarms caused by the appearance of some Algerine men-of-war in the Channel. One of them, after capturing several foreign prizes, put into Harwich to refit, relying on the late treaty of peace and alliance between England and Algiers. Her presence there was a great embarrassment to the Government, for the local authorities, at a loss what to do with her, yielded too readily to an insular instinct to clap her dusky crew into jail and seize her cargo. Pepys intervened and instructed the Mayor of Harwich to supply the needs of the stranger at moderate rates, "they being the King's allies", but to rescue, firmly but tactfully, any English slaves found among the crew. "I am apt", he wrote, "to believe the King will not think it anywise fit that, having had the fortune to be brought near their own country, they should be continued and carried out again in that condition, but . . . will rather find some other way to have their ransom paid in case their own friends are not able to do it."

The subsequent negotiations brought the captain and master of the Algerine to London, where they were interviewed by the King and Cabinet. The Sunday evening's entertainment which their visit

afforded was described by Pepys with obvious
enjoyment in a letter to Mr Sandford. "They
appeared very much unprepared either what to ask
in reference to themselves (the young one, who is a
seaman, insisting upon a supply of stores, while the
old one who is a soldier would allow that they
wanted nothing but provisions and a pilot) or what
to grant in reference to the King's demand of his
subjects, then slaves." In the end the matter was
referred to the arbitration of a London merchant
experienced in such matters. Meanwhile the
Commander-in-Chief in the Straits was instructed
to represent the inconvenience of the whole irregular business to the Dey of Algiers. The affair was
finally closed by a promise from that friendly despot
that any of his captains henceforward entering the
Channel should be promptly and pacifically
hanged.[9]

Occupation of a less exciting nature was afforded
that summer at York Buildings by an elaborate survey, carried out in conjunction with Trinity House,
of the encroachments made by private trespassers on
the banks of the Thames between London Bridge
and Cuckold's Point, and by the examination of
plans for a public hospital for relieving old and
bringing up young seamen—the germ of the royal
foundation at Greenwich in the next reign. The
Victualling Commissioners, to whom during
Pepys's absence in Tangier the feeding of the Navy
had been entrusted by the late Lords of the Admiralty, found themselves subjected to his searching
scrutiny. For Mr Secretary, however severe and
occasionally unfair to highly placed commanders
and officials, always looked with a jealous eye on
every tendency to starve the plain sailor of his just
portion.[10]

A slightly comic element made its appearance

about this time in the Admiralty Letter Books with
the rival claims of two ingenious projectors, each of
whom had invented a new sea-pump. Sir Samuel
Morland, who had been Pepys's tutor at Cambridge,
had in the course of years acquired almost a monopoly of government inventions, though he had
somehow contrived to remain in a state of perpetual
and clamorous impecuniosity which no reward
could long alleviate. He was now challenged in his
most sensitive part, the naval pump, by a persistent
and avaricious baronet from the far end of Scotland
named Sir Robert Gordon who submitted a pump of
his own to the Admiralty. At first there was some
difficulty in making this engine work, and then only
with such a noise as to be almost unbearable. Indeed
during the summer of 1686 Sir Samuel Morland
formed the habit of attending its trials, which took
place in the early hours of the morning in St James's
Park, in order to see it fail.

But on a further trial at the beginning of
November Sir Robert's pump proved so unexpectedly successful that Morland was driven hastily to
invent an entirely new one of his own. This he
submitted after a few days with a long letter to the
King claiming that it was cheaper and more lasting
and able to be worked by fewer hands than any
"other pump whatever, though all the engineers in
the world should contrive together to contrive it".
He accordingly offered to submit it to a trial with
any other chain pump and Sir Robert Gordon's in
particular. The plans of this wonderful machine and
the correspondence to which they gave rise were all
passed to Pepys, who for several weeks suffered
many explanations from his old tutor. He was also
the ultimate recipient of the petitions which Morland was in the habit of slipping into his sovereign's
hands as he passed down the corridors of Whitehall.

These generally took the form of peremptory demands:

1. That this may be the last trial, and a final end put to all disputes.
2. That your Majesty will send positive orders to Sir Robert Gordon to forbid him to imitate any part of my last engine or model, particularly the drum capstan, but above all the counterpoise. . . ., being the principal part of my invention whereby I pretend to outdo him or others. . . .
3. That when he has finished and fixed his engine, he may have order to quit the place, and I free liberty to go and set up an engine to be tried together with his, that so I may not be disturbed, as I was before the last trial, by both Sir Robert and his workmen and treated with very undecent language. . . .
4. That your Majesty will speedily order me a reimbursement of the £200, I being in very great want of it.*

In the end it was found necessary to set apart two separate ships for the scene of these experiments owing to the suspicions entertained by the rival inventors of each other's honesty.[11]

The controversy was still raging in the following spring, though by that time with such advantage to Sir Robert that poor Morland spoke of committing suicide. The scene of battle had now shifted to York Buildings and the Navy Office, which were perpetually bombarded with requests from the successful inventor for rewards and the defrayment of his expenses. To secure these, Sir Robert even tried to bribe Pepys, explaining with the innocent effrontery of his race that the £1000 which he had expended on his invention had hitherto prevented him from making a suitable acknowledgment. He added that one of the most acceptable features of the royal bounty when it came would be that it would give him the chance "of requiting in some measure those obligations I lie under by the constant trouble you were

* Nov. 19th, 1686. *Rawl. MSS. A.* 189, f. 53.

pleased to give yourself".★ "Sir," replied the great
Secretary, "I am obliged to you for your courteous
expressions. . . . But (as I said to you on the like
occasion the other day) I . . . assure you that I never
yet suffered myself to rob his Majesty of any part of
the thanks due for his favours to private persons and
will not begin to do otherwise in the case of Sir
Robert Gordon. To whom, if I have in any wise been
serviceable, I think myself abundantly rewarded for
it by the industry I have seen him use to render
himself so to the King, my master." And he enclosed
a warrant for £318 on the Treasury, or about a third
of the sum which the baronet had claimed. Within a
fortnight he was receiving complaints from Captain
Shovell about the pump's imperfections.[12]

At the end of the first six months of the Special
Commission's existence, Pepys and its members
attended the King and Lord Treasurer in the Treasury Chambers to report progress. Though they had
been compelled to add a supplementary £23,081 to
Pepys's original estimate, they had already accomplished much of which they could be proud, and
were. On taking over the work of the old Navy
Board in April they had found "nothing a'doing in
the Yards" beyond some leisurely repairs to two
ships of the line. They had now gone so far as to put
all thirty new ships out of any danger of sinking.
Moreover they had issued and were enforcing
orders that would prevent their ever falling again
into so lamentable a state, the result, as they stated,
of "an unpardonable degree of negligence and
ignorance". At the Yards they were employing once
more the full complement of workmen without
resort to the press-gang or any interference with the
work of the ordinary shipbuilding yards. They had

★ Sir R. Gordon to S. P., May 16th, 1687. *Rawl. MSS. A.* 189, f.
131.

contracted for £90,000 worth of goods. By Lady Day 1687, they reckoned they would be able to set to sea, if need be, a fleet of sixty-five vessels, including three 1st rates, seven 2nd rates, twenty-one 3rd rates—that is thirty-one ships of the line—and twenty-five 4th rates. The success of the first stage of their work had exceeded everyone's wildest hopes. It was no wonder that the King praised them. Yet to Pepys's experienced eye it was plain that the bulk of the work was being done by two only of their number—Will Hewer and the great naval architect, Sir Anthony Deane. For all his careful choice of them and "daily eye and hand upon them", the rest, "what with the laziness of one, the private business or love of pleasure in another, want of method in a third", had already proved themselves little more than passengers.[13]

Possibly the swift success which attended the Special Commission on the Navy had some influence on the royal decision to set up another and more questionable Commission. During the summer of 1686 two great political questions were put to the test—could the King as statutory head of the national Church use his supreme ecclesiastical power to benefit a religion antagonistic to that Church, and could he as ruler of the State use his prerogative to suspend the Law? To attain his ends—the emancipation of the Roman Church in England—he attempted both. Feeling as a Catholic unable to exercise in person the ecclesiastical rights vested in the Crown by the English reformers of the sixteenth century, he resorted to an Ecclesiastical Commission of subservient prelates and lay politicians, presided over by Lord Chancellor Jeffreys, to silence criticism of Rome in the Anglican pulpits. At the same time, by dismissing several of the more independent judges★

★ "Our Judges sit very loosely upon their benches." April 17th, 1686. *Ellis Correspondence* 1, 104.

and replacing them by more complaisant lawyers of
his own choosing—one of them, curiously enough,
a brother of Milton the poet—and then bringing a
test case against a Catholic office-holder who
pleaded the royal dispensation for his breach of the
Test Act, he secured a judicial *obiter dictum* in favour
of his right to dispense with the penal laws against
his Catholic subjects.

What King James's Protestant subjects thought of
these events was becoming every day more clear.
The judges on circuit were received with conspicu-
ous coldness by the Anglican gentry, while the
Catholic chapels of the foreign ambassadors were
insulted by the mob. At one of these the hot-headed
apprentices pulled down a cross and, affixing it to
the nearest pump, paid mock obeisance to it. They
would have no wooden gods worshipped in their
city, they cried, as they laughed and hallooed around
it. And when the flustered Lord Mayor arrived to
restore the peace, he was greeted with scornful
shouts of "What! is the Lord Mayor of London come
to preach up Popery!" It made things very awkward
for the authorities.[14]

Through these gathering clouds, Pepys pursued
the tenour of his way—a very great man. His power
was patent to all, and it was not the less respected
because he scrupulously refrained from using it in
whatever did not concern his own business. In the
Navy and all that appertained to it his word was law.
His influence was exercised in a thousand unobtru-
sive ways, and nearly always in useful or kindly
ones, whether it was to get the Astronomer Royal to
defend a treatise on Navigation which was being
unjustly criticised, or to secure the payment of past
debts to the half-ruined Victualler, Sir Dennis Gauden, or to champion, at Mary Evelyn's request, the
cause of a too blunt tarpaulin captain who had fallen

foul of a Court lady while transporting her home
from her husband's embassy in Constantinople.
"But this mishap", Pepys warned Captain Fowler
after he had secured the King's pardon for him, "you
will not be able to avoid no more than anybody else
that has a quarrel with a fair lady, that her report will
prevail amongst the ladies, whatever it does elsewhere. As an instance of which you must know that
my Lady Trumbull has had such impressions made
upon her concerning you from the account she has
met with of your goodness knows what usage to my
Lady Soames, that you may as well expect to persuade a child to meet a bulbeggar in the dark as my
Lady Trumbull to venture herself in a ship with
Captain Fowler. So that the King has been prevailed
withal to appoint another ship for that voyage and
(as far as I can judge) I don't think you have any
reason to be sorry for it, nor consequently (seeing
that it is over) to give yourself any more care about
the differences between my Lady Soames and you,
the King not having been pleased upon all this noise
to express any change of his opinion touching your
capacity of serving as a seaman. And for a courtier I
don't think he ever took you for any or thought the
worse of you for not being one."* It was the wife of
Pepys's old Tangier acquaintance, the timorous Doctor, now knighted and made English Ambassador to
the Ottoman Porte, who was so reluctant to entrust
herself to the honest captain.[15]

Not that Pepys, though ready to overlook the lack
of a courtier's gallantry in another, was ungallant
himself. One of his many minor acts of kindness that
year was to place a yacht at the disposal of Nell
Gwynne, now fallen from her former state and fast
nearing her end. And he was both a courtier and a

* S. P. to Capt. T. Fowler, Dec. 22nd, 1686. *Pepysian MSS.*, *Adm.
Letters* XII, 406–7.

virtuoso. He corresponded with Sir Christopher
Wren about an old sail which he lent to help his
friend Signor Verrio paint the ceiling of the Chapel
Royal,★ and took a great deal of trouble to procure
specimens of the vegetables and plants of New England to please that prince of gardeners, John Evelyn.[16]

As in the past Pepys's influence was at the disposal
of his friends and relations in the Service, provided
always that they merited it. That, however, was
essential: no degree of kinship could excuse a breach
of duty. When his humble cousin, Thomas Alcock,
carpenter of the *Elizabeth*, was accused—it trans-
pired falsely—of embezzlement, the grim Admiralty Secretary let his superior know: "By God's
grace if you find the least umbrage of a miscarriage
of the same kind in him he shall soon make a vacancy
instead of filling one". In the winter of 1686–7, he
had three youthful protégés at sea, his nephew
Samuel Jackson, young Holmes, the son of his old
friend Sir Robert, now in the East Indies, and Peter
Skinner, son of his erstwhile beloved house-
companion Mary Skinner. Peter was always thanking his patron for his favours, which included, it
appeared, not only instruction in navigation, but a
view of the world and Captain Fowler's fatherly
chastisements: "I desire your Honour's excuse for
the weakness of so green a youth, . . . but hope time
and your Honour's patronage and encouragement
will spring forth a more fragrant fruit in him."[17]

Pepys's other and younger nephew, John Jackson.
now aged 15, was not intended for the sea. In June
1686 he entered him as a Pensioner of Magdalene College, Cambridge, under the tutorship of

★ He was careful to chose one that would "not be at all the worse
. . . by its being spotted or smeared with the painter's oil colours."
Pepysian MSS., Adm. Letters XII, 244.

Mr Millington—an act of piety which the Master of the College gratefully described in a letter of appreciation as "crediting us with the education of your nephew". John Jackson himself paid tribute to his uncle's kindness in a Latin epistle written in a large flowing hand beginning *"Vir Noblissime et Amplissime!"* The reports of him were most satisfactory: "innocent, modest and diligent", was the Master's exordium, while his tutor described him as "very tractable and docile, endued with solid parts and good memory". The Jackson estates at Ellington still occupied a good deal of Pepys's scanty leisure: in November 1686 some of the leases fell in and he was asked by Peterhouse, the landlords, whether he wished to renew them. It was characteristic of his method of evading inconvenient issues that he delayed for so unconscionable a time before committing himself to a definite answer that the college was driven to expostulate.

As though the concerns of his own younger kin were not trouble enough, Pepys continued to care for the children of his friends. When Ned Southwell finished his education in London at Christmas, Sir Robert, his father, wrote gratefully from King's Weston to his old acquaintance and fellow civil servant thanking him for all the wise and loving service he had done the boy: "I do acknowledge them to be very many and more perhaps than you think I know." And thereafter Pepys followed his pupil's career with eager interest. "If country wishes and country gratitude could do you any good", Sir Robert told him, "the young man and I will be answerable for your welfare. He is going to Oxford till Michaelmas next, having met with a tutor to our mind who then intends to leave the place. 'Tis one Mr Lane of Merton College who intends to follow the Civil Law and in the interim to pour in logic as

fast as his disciple can swallow. From thence I intend
him for Lincoln's Inn and to take his fortune in the
Law. I had thoughts of travel and preparations for
the like service his father trod. But the ground being
grown too slippery . . ., let us venture him into
Westminster Hall, where the cats fall always on their
legs."

The slippery ground to which Southwell referred
so ominously was caused by the increasing tempo of
the King's religious policy. Determined to emanci-
pate his Catholic subjects at the earliest possible
moment, and believing compromise to be weakness
and weakness ruin, James was now proceeding ever
more swiftly down the perilous path of dismissing
his Anglican and high tory Ministers and replacing
them by those—the representatives of a tiny
minority—who shared his desire for toleration. In
the autumn five Catholic peers, who had suffered
with him under the Popish Terror, were admitted to
the Privy Council. At Christmas the champion of
the cause of Anglican exclusiveness, Lord Treasurer
Rochester, was given the option of entering the
Catholic communion or laying down the white
staff. He chose the latter, and the Treasury, like the
Navy and the Church, was put into Commission
with a Catholic, Lord Belasyse, among its members. The King explained to his brother-in-law that
it was not lack of trust or of gratitude that caused
him to dismiss him, but the impossibility of carrying through his policy of suspending the Test Act
and the oaths of religious conformity under a Minister who regarded their continued existence as the
keystone of national policy.

To the ordinary Anglican loyalist it seemed as if
the solid earth was crumbling away. "I could not
have believed", wrote Evelyn who watched the
Jesuits in their rich copes officiating at the altar at

Whitehall, "I should ever have seen such things in the King of England's Palace, after it had pleased God to enlighten this nation." A month later, in the January of 1687, the good man was in despair at what he saw: "Popish Justices of the Peace established in all countries of the meanest of the people; Judges ignorant of the Law and perverting it—so furiously do the Jesuits drive, and even compelling Princes to violent courses and destruction of an excellent government both in Church and State. . . . The Lord Jesus defend his little flock, and preserve this threatened church and nation!"[20]

Chapter II

His Orders Hold

"So this man—prescient to ensure,
(Since even now his orders hold)
A little state might ride secure
At sea, from foes her sloth made bold."

Kipling, *Pepys Tercentenary Poem,* 1933.

The common people had a ruder way of expressing
their disgust. When a new Catholic chapel was
opened in the City and, in defiance of law, thrown
open to all and sundry, the Lord Mayor, fearing the
wrath of the London mob, which, as a contemporary put it, had "as a weak a pretence to prudence
upon such occasions as any mobile in the world",
sent his officers to lock the doors. For this he
received a public reprimand in the Council, and the
chapel was reopened under protection of the Militia.
Whereupon there appeared on Sunday in time of
service "a heedless prentice" who stood about the
place, we are told, "laughing and staring. An officer
bade him go out since he appeared not by his
behaviour to be of that religion. He said he would
not go out, and if they said much to him, he would
break their crosses and juggling-boxes down,
whereupon a riot seemed to form." The interrupter
without difficulty evaded the half-hearted attempts
of the authorities to arrest him, and, lying in wait
after service for the priest, gave him a thrashing and
threw him into the gutter. And though the Lord
Mayor was brought again before King and Council

35

and the City threatened with military occupation if it could not keep the peace better, it made no difference to the attitude of the untutored populace. For the rude and valiant natives of this intolerant island were clearly of the opinion that the Bishop of Rome had no jurisdiction in the realm of England.[1]

This was the period of what became known as "closeting", when the King in his zeal made a practice of withdrawing into his private closet with the functionaries of Church and State, and there frankly discussing with them, high and low alike, his revolutionary plans for equalising all creeds before the Law. If they replied that their scruples must prevent them from obeying the royal will in a policy directed towards removing the penal laws and the oaths of conformity, they were told that the state of their health or the King's service necessitated their retirement. Pepys, who was never a zealot for any one creed or dogma and whose own sufferings under persecution had given him views on toleration far in advance of those of most of his contemporaries, had no quarrel with his sovereign's desire to end the era of persecution. He was only restrained by his sense of caution. But as it was not his way to allow prudential motives to interfere with the discharge of his official duties, and as he never meddled in politics outside his own department, he remained at his post, advising his master in all matters appertaining to the sea and keeping quietly outside the little inner ring of zealots and careerists who, under Father Petre and Lord Sunderland, were egging on the King in his desperate race to jostle his subjects out of their deepest prejudices and habits of thought.

To those of his fellow officials whose religious views or fears disabled them from accepting the course of events with his own calm detachment, Pepys extended all the help he was able. When his colleague, Sir Phineas Pett, was threatened with the withdrawal of the royal support at the forthcoming parliamentary election, he boldly stood up for him at the next Cabinet meeting. And his influence was such that he was able to quiet his Majesty's scruples as to Pett's ability to serve him. It was this generous and Christian readiness to use his hard-earned influence not to advance himself further but to help those who were in the shadow that caused him to be solicited so often in this troubled time. Sir Matthew Andrews, his fellow Governor of Christ's Hospital, turned out of the Commission of Peace after nineteen years' service, and Captain Langley, deprived of the Mayoralty of Harwich, were among the many who sought his aid.[2]

Early in the New Year a more serious offender against the overriding royal will wrote to Pepys in a sad dilemma. It was his old red-nosed friend, Dr Peachell, Master of Magdalene, Cambridge, who had had the misfortune to be chosen Vice-Chancellor at the very moment that the King had resolved to apply his dispensing power to the Universities in order to secure the admission of deserving Catholics to Fellowships and degrees. As Oxford and Cambridge were the corner-stones of the Anglican hierarchy and the exclusive nurseries of those who moulded public opinion from the pulpit, this was a serious matter. In an agony of mind poor Peachell related what had happened: how the King had been pleased to direct a letter to him as Vice-Chancellor to admit one Francis Alban, a Benedictine monk, without administering the statutory oaths; how, unable to decide whether it was better to disobey the King's letter or his laws, he had prayed God to direct, sanctify and govern him in the ways of His higher laws. For a smack of the old pre-Restoration piety of phrase still hung about Peachell for all his love of the bottle. Now, feeling it "unmannerly to importune his Sacred Majesty" further and "strain his friends against the grain", he had decided to obey his conscience, incur the King's displeasure and cast himself upon his princely clemency.

But such martyrdom did not come easily to the good Doctor. "Worthy Sir", he told his old pupil, "'tis extraordinary distress and affliction to me after so much endeavour and affection to his Royal person, Crown and Succession, I should at last by the Providence of God be exposed to his displeasure. But I must commit myself to the great God and my dread Sovereign, the Law and my friends, none of which I would have hurt for my sake, but desire all favour and help they think me capable of without hurting themselves. For if I do ill, 'tis not out of malice but fear of the Last Judgment, and at the worst through involuntary mistake. Sir, I am sorry I have occasion to give you this information and trouble. But you will pardon, I hope, if you cannot help."[3]

Pepys could not help. But when Peachell came to London in the spring to explain his refusal to the Ecclesiastical Commissioners, he refused to cold-shoulder him and earned the unhappy man's gratitude for the frank and friendly way with which, when all were shunning him, he greeted him in the royal Withdrawing Room. But more than that he could not do. Deprived of his Vice-Chancellorship, suspended from his Mastership, Peachell was dismissed by Lord Chancellor Jeffreys with a terrifying admonition "to go away and sin no more".[4]

"The Laws of the Land and the oaths we lie under are the fences of God's church and religion," Peachell had written in his agony, "and I cannot suffer myself to be made an instrument to pull down

those fences." Many an honest Englishman felt the
same. But when in the spring of 1687, the godless
Rear-Admiral of England, Arthur Herbert, pleaded
his conscience as a reason for refusing to promise the
King his support for his attack on the Test Act, it
was plain to the discerning that the time had been
reached when it was no longer to a prudent man's
advantage to obey the King. But possibly Herbert's
dismissal was the result not so much of his hitherto
unsuspected religious scruples as of Pepys's report on
his financial misconduct during his Mediterranean
command. It appeared that he owed the Treasury
over £4000 and was entirely unable to account for
the slaves whom he had starved and sold. And a
further enquiry, instigated by the King, had been
ordered into his accounts as Master of the Robes.[5]

It is just possible that in this uncertain time Pepys
may have toyed with the idea of apostasy. Among
his friends were such devoted Catholics as Lady
Throgmorton and Lady Tuke, and at the Pearses'
house he sometimes used to meet the learned Dr
Philip Ellis* who later became Roman Catholic
Bishop of Aureopolis and the King's Agent at
Rome. But his sympathy for his royal master's professed ideal of religious toleration needs no such
improbable supposition to explain it. It was in keeping with the whole bent of his mature mind. Among
Pepys's papers of this year are some private theological writings of Sir William Petty, procured for
him by his friend Southwell, and to which we know
that he attached particular importance. They incline
towards freedom of conscience and absolute equality for all Christian sects before the Law. "As to
controversies", ran a passage in one of them, "he

* Ellis's relations were always expecting to see him with "some
badge of a more eminent character, as a gold cross before or scarlet
skull-cap behind". *Ellis Correspondence* 1, 239.

thinketh it safe and decent to hearken to them who
sit in Moses' chair, and that every soul be subject to
the higher powers, and that two or three met
together in the name of God do make a competent
church, and that *Vox populi* is *Vox Dei*." It is not
unreasonable to suppose that these were also the
religious views which Pepys in his middle-age, and
after his long and harsh experience, had come to
accept. They are certainly not the tenets of the
Catholic Church. But they tally almost exactly with
certain of those which Pepys's old acquaintance of
Seething Lane days, William Penn the Quaker, now
in high favour at Court and unworthily suspected of
popery elsewhere, was so industriously preaching to
an unconverted England. They are those which
future generations have come to accept as rational
and wise.[6]

That Pepys, therefore, raised no conscientious
opposition to the King's policy, however ill-timed
he may have thought it, and that he entertained at his
house men who did their best to further it like the
time-serving Bishop Cartwright of Chester, is no
proof, as some have supposed, of lack of courage or
religious conviction on his part. It is almost certain
that he believed his master's immediate and declared
object to be a right one, though he may well have
doubted the practicability of his methods.[7]

Nor can fear of losing his post have been any
reason for his acquiescence, for in the winter of
1686/7 he was far from well, believed a collapse of
his over-taxed powers imminent and looked forward to an early release from office. Repeated pains
in his kidneys made him afraid of a return of his old
disease, the stone. A little before Christmas he told
his tiresome brother-in-law, Balty St Michel, not to
rely on his continuance in high place for much
longer. "It was not without very much ground that

in one of my late letters of general advice to you, I cautioned you against depending upon any support much longer from me, I then feeling what I now cannot hide; I mean that pain which I at this time labour under (night and day) from a new stone lodged in my kidneys and an ulcer attending it, with a general decay of my stomach and strength that cannot be played with long. Nor am I solicitous that it should." And he cautioned his brother-in-law to beware of improvidence, lest the long friendship he had shown him should be wasted and his family be left once more at the mercy of a cruel world.[8]

Pepys's fears for his health proved for the present groundless. The stone subsided, and during the next two years he suffered from little more than a rheumaticky shoulder and an old trouble with his eyes. But his fears of Balty's reckless extravagance were speedily justified. Before the end of January he had to intervene to save him from arrest at the suit of a lady creditor who was dunning him on the score of a fine saddle long unpaid for. In his reply to Pepys's letter of reproach, Balty paid an eloquent tribute to what he called his "great goodness and kindness in stopping the clamours of that nasty woman about the saddle" but dismissed it none the less as a small matter, to be explained by his large family, his former unemployment "and many other grievous causes". "It is therefore", he went on, "extreme grievous to me to have from such a blessed person such an expression as in the beginning of your said letter. . . . And although you are pleased to say that you hear of my continued extravagant expenses, I hope it is but the effect of your generous and kind conjectures, being confident that . . . none but the blackest envy and malice (on which curses attend) can accuse me."

Pepys replied with sorrowful dignity. His

brother-in-law, he well knew, was incorrigible:

Brother,

I have received your letter of the 24th and have said my say. Upon your own head be it if in deceiving me you at length find the effect of it to the ruin of your family. I am sure I have nothing to lead me to these jealousies concerning your conduct but my fears on their and your behalf. . . . Nor have I my information but from them that bear you good will; besides that your running on the score of this saddle seems very little to consist with the good husbandry you would be thought to walk by. But I have done; and shall be glad to see you, and without anger as you call it, though it deserves another name; it being too painful a thing to write at all, and much more upon a subject so unpleasant to me as this is.*9

Only a fortnight after the despatch of this solemn document Pepys learnt from Balty's clerk that his master was in trouble again. This time it was undeserved misfortune. "This afternoon about one, his lady fell in travail and was about two delivered of a son; but the birth of the child became the death of the mother, for within a quarter of an hour after, her soul expired; and hath left a husband and numerous family bleeding under (I think) the saddest accents of sorrow I ever saw." The poor neglected woman had had her revenge at last.

Pepys comforted his brother-in-law by return with the stately condolences of the seventeenth century. He took the occasion to add some further good counsel, which Balty's clerk, who lacked nothing of his employer's eloquence, acknowledged with fitting humility and gratitude. "He returns your Honour millions of thanks for your great kindness and generous favours . . . which he will own to his life's end and endeavour strictly to observe and obey those excellent advises you are pleased to administer; which having said, a deluge of tears again over-

* S. P. to B. St Michel, January 27th, 1687. *Rawl. MSS. A.* 189, f. 225.

whelming him, could add no more." Balty himself was able to write a few days later; he should, he assured his protector, to his life's end study to obey his commands and follow every one of his counsels. "I am, Sir, stopped with a torrent of sorrowful lamentation, for, oh God, I have lost, oh I have lost such a loss that no man is or can be sensible but myself. I have lost my wife, Sir, I have lost my wife; and such a wife, as your Honour knows, has (may be) not left her fellow."★ Poor Balty's recognition of the fact seemed a little tardy.[10]

February 1687 saw another of Pepys's friends in trouble—not from the loss of a wife but from taking one. Sir Samuel Morland, who was wont to alleviate his recurrent insolvency by the rapid invention of some new wonder—his latest was a naval gun-carriage—suddenly embarked with reckless haste on a novel method of bettering his condition. "Being", he told Pepys, "almost distracted for want of monies, my private creditors tormenting me from morning to night and some of them threatening me with a prison, . . . there came a certain person to me whom I had relieved in a starving condition and for whom I had done a thousand kindnesses, who pretended in gratitude to help me to a wife who was a very virtuous, pious and sweet dispositioned lady and an heiress who had £500 p.a. in land of inheritance and £4000 in ready money, with the interest since 9 years, besides a mortgage upon £300 p.a. more, with plate, jewels, etc." This catalogue of charms turned out a complete fraud, for the lady proved no better than the generality of her kind and, indeed, rather worse, for besides being penniless she was a whore and diseased at that. All this, as he poured it out in his letter to his worldly-wise friend at the Admiralty, he had discovered too late: by

★ B. St Michel to S. P., Feb. 14th, 1687. *Rawl. MSS. A.* 189, f. 316.

charms or witchcraft he had been "led as a fool to the stocks and married a coachman's daughter, not worth a shilling and one who about nine months since was brought to bed of a bastard".

Thus, in addition to being practically bankrupt, poor Morland had become the jest of London. Having laid his sad case before the Spiritual Court, he begged Pepys for the sake of old acquaintance and Christian charity to speak to the King and get him to move his proctor on his behalf. "A flood of tears blind my eyes and I can write no more."[11]

Pepys did what he could and consulted the Judge of the Admiralty Court. But he found that the opinion of the town was against his foolish old tutor, and that there was little chance of finding any legal ground for nullity. Six months later, in November 1687, Morland was besieged in the poor hut in which he sheltered near Hyde Park gate by "rude fellows" with orders from his wife's proctors to take him alive or dead. In the following spring he was being dogged by bailiffs on the score of her debts. Throughout the sordid affair Morland turned perpetually to Pepys to help him, until the lady's brazen and open adultery at last gave him the freedom of divorce.[12]

Morland was far from being the only person who came to Pepys for help. Some of the greatest in England did so. The University of Cambridge, threatened with the embarrassment and scandal of a State lottery in the town, besought his intervention: so did Oxford when the Stationers' Company tried to deprive it of its ancient privilege of printing Bibles. Nor did they appeal in vain. In such matters the despotism of King James could generally be tempered a little by the good sense of his friend, the Secretary of the Admiralty. Sir Robert Southwell, at whose instance Pepys secured the release of a poor

Huguenot seaman from a French galley, thought him the most powerful man in England, "and perhaps in the world", he added, "when I see who, against his will, you could force to be guilty of one good action. Whether Father le Chaise"—King Louis's Confessor—"will not stick on your skirts for this odd prank, I leave you to consider."[13]

His old companion and rival, John Creed, desiring to be an Elder Brother of Trinity House; Lord Chancellor Jeffreys, who signed himself his most entire affectionate friend and servant and wanted a post for a protégé; Dr Mills in search of a Prebendal stall; Evelyn troubled by the smell of the mud in the Deptford docks; Sir William Petty anxious for royal sanction for the publication of his studies on statistics and political economy, all turned to Pepys. "I thank God", was Petty's grateful verdict, "that his Majesty appointed you to examine these my opinions." When Bolingbroke became First Lord of the Treasury the ladies of Covent Garden are said to have cried out in jubilation, "Five thousand a year, girls, and all for us!" Learned men had similar reason to rejoice when Pepys was in power. Dr Nathaniel Vincent had only to ask to receive twenty-five guineas that he might enrich his "little study" with an expensive work of reference. Even a female poet— a poor widow—who enclosed her verses and a litany of her wants did not go away empty. And the Fellows of his old College at their audit dinner feasted by Mr Pepys's grace on a doe from the royal forests.[14]

The learned recompensed the great Secretary by flattering him. More than one author that year dedicated his book to him—Dr Richard Cumberland his work on Jewish Measures, charmingly inscribed "for that good affection being begun in your youth thirty years ago in Magdalene College", Captain

Greenville Collins his Chart of Harwich and its adja-
cent coasts, Nathaniel Vincent his *Conjectura Nautica*
and Francis Willoughby his *Historia Piscium*. As
President of the Royal Society Pepys bore the cost of
sixty of the plates of this last work, and the Society
graciously ordered "that a Book of Fishes of the best
paper, curiously bound in Turkey leather, likewise
five others bound also" should be presented to him.
And the greatest of all seventeenth-century scientific
works, Mr Newton's *Principia*, went out to an awed
but puzzled world with his name as *ex officio*
licenser, on its title page:

Imprimatur, S. Pepys, Reg. Soc. Praeses, Julii 5 1686[15]

★   ★   ★

Yet Pepys was greatest by far in his capacity as
plain Secretary of the Admiralty. Thence all his
honours sprang. What he had won by virtue of
penmanship, method and precedent he continued to
maintain by these weapons. Among certain notes in
his own hand, written about this date and entitled
"Momentalls", is an entry which shows how zealous he still was to enhance the stature of his office:

Lord Admiral's Duty.
   Secretary Admiralty and his office to be certain, depending
on the Crown, not the Admiral, and his work and duty
adjusted.

Nor would he tolerate any suggestion that he did
not personally supervise the work of his office even
in its most minute part. When at the end of 1686 one
of his senior clerks, Walbanke, died, and his old
friend, Mrs Pearse, the Surgeon-General's wife,
sought the vacant post for her son, Pepys addressed
to that young gentleman a letter which summarised
his reaction to any suggestion that one of his subordinates could in the smallest degree be indispens-
able. Not having seen the light before, it is worth

perusal as a perfect expression of that high bureaucratic pride which was so characteristic a part of
Pepys's legacy to the Civil Service of his country:

Mr Pearse,
    Pray (whatever be the issue of your present desire) don't
forget the right you have to be always welcome to me. . . .
Wherefore don't any more treat me as you have done now at
that distance that does not become me to receive from one that
I esteem so nearly as I do you.
    . . . I am far from forgetting the proposition made earlily to
me by my excellent Lady, your mother . . . in prospect of Mr
Walbanke's death. Nor have I escaped many solicitations . . .
since yesterday morning, not only from the Navy Office but
from potent hands at Court, both the one and the other
grounded upon a mistake people had been led into of Mr
Walbanke's mighty sufficiences by his being admitted to be
indeed the do-all to the late Commissioners at Derby House.
Whereas I never thought fit to rely on his clerkship for the
drawing up of one letter or paper of moment in my life, nor
have felt any want of him during his long absence, poor man,
by sickness at a time wherein matters of more importance to
the Crown have been transacted in reference to the Navy than
ever passed this office since England had a Navy. Not that he
wanted talents very useful in their kind relating to the keeping
of the books, marshalling the papers and examining of passes
and divers other things wherein time only had made him fully
master of the methods of the office, and he his brother by his
continually employing him for many years under him. So that
the affairs of this office are no more affected by his death than
they would, were he still alive or had never been born.*[16]

Every month that Pepys sat in his office at York
Buildings frowning his disapproval at any deviation
from his rules—his portrait painted about this time
by Godfrey Kneller reveals the frown as an appar-
ently permanent feature of his expression†—those

* S. P. to J. Pearse junior, December 16th, 1686. *Rawl. MSS. A.*
189, ff. 261–3.
† Yet in a painting of him in my possession sent to Sir William
Booth in the closing years of Pepys's life, the frown has vanished and
the softer lines of youth have revived in the mellow twilight of
retirement.

rules became more firmly established in the professional consciousness and habitude of the Service. Every captain at his potent bidding now sent to the Admiralty before each voyage his Certificate of Readiness for Sea, at each port of call his Abstracts and when the voyage was over his Journal. For only when these were received regularly were wages and allowances paid. After a while observance of these formalities began to become second nature—the administrative and liturgical ritual, as it were, of the Navy.[17]

Like the men of the past who founded the great monastic orders whose history he so loved to study in his leisure, Pepys's plan was to make a rule for all things, great or small. From that unresting brain came a perpetual flow of rules of every kind: for a clear method of dividing prizes between officers and seamen, for pensioning naval widows and orphans, for regulating the issue of rum and brandy. A rule now became sacred because it was a rule and not merely on account of its intrinsic importance; it was only to be broken when the unforeseeable necessity of the King's Service made it imperative to do so. Its wisdom was not to be called in question.

Nor was its enforcement by Pepys's office to be regarded as a matter of personal grievance or affront by those holding the King's commission. "Sir," he wrote to the captain of the *Assistance,* who had complained about his allotment of guns, "I have received yours of the 6th inst. And though it be what nothing but your own saying so would have made me believe, yet because you have said it, I will believe that you did not know there was any Establishment of Guns in the Navy, that the number and nature thereof to each ship were not reduced under a known and regular Establishment. But I must beg you to alter your mind so far concerning me as to

SAMUEL PEPYS, Secretary of the Admiralty, aged about 54
*(From a portrait by Kneller at
Magdalene College, Cambridge)*

Gravé par A. Trouvain Avec Prvilege du Roy 1694

Jacques 2.ᵈ Roy d'Angleterre.

se vend a Paris chez le dit Trouvain rue St. Jacques au grand Monarque venant les Mathurins

JAMES II in prayer
(From a coloured engraving in
the Pepysian Library)

think that I can do my duty to the King in taking
notice (as he both commands and expects it from
me) of all things wherein the discipline and good
order of his Navy is concerned, without the least
want of good will and respect to the persons to
whom the same relates. This, I assure you, is true in
your particular case, to whom I will be found so on
all occasions. And I am sure I have been as forward
to do all offices of kindness as you (by a mighty
mistake) would seem, from this honest freedom of
mine in the execution of my duty to the King, to
collect the contrary. Which if everybody should do,
to whom on like occasions I never fail to exercise the
same necessary and friendly liberty, I should have a
weight upon me much less easy to bear than all the
work of my office besides." For step by step) in days
when gentlemen drew their swords at a verbal
slight, Pepys had to educate his high-spirited contemporaries in the formalities and ungrateful necessities of official correspondence. He did so with all
the courtesy that was compatible with unswerving
firmness.[18]

There was no avoiding Mr Pepys's way. If an
officer, however highly placed, had occasion to
come up to town on his private occasions, he must
apply to the Admiralty for the King's formal consent.★ He was expected to do so in a set petition,
stating the exact reasons for which leave was needed
and the number of days required. It all sounds so
natural and normal to us: it did not seem so to the
men of that time. Once a captain, unaccustomed to

★ "Sir. I received yours of the 9th inst., and did immediately move
his Majesty in your desires herein for leave to continue in town ten
days longer on score of your health, which he was very graciously
pleased to grant, as you will find by the enclosed warrant. To which,
praying you to be referred, I remain, Your most humble servant,
S. P." S. P. to Sir R. Strickland, March 12th, 1687. *Pepysian MSS.,
Adm. Letters* XIII, 6.

the new regime, arrived unexpectedly in the Downs from the West Indies, having abandoned his station in a pet after a quarrel with the Governor of one of the islands. The letter in which Pepys informed the offender of his horror and of the impending certainty of an enquiry and court-martial is a little epistolary masterpiece:

Sir,

I have received yours of the 2nd inst. from the Downs, and cannot but congratulate you your safe arrival there with one of his Majesty's ships, though I must own myself wonderfully surprised with the tidings of your being there. Nor is his Majesty himself (to whom I immediately communicated it) less earnest to know the true grounds of it, which both for his satisfaction and your own justification it will be necessary that you enable me without delay to give him. For the coming home of a ship from a station to which she was purposely and at great charge sent . . . will necessarily call for some good reasons to justify it. . . . His Majesty has been pleased to tell me that he will have the matter fully enquired into, as becomes a proceeding extraordinary. . . .

"I thank you", he added, "for the account you give me of that which you call a fiery vapour falling upon you, the effects whereof are very wonderful and indeed not at all less surprising than your being here to relate them." None knew better than Pepys how to rebuke ignorant presumption with a velvet touch. [19]

He knew, too, how to rebuke it in the great. The rules he enforced to preserve the respect due to the King's flag were flaunted in the spring of 1687 by the papist Sir Roger Strickland, who had now succeeded Herbert as the royal favourite in the Service. With the high temper of his ancient race, Strickland had set his heart on flying a Vice-Admiral's flag during a voyage to the Mediterranean in which he was acting as second-in-command to the young Duke of Grafton, even though only a small force of frigates was employed. This Pepys sternly opposed until he learnt that the King in a weak moment had been induced by Strickland's importunity to promise it. He thereupon withdrew his opposition but wrote that officer such a letter with the coveted warrant as must have turned his triumph to rage:

I am loath it should be thought possible that any degree of friendship or other consideration whatever could prevail with me to mislead his Majesty by one word of mine to the granting a thing so extraordinary, so irregular, and unjustified by any practice past, and unlikely to be ever imitated in time to come, as this which you have thus contended for of having two of the top flags of England exposed to sea in view of the two greatest rivals of England for Sea Dominion and Glory (I mean the Dutch and French) with no better provision for supporting the honour thereof than six ships, and two of them such as carry not above 190 men and 54 guns between them. And this too obtained through mere force of importunity by one who but in September last charged Captain Priestman with turning the King's flag into ridicule in putting up but an unusual swallow-tailed pendant.

Lest the royal favourite should charge him with disloyalty to his master's wishes, the uncompromising Secretary went on: "However, as much as I do with this my usual plainness unbespeak the thanks you might otherwise conceive due to me on this occasion"—one fancies that Pepys must have smiled as he postulated this improbable contingency—"this much I shall take to myself of the merit of having done you justice therein, that from the instant his Majesty was first pleased to tell me of the promise he had been prevailed with to make you touching the Flag, showing me at the same time his being not at all less sensible than myself of the irregularity of the thing so granted, I have never made it my part officiously to inculcate anything to him that might interrupt the resolution he had thus taken in your favour, as well remembering that his Majesty is

master of his own orders and can as well dispense
with as make them, and, above all, that it is a virtue
much more becoming a Prince to do violence to
himself by dispensing with an order than grieve a
good servant by a breach of a promise." And he
ended this stinging communication by advising
Strickland to thank the King for the privilege but to
refrain from using it.[20]

The same jealous vigilance for the King's honour
characterises Pepys's correspondence in another
much-disputed matter—the immunity of naval
officers and officials from arrest for debt. He would
neither allow the King's prerogative to be overrid-
den by insolent bailiffs and creditors, whom in any
case of contempt he summoned to York Buildings
to explain themselves, nor his justice to be called in
question by any avoidance by public servants of
their private liabilities. Those who tried to do so
were quickly undeceived, their papers being
endorsed by a curt "Left to the Law" in the Secretary's hand. Nor would he tolerate in the Navy the
practice, tacitly allowed in every other branch of the
public service, of payments by incoming holders of
offices to their predecessors. He himself, he once
stated, might have made £40,000 by such an abuse of
the King's favour, and he would never concur in
suffering others to do what nothing could tempt
him to do himself.[21]

For the essence of Pepys's rules was that no one
was allowed to break them. One of his finest letters
of this period is that to the two naval officers he most
cared for and trusted, Sir John Berry and Sir John
Narbrough, reproaching them for having given an
old friend a Lieutenant's commission contrary to
the regulations laid down in his Establishment of
1677. Least of all would he allow any deviation in his

own office from the rectitude he enforced on the Service. When in the summer of 1687 his favourite clerk and disciple, Josiah Burchett, confidant and companion of all his recent journeys and an inmate of his household, offended against his stern regimen, he was summarily dismissed from it. Nor could all Burchett's repeated entreaties turn Mr Secretary's heart. "I know well enough", the young penitent sadly confessed, "that whatever you do, you do by the rules of justice."★ Sometimes it seemed to those about him that this great man was too severe and unbending.[22]

But Pepys's task was to build a vessel stout enough to withstand the changing waves of individual feeling. And all its hundred and one urgent needs of the moment, as well as its greater ones of the future, were his care. His lot it was to send out squadrons and appoint captains, to confer with the Navy Office and supervise the Special Commissioners, to enquire into complaints and punish offenders, to reward the diligent and arbitrate in disputes. The applications for yacht-passage across the Channel, the appointment of properly qualified chaplains to every ship, the leakage of British seamen through the inducement held out to them by the shipping agents of foreign states, were alike his concern. Nothing was too small for his eye. Seventy-six pages of one of his many volumes of administrative papers, now preserved in the Bodleian Library, are concerned with his own personal examination during 1687 of the wrong suffered by the purser of the *Suffolk* at the impetuous hands of the Master Atten-

★ J. Burchett to S. P., Aug. 8th, 1687. *Rawl. MSS. A.* 189, f. 1, printed in *Howarth*, 181–2. In after years Burchett was to become what was virtually the first permanent Secretary of the Admiralty, M.P. for Sandwich, which he represented in Parliament for half a century, and the historian of the Navy.

dant at Chatham, his old acquaintance, Captain Vittles.★[23]

The principal naval events of the year 1687 were the presence of the Algerine fleet in the Channel in June, the Duke of Grafton's voyage to the Mediterranean and the despatch of Sir John Narbrough to the west. The first was occasioned by a naval war between Algiers and England's ancient rivals, the Dutch. The presence off the British coasts of African corsairs, rendered desperate by poverty, caused great anxiety to the government. When they first appeared Pepys thought it almost inevitable that some untoward act of "that heady and faithless people", as he termed them, would lead to a rupture. Afraid of the loss that would follow to the Levant and Turkey merchants, he warned his old and much-loved friend, James Houblon, the great Whig and Huguenot merchant, to look to his trading ventures.† But by the exercise of considerable tact on the part of all concerned, the danger was averted, though not before British seagoing opinion had been outraged by large numbers of derelict and rifled Dutch ships driving helplessly about the narrow seas. At one time Pepys had had to address a severe rebuke to the officers of Pendennis Castle, who, regardless of the treaties with Algiers, seized and jailed the crew and confiscated the powder of an Algerine prize driven into Falmouth by stress of weather.

The most delicate situation of all arose in the middle of June, when Sir Roger Strickland was ordered to sea with a hastily collected squadron to

---

★ *Rawl. MSS. A.* 177, ff. 1–76. The award was promulgated on Jan. 4th, 1688, over two years after Vittles had struck John Trevor over the head with a boat-hook for attempting to go on shore contrary to his orders.

† Later one of the founders of the Bank of England.

perform the double function of preventing the
Algerines from returning with any British subjects
who might have been captured from Dutch ships
and of enforcing a salute from the French fleet,
which was hovering in the Channel under Monsieur
de Tourville in search of escaping Huguenots.* For
a week or two the country was on the verge of war.
Fortunately both tasks were accomplished without
resource to blows. It was quite a little triumph.
Pepys himself secured the release of some unfortunate French Protestants who had been captured by
the Algerines while crossing in a Dutch vessel to
Holland. They dared not, he told the Admiralty
Judge, claim their privilege as French subjects to
secure their release for fear King Louis should com-
pel the Algerine Government to deliver them "from
their captivity in Africa to a more severe one under
himself at home". Pepys even succeeded in persuading his sovereign to stretch the laws of denization by
claiming them from the Moors as British subjects.[24]

After this unwelcome incursion, the Duke of
Grafton, who was about to sail with the new Queen
of Portugal to Lisbon, was instructed to extend his
voyage into the Mediterranean. The visit of a British
fleet had a sobering effect on the authorities at
Algiers and secured a confirmation of existing
treaties. The expedition was chiefly notable for
being based strategically on Gibraltar, whence
Pepys victualled and controlled England's distant
ships. He had some fears lest the place might be
taken by the French, who had also established a

* ". . . which squadron will I doubt not (with God's assistance)
suffice to support his Majesty's honour in these his seas against
anything that shall be offered in diminution of it by Monsieur Tourville, it being his Majesty's expectations that his honour be asserted,
and is in no doubt but it will effectually be so." S. P. to Sir R.
Strickland, Sunday night, June 12th, 1687. *Pepysian MSS., Adm.
Letters* XIII, 136.

victualling station there, before his chance should come to seize it for England.[25]

The expedition to the west was of a different kind. For some time past there had been talk of fabulous treasure in a Spanish wreck which had lain for nearly half a century near the shoal of Bahama off the coast of Hispaniola. A small stock-company of Gentlemen Adventurers, including the Duke of Albermarle—son to the stout old fighter of Pepys's youth—and Sir John Narbrough, had sent out two small ships to investigate. Early in June 1687 they returned to England with the first instalment of the treasure amounting to over a quarter of a million— equal in those days to a fifth of the national revenue. Few, if any, like enterprises can ever have yielded so rich a return: it is reckoned that the shareholders received £10,000 for every £100 invested. And the remainder of the treasure was still to be reclaimed. On Tuesday, June 14th, the four chief partners waited on the King and Council in the Treasury Chamber at Windsor, where Pepys in attendance took notes. It was agreed that the government should lend them a fully-manned and equipped frigate for a year and the services of Sir John Narbrough to command it, in return for a fifth of the treasure if under £150,000 and a third should it prove more.[26]

In the autumn Narbrough sailed for the West Indies. He was followed a few weeks later by the Duke of Albermarle who was sent out as Governor-General of Jamaica to consolidate the trans-Atlantic empire fast forming in these islands and along the eastern shores of North America. Much about the same time Pepys was employed in working out plans for a further western expedition to suppress the English pirates, who despite many efforts to bring them under the heel of authority were still spasmodically terrorising the Spanish Main and South Seas to the profit of the colonies but the scandal of the civilised world. He reported that a force of five frigates manned by 725 men at an annual cost of £33,930 would be needed if the work was to be done properly. Many years later he entertained—with great pleasure—one of the most famous of the pirates whom he was seeking to destroy as an honoured guest at his house in York Buildings. From the other side of the globe his correspondents sent him news of England's growing concerns in India, where a tiny squadron under his friend Sir John Wyborne was assisting the East India Company to put down the interlopers.[27]

Through the old problem of money still made itself felt, the mists of imminent bankruptcy which had darkened the path of every naval project through all Pepys's twenty-seven years of experience were at last beginning to lift. Save when a temporary stop was caused by the change at the Treasury at the beginning of the year, the cash payments required for the work of the Special Commission continued regularly at the rate of £7000 a week. Early in the year additional sums of over £40,000 were allowed for new storehouses and dry-docks at Chatham and Portsmouth. The Navy debt, reduced by over £30,000, stood in January 1687 at no more than £171,836. 2s. 9d. The repairs of the battle fleet were pushed rapidly forward, and during the summer four new frigates were launched. Soon the country would have a Navy which could bid defiance to, and perhaps master, any in the world.[28]

Chapter III
Pleasures of a Virtuoso

"We eat with great pleasure, and I enjoyed myself in it with reflections upon the pleasures which I at best can expect, yet not to exceed this; eating in silver plates, and all things mighty rich and handsome about me. A great deal of fine discourse, sitting almost till dark at dinner, and then broke up with great pleasure, especially to myself."—*Pepys's Diary,* Nov. 28th, 1666.

King James the Conqueror had made up his mind to conquer England. His father had died because he could not make up his mind, and he was not going to fall by the same mistake. His whole life had shown him the advantages of being resolute. He had spent the first years of it in civil war and exile, yet had returned triumphantly with his brother to England without yielding an inch of principle. Later, to the terror of cowards and trimmers, he had openly declared his reconciliation to the Catholic Church and had again refused to compromise, with the result that, after a further period of persecution, proscription and exile, he had seen his enemies defeated and ruined and all that he had so courageously stood for universally acclaimed. Since his accession he had smashed Monmouth, Argyll and the Whigs, had set the Navy on its feet and doubled the size of the army. If the Cavalier Party and the Anglican Church, who had once stood by him, now chose to stand in his way, so much the worse for the Cavalier Party and the Anglican Church.

Protected from the salutary sting of criticism by

both his position and the bent of his temperament, and spurred on by his priests and the inexperienced Catholic politicians at his side, James seemed to have no doubts. He had tamed war-like and covenanting Scotland; he could tame England. His third kingdom, Ireland, being predominantly Catholic, needed no taming. The armies he was raising there under the papist Lord Deputy, Tyrconnel, could be used later if any of his English subjects were so foolish as to imitate Monmouth. Right and reason were clearly on his side. As a devout Catholic it was his divine mission to help the faithful men and women who had stood fast by their Faith under the persecutions of the cruel laws which were now administered in his name, to relieve them from humiliating disabilities and to give them their share in the civic privileges of their country. As a just sovereign it was his duty to give all his subjects of whatever creed the right to worship God in their own way and to utilise their talents regardless of discriminating oaths and tests. And if some of them opposed freedom of conscience for their own selfish reasons, he must enforce that freedom.

In the course of the three years of his reign, therefore, the King performed a complete *volte-face*. The Tories and high Churchmen, who before his accession had been his best friends and were now passively resisting his repeated wishes for the abolition of the religious tests, should be given a taste of his displeasure. The persecuted non-conformist minorities whom he had formerly defeated with their aid should be raised from the dust and given executive office with the despised Catholics. The second anniversary of his accession was marked by a widespread pardon of forfeitures and penalties incurred by Dissenters and Whigs, and the promise of liberty of conscience to all. Meanwhile the tory press was muzzled and the chief tory magistrates of London replaced by Whigs and Dissenters. In April, after Parliament had been again prorogued for a further six months, a royal Declaration "for a general toleration of all religions" was issued, suspending the penal laws and dispensing with the oaths and tests for admission to civil and military office.

Throughout the summer of 1687 the new policy was pursued relentlessly. *Mandamus* letters were sent to both Universities for the admission of papists to degrees and Fellowships: those who opposed the royal will were suspended like the laws. A crop of conversions to the Catholic Faith in high places followed. "All goes redwise", was the catchword of the hour. The man in the field and the street watched with horror the growing size of the King's army, the great summer camp at Hounslow and the admission of Catholics to high military office. Even the frowning guns of the Tower of London were now placed under the orders of a papist.

Yet so long as the penal laws remained on the statute book, the King was aware that the whole fabric of toleration and religious equality which he was trying to create rested precariously on the royal prerogative. Should anything happen to him, and his Protestant daughter and her sombre Dutch husband inherit his power, the old, harsh laws would again be enforced. If his system was to endure they must be repealed without delay. A tory Parliament had refused to do so, and had since been prorogued. A non-conformist Parliament might act differently. A non-conformist Parliament there should be.

The closing years of Charles II's reign had shown how easily the electoral machinery of the country could be altered to return a Parliament of a new complexion. The same methods were now employed to reverse the policy of those years and ensure

that the electoral corporations, which had returned
Whigs in 1680–1 and Tories in 1685, should in 1688
return a solid *bloc* of enemies to the Anglican monopoly. On July 2nd, 1687, the existing Parliament
was dissolved. At the same time steps were taken to
replace the tory office-holders in the counties and
parliamentary boroughs with new men favourable
to the royal policy and to alter the constitution of the
electoral corporations. What *Quo Warranto* had done
once, *Quo Warranto* should do again.[1]

In the late summer of 1687, the King made a
Progress through the western midlands to prepare
the ground for the revolution he was planning. He
began by a visit to Portsmouth on August 16th.
Here Pepys attended him while he inspected
fortifications, discussed plans for new forts and
tested an engine of Sir Samuel Morland's. Two days
later, on his return to London, the Secretary of the
Admiralty was summoned to join the Court again at
Bath. Hence he accompanied it to Gloucester, where
he transacted Admiralty business on the 23rd—Sam
Atkins, his faithful Puritan clerk, had been left in
charge at York Buildings—and on the following day
to Worcester.[2]

At this point Pepys's brief part in the royal Progress came to an end. He was probably not sorry, for
his chief friends in the place—Dr Reynolds, the
Bishop, his "cousin Nan", wife of the Cavalier
Fisher who entertained him, and the learned Dean,
Dr Hickes*—being all Tories, were all out of
favour. Hickes, who read the King an Address in the

---

* The great scholar and future non-juror who was to administer
the Sacrament and Absolution to Pepys on his death-bed in 1703 and
who wrote of him: "The greatness of his behaviour in his long and
sharp trial before his death was in every way answerable to his great
life, . . . and I never attended any sick or dying person that died with so
much Christian greatness of mind or a more lively sense of immortal-
ity."

name of the Dean and Chapter, was not so much as answered. The only people in the most royalist city in England who appeared to be in his Majesty's good graces were the Presbyterians.

Pepys's method of dropping out of the Progress was characteristic. "To tell you the truth," he explained on his return, "I was got with Mr Dean of Worcester into the Library among the manuscripts and pored away my time till (at my going out) I found nobody left in the town but myself." Leaving the Court to pursue its missionary pilgrimage to Chester, he returned to London and his own business, stopping a night at Oxford on the way and sending from his inn to Merton College for young Ned Southwell whom he just missed. He was back at the Office on the afternoon of the 27th.[3]

★   ★   ★

With every year Pepys was growing more of a philosopher. When the disturbing pressure of outside politics became too great he drew himself more closely into the inner citadel of his work and his love of study and scholarship. Among what he described as his "By-Notes Private" for that winter is an entry which reveals that in the midst of business and civic alarms he was pursuing his researches for a life of Lord Sandwich. Other evidence shows him still accumulating information for his history of the English Navy, "with hopes", he told an informant, "to ease posterity for my time of the difficulties that my predecessors have left me under to recover any certain knowledge of the history of theirs". All historical learning was grist to his mill: that year he added to his library an index of the letters and manuscripts of the Reformation belonging to the Dutch Church in London.[4]

His library continued to grow. It was already

passing out of the stage required by a cultured
gentleman for his private reading into that of a
remarkable collection of rare and beautiful books
and manuscripts. In the shops of Little Britain—that
"plentiful and learned emporium of authors"—the
virtuosos of the later seventeenth century were wont
to gather to examine the latest sheets from the printing presses and discuss them with those "knowing
and conversible men", the booksellers. In such
company the small erect figure and dark features of
the Secretary of the Admiralty must often have been
seen: here, whenever his naval occasions permitted,
he would buy a Turkish history, a volume of Scottish Ballads, Dean Hickes's latest book or a Greek
folio for his cousin Gale. His favourite bookseller
was Robert Scott, the king of Little Britain, who
loved, as he told him, to find a perfect book for him.
When Scott acquired a copy of the "old Ship of Fools
in old verse, yet so very fair and perfect that seldom
comes such another", he let Pepys have it for eight
shillings, though it had never been sold before under
ten.[5]

Pepys was not only a collector of books. Anything rare and curious interested him, provided the
sum demanded was not too princely. In October
1687 he was offered a complete set of Roettier's
medals for £42 by a friend. He made enquiries about
the globes of the great Dutch master, Blaeu—the
finest of their kind in the world. Since his death they
had been in the hands of Joannes van Keulen the
Amsterdam globe-maker. Demanding only the
very best, Pepys ascertained that a globe of 26 inches
diameter with fannered frame could be bought for
250 guilders or £22. 14s. 6d.[6]

He could afford these luxuries now, for his
fortune was greatly increased by the emoluments of
his Office. On November 19th he accounted for

£2622 received in fees for passes during the past three and a half years, leaving a residue of £4378 due from the Crown to bring his salary up to the agreed £2000 p.a. For this sum a royal warrant was issued to the Navy Board. It did not include the Admiralty fees for new appointments, which ranged from £5 for Master Shipwrights, Storekeepers and Clerks of the Cheque, to 10s. for Midshipmen, Volunteers and Chaplains. It would probably be no exaggeration to say that Pepys was enjoying the equivalent in modern purchasing power of an income of at least £50,000 p.a. free of tax, with all his expenses including the rent of his house paid.

Yet when his fortune is compared with that of his friend, Sir Stephen Fox, who as Paymaster to the Army acquired a King's ransom from the nation and laid the foundations of a great house, one is struck by Pepys's moderation. He might have made himself one of the richest men of his time. A quarter of the State's expenditure and an even greater proportion of its patronage passed through his hands, and in his own department he was absolute master. He preferred to be modestly comfortable, surrounding himself with the beautiful things of which he made himself the custodian and trustee for posterity. The public's money he enjoyed by spending it on the public's occasions better than anyone else could have done.[7]

In the early months of 1688 such time as Pepys could spare from affairs of State was occupied in the business of moving his home and office from No. 12 to No. 14 Buckingham Street, of which he took a lease for himself and the Admiralty from Will Hewer.* No. 14 was the finest house in York Build-

---

* The house still belonged to Hewer at the time of his death in 1715. (*L.C.C. Survey of London* XVIII, Part II (*Strand*), 71 *n*.) Its assessed rental in 1696 was £200 p.a.

ings, newly completed at the south-west end of the street on the site of Lord Willoughby's burnt-out mansion. It thus fronted both street and river, standing almost immediately above the beautiful stone water-gate past which the waters of the enembanked Thames still flowed. Between it and the river wall was a walk planted with trees where Pepys and his neighbours employed an honest gardener.*[8]

The outside of the house Pepys beautified at the King's expense. Over the main door facing the Thames he had a shield carved by Mathias Fletcher, Master Carver of the Deptford Yard, containing the Lord High Admiral's anchor with the imperial crown and ciphers, eight feet deep by six broad and costing £30. Above them he had displayed the Royal Arms set in the midst of the pediment, fifteen feet long and nine in height and costing £73. 15s. so that all the boats on the river could see who and what dwelt within. To enhance the effect he had them gilded and coloured.[9]

Pepys took a good deal of trouble in furnishing his fine house. He got James Houblon to negotiate the purchase of £80 worth of tapestry for its walls; after much ado the great merchant secured two pieces of eight by four ells at 25s. 6d. an ell, a reduction of twenty-five per cent on the usual price—"a pennyworth", as he called it. The office also came in for attention: before the move Pepys had made a general review and arrangement of his loose papers, and the shelves of the presses which lined the walls of the clerk's office were now filled with neatly docketed

* To S. P. from Peregrine Bertie, May 23rd, 1688. "About the Walk and Trees in York Buildings." "Mr Pepys. This is to let you know that Mr Euers did imploy the bearer, John James, to look after the trees and walk, and many of us did give our consent to it. And if he has not offended you, I should for my part be glad he continued in his place, for he is an honest man and fitter for that employment than any." *Rawl. MSS. A.* 179, f. 78.

bundles. To these were added as soon as he was established in his new quarters a splendid collection of maps and plans, which were sent down from Whitehall by the King in parcels—a Spanish map of Africa, charts of the Philippines, Java, Japan and the East Indies, a print of Speed's of the Earl of Essex's attack on Cadiz, a map of Sebastian Cabot's, a draft of the pinnaces belonging to Henry VIII's fleet and much else. They were intended to adorn the Admiralty, but somehow most of them found their way ultimately into Pepys's private collection.[10]

Over his household Mary Skinner, who had first come to live with him a year or two after his wife's death eighteen years before, appears to have presided in some capacity not quite clear: it is not even certain whether she was living with Pepys or not at this time. She is certainly mentioned on more than one occasion as concerned in his domestic arrangements.* In a letter to the Governor of Barbados written in March 1688 Pepys acknowledged "the fruit which my friend Mrs Skinner has received of your kindness to her at my instance, whereof she is most sensible". Those were the days "when keeping was in the fashion", and friendship as between man and woman was a wide term. Mary Skinner cannot have been wholly in charge for him, for in the fall of 1685, he had sought a professional housekeeper. Mrs Evelyn, a great authority on such matters, claimed to have found an ideal one: "such a one as I am sure so good a master deserves. . . . She is very neat, an excellent housewife, not ungenteel, sightly and well-behaved, yet of years to allow the necessary experience and prudence to direct in a family

* She was the daughter of a respectable but declining City merchant to whom Milton addressed a sonnet; her younger brother had incurred political odium by being the great republican poet's last amanuensis.

and preserve respect." In the end Pepys, perhaps wisely, had chosen a protégée of James Houblon's, a Mrs Fane, whom that discerning merchant had known "from her bib upwards".[11]

Mrs Fane had all the virtues save one. She was knowing, faithful and vigilant, a strict home-keeper, which much endeared her to Pepys, and an excellent sick-nurse. But she was also a shrew with a bitter tongue that at times made the household in Buckingham Street very far from the peaceful place that Pepys would have it. After eighteen months of her despotism, he put his foot down and dismissed her. There followed an uneasy interregnum of a few weeks during which he hastily summoned one Judy Robbins from Chatham, though whether the same Mrs Robbins, daughter to old Delks the waterman, with whom he had toyed so voluptuously in his office one August twenty-two years before, history, discreet Muse, does not relate. The lady came, for she could not bear, she said, to hear what ill-carriage his honour Mr Pepys had received from his servants. But lameness and increasing years had rendered her less stirring and serviceable in the managery of a house than once she had been, she explained. Mr Homewood, Clerk of the Survey at Chatham, to whom Pepys had written to enquire about her, informed him privately that, though she still ans-wered the character of a careful, diligent and house-wifely person, she would probably be unable to stay as he had reason to believe her secretly married to the gentleman whose house she kept at Chatham.[12]

The crisis ended in Mary Skinner's persuading Samuel to give the bitter-tongued Mrs Fane another chance. Mrs Edwards—the Jane Birch of former days—was unable to aid him in this emergency as she had often done in the past, since she was now looking after Will Hewer's new house in Villiers

Street a few yards away. She seems to have still had a good deal of influence with her old master, for it was through her that the clerk Josiah Burchett, still unforgiven, made a last despairing effort to recover his favour.* His "good old Mistress" he called her. Her son, Samuel, then aged 15, was one of the forty children from the Mathematical School who were presented to the King on January 1st, 1688, by the Lord Mayor in the presence of Pepys and his fellow Governors of Christ's Hospital.[13]

One familiar inmate was lacking now from his home—the gentle singing master, Morelli.† On his father's death he had left Pepys's protection and returned to Hainault to look after his mother and sister and his little estate. He had found the former dead and the latter wasted by Louis XIV's wars of conquest. Hearing that his Britannic Majesty was about to form a chapel of musicians, he had written to his old patron to beg him to secure his admission. But on his return to England Pepys refused to see him. It seemed that the young man, greatly improvident, had contracted a secret marriage. This was

* See a letter in Burchett's beautiful sloping writing of April 23rd, 1688, and addressed to Mrs Edwards at Mr Hewer's house in Villiers Street in York Buildings. "Mrs Edwards. Though I have many times of late attempted to cast myself at my honourable master Mr Pepys's feet to beg his pardon and compassion, yet whenever opportunity offered itself, the fear that seized me rendered me wholly unable to do it. I am afraid his Honour thinks 'tis pride that keeps me from it, but God knows 'tis so far from that that I would gladly do anything that might procure me but never so small a portion of his favour, it being the only thing that can make me happy in this world. For my devotion to his service is such that 'tis not in my power to seek after anything else. Whereby I am reduced to so poor a condition that 'tis next akin to starving. . . . For God's sake by my solicitor." *Rawl. MSS. A.* 179, ff. 20–1.

† There is an interesting reference to Morelli in Roger North's autobiography as the "Italian" singing master who taught North's pretty cousin to master "that puzzling instrument, the lute" and to sing to her own accompaniment "after the Italian manner". R. North, *Lives of the Norths* (1890 ed.) III, 29.

an offence which the autocrat of York Buildings found it particularly hard to forgive. Possibly it was with a favourite servant.[14]

In York Buildings Pepys entertained his friends and took his seemly pleasures. The sound of music so familiar to No. 12 now came nearer to the waterside: passers-by on the river must have often heard it of an evening borne to them from the tall balconied windows whose silver sconces twinkled at them through the leaves. Pepys loved to give his guests a concert. In the April of 1687 Evelyn listened to the famous singer Cifaccio, esteemed the first in Europe, performing before a select company at Admiralty House, extending and loosing his notes with incomparable softness and sweetness, though for the rest, the fastidious gentleman noted, he found the Signior "a mere wanton, effeminate child, very coy and proudly conceited". It was certainly a feather in Pepys's cap to have secured him to grace his private concert, for Cifaccio disdained to show his talent to any but princes. Lady Tuke had beguiled him into coming by telling him that her friend, Mr Pepys, was a great lover of music and had the best harpsichord in England, which, Evelyn recorded, "he touched to his voice rarely well". (Lady Tuke was careful to caution Samuel not to offer the great man a present as some had had the presumption to do.) Cifaccio was so impressed by this that he brought the incomparable Baptist★ along with him to play this noble instrument.[15]

Pepys delighted to be thus at ease with those he loved. Perhaps he was happiest of all when he could entertain James Houblon on a fish day to a dish of ling and a merry afternoon of good talk and banter, or spend a cool summer's evening with him on the

★ ". . . that excellent and stupendous artist." Evelyn, *Diary*, Jan. 28th, 1684.

river—"when we may despise the sun". The stately
pair loved to stroll under the trees of St James's or
drive together in Pepys's coach in Hyde Park. The
comradeship between these two—bureaucrat and
merchant, Tory and Whig, Englishman and
Huguenot—grew with the years. "If I hear not from
you by pennypost", wrote Houblon in one charm-
ing note, "I'll not fail you at your house at seven in
the evening tomorrow, when you shall dispose of
me as you please, as you always shall and of all that I
have." The whole Houblon family was included in
the friendship: in the summer of 1688, Samuel gave a
favourite riding pad to Wynne Houblon, the husband of his beloved Sarah. "I don't extremely wonder at the greatness of your noble present, 'tis so like
Mr Pepys", the gratified man replied. "But Sir, not
to detain you too long from your extraordinary
affairs, permit me to entreat you to consider a little
farther before you part with so good a servant as
your horse may be to you."[16]

Another friend, almost equally beloved, was Sir
Robert Southwell. From his Gloucestershire home,
King's Weston, he wrote often to his old colleague:
"we are here among the trees and sometimes joining
our heads to understand the useful things of this
life". One of his letters, just before Christmas 1687,
brought the sad news of the death of another friend,
the much admired Sir William Petty, whose writings, theological and economic, Pepys so carefully
enshrined in his collection.★ Death was already
growing busy among his circle of friends; good,

★ He did not, however, include Petty's solitary essay in verse; the
lines he wrote to his six-year-old daughter:

>   "My pretty Pusling and my daughter Ann
>   That shall be countess, if her pappa can.
>   If her pappa cannot, then I make no doubt
>   But my little Pusling will be content without."

kindly-faced Sir John Buckworth, his fellow fen-
man, went the same December, and in the next July
Sir Dennis Gauden, the Victualler, whose father had
given him his first pair of silver flagons nearly a
quarter of a century back.[17]

Presents still came for Pepys, though of a different
kind. Will Howe—"that pretty and sober fellow"
now grown into a colonial Judge—sent him sweet-
meats and refined sugar from Barbados, where he
was a councillor and a great man. Lady Wyborne
sent from Bombay a velvet carpet and her husband a
fine plain cane, a jasper antonia stone and fifteen
little birds for Pepys's aviary; the purser of the *Charles*
galley at Gibraltar a "present of sweet waters" com-
prising "two half chests of flourences, two boxes of
essences and six flasks of orange-flower water".
From Ireland came a gift of usquebaugh, and from
Jersey red-legged partridges and barrels of pickled
carp; "the only things", the donor, Sir Philip Car-
teret explained; "this poor island can afford which
are not in greater plenty in England", adding that
not all the birds and fish in the island would be
enough to do Pepys honour. He asked him to present a few of the former to the King if he thought
them worthy of his acceptance.[18]

★   ★   ★

Carp and partridges were not the only things Sir
Philip—kinsman to Pepys's old friend and patron,
the Navy Treasurer—sent him. In the letters that
accompanied them were answers to questions that
the Admiralty Secretary had put to him about the
naval and military strength of France: how Monsieur Vauban, the great engineer, had been visiting
all the harbours of Normandy and Brittany and
what vast works were being set in train at Granville.

It looked like a threat to the Channel Islands. News of much the same kind was reaching Pepys from other sources. For England's southern neighbour was dreaming of universal empire. Thoughtful men everywhere feared that her armies would soon be set in motion against Rhineland and Netherland and her new navies put to sea to challenge command of Mediterranean and Channel.[19]

But James II of England, unlike his subjects, had no fears of France. No sovereign, as Ranke said, was ever less concerned with the balance of power. For support in domestic crisis, should his bold projects miscarry, he looked for help to his Catholic cousin, King Louis. If a European conflagration was again to come—and all Lousis's motions made it imminent— the Crown of England was more likely to side with France than against her. Besides England had a naval and commercial rival of older standing than France, against whom King James had twice led her fleets and Pepys seven times set them to sea. To many older men, who then as now viewed the world through the eyes of their youth, the Dutch still seemed the natural foes of England. It was only the younger generation who could fully realise that what Holland had once been it would never be again,* and that it was with France that their country would have to reckon in the future.

A faithful servant of King James could be excused for regarding the Stadtholder of the United Provinces as a man to be watched and feared. For, though his nephew and son-in-law, he was the champion of all those who opposed the religious and

---

* In March 1687 Pepys received information from Amsterdam that since the last war the Dutch had lost almost their entire Baltic trade to England, and that they now sent only 80 ships to the Levant where before they had sent 200. *Rawl. MSS. A.* 189, f. 292.

political aims of the King of England. If there was to
be an alliance against France, William would be its
mainstay: if there was to be foreign support for the
political malcontents in Britain, William would be
behind them. Already Holland was sheltering rebels
like Locke and Burnet as in the past it had sheltered
Shaftesbury, Monmouth and Argyll. It was natural,
therefore, that the Secretary of the Admiralty should
keep a careful watch on its coasts and harbours,
though he also did so, as we have seen, on those of
France.[20]

There was no doubt that the Dutch were making
preparations. As early as March 1687 Pepys was
informed by the Marquis d'Albeville, King James's
Irish envoy at the Hague, that at Amsterdam the
butter-boxes, as the Dutch were popularly called, had
four lines of thirteen vessels each, all in good condition and ready to sail at two days' notice. Many of
them were ships of the line. The magazines and
stores were full and all the shipyards busy.[21]

They were busy in England too. Throughout the
year 1687 and the ensuing winter the Special Commission, its burden borne by Hewer, Deane and
Pepys—its "worn, unassisted Secretary", as he
afterwards described himself—went vigorously
ahead with its work. Already the end was in sight.
By the spring of 1688 the greater part of the battle
fleet, given up for lost three years before, had been
repaired. To maintain it in good order an additional
dry-dock was being built at Portsmouth capable of
receiving the largest ships of the line and measuring
250 by 68 feet with a depth of 24 feet 3 inches. New
storehouses were already built or rising in all the
dockyards, and the stores and magazines filling fast.
"Mr Pepys", wrote his neighbour, Lord Ailesbury,
"put the ships and docks in the greatest order
beyond what can be expressed." Another year and

the work of restoration would be complete. By the
Christmas of 1688 Pepys hoped to be able to make
the King a present of the finest fighting fleet England
had ever known.[22]

He was laying plans for the distant future too.
Among the State papers of the year 1791 is a letter
written at the instance of that formidable administrator, Sir Charles Middleton, afterwards Lord
Barham, referring to an important proposal for
improving the durability of ships which he had
found among the official correspondence of over a
century before. It appeared that in 1687 Mr Secretary Pepys, who had been beguiling his leisure hours
by reading Dr Plot's *Natural History of Staffordshire*,
had been struck by a passage describing the method
of felling timber in that remote county. This differed
from that in use in the royal forests of the south,
where the trees were cut in the spring as soon as the
sap was up and subsequently bark't as they lay pros-
trate. But it seemed that the wise men of Staffordshire from time immemorial had bark't their trees in
the spring and left them standing throughout the
summer to fell them in the late autumn when the
juices that bred worm and decay were no longer
active and the cut saplings able to endure as long as
the heart of the tree.

In reading this passage Pepys recalled that King
Charles I's *Sovereign of the Seas* had been built of
northern timbers, and that to this fact "that extra
degree of lastingness" observable in some of her
beams (for the ship was still in commission after half
a century's service) might be imputed. Accordingly
he got Dr Plot, who was a fellow member of the
Royal Society, to prepare a paper for the royal eye
on the most seasonable time for felling timber*—as

he did another on the corrosion of guns and the decay of cables and hawsers—the result of a visit paid by this ingenious philosopher to the Yards at Chatham. He then instructed the Commissioners of the Navy to take the first opportunity of experimenting on these lines. For by industry, method and constant endeavour it must be possible, Pepys held, to bring the Navy to such a state of perfection that it would surpass all others and be susceptible of no further improvement.[23]

Yet in the last resort the Navy like everything else that belonged to England was dependent on the King's policy. And by the end of 1687 it was clear that the royal hand on the helm was heading the ship of State towards the gathering storm.

Chapter IV
The Gathering Storm

"In power, as in most other things, the way for Princes to keep it, is not to grasp more than their arms can well hold."—Halifax, *The Trimmer*.

Pepys's plans, like other men's, were at the mercy of his fellow mortals' folly. Great events, moved by causes which he could not control, were about to sweep his schemes into dusty pigeon-holes and his name, for a while, into limbo. The opening of the year 1688, which was to bring his reform of the Navy to completion, saw Louis XIV pressing his cousin James to aid him in his European ambitions in return for the assurance of ultimate help from France if his own perilous projects in England went awry. Once again the joint enemy was to be Holland, whose destruction was to coincide with the establisment of toleration in England. It was to Holland that Pepys had just hopefully sent his younger and cleverer nephew, John Jackson, to complete his education.

Louis was on the verge of embroilment with the Dutch over the rather dubious affairs of his ally Denmark. He wanted James to use his fleet in conjunction with his own to prevent a junction of the Dutch and Swedish fleets against that country. This was a great deal more than James was prepared to do, for he knew that his own battle fleet was not yet ready for a naval war. Nor had he any desire to repeat the errors of 1672. The most he would agree to was to fit out a small squadron in the spring to

make a joint, though pacific demonstration with the
French fleet. This would serve as a warning to the
Dutch, who had angered him both by opposing
English commercial claims in the East Indies and by
delaying the return of certain English regiments
which he had lent his son-in-law. They were also
giving shelter to many of his own rebellious subjects, including Pepys's old adversary, William Harbord. [1]

In the routine of the Admiralty, therefore, a hint
of warlike preparations began to appear during the
opening weeks of 1688. Old ships were examined
for conversion into bomb vessels and the size of the
Channel Guard was slightly increased. Pepys, sub-
mitting the usual annual project, made provision for
a force of 4035 seamen. They were to be disposed in
one 3rd rate, nine frigates and three yachts in the
Channel, a guard-ship each at Portsmouth and
Sheerness, two frigates in the Channel Islands, eight
in the Straits, one in Ireland, two in Virginia and
three in the West Indies. The total did not include the
ships lent to the East India Company. At the same
time the Catholic Sir Roger Strickland was raised to
Herbert's vacant place as Rear-Admiral of England,
though to Pepys the new appointment can scarcely
have been much more welcome than the old.
Shortly afterwards orders were given to fit out
twenty ships for sea. [2]

These preparations were soon magnified in Holland, where they were quickly followed by retaliat-
ory and far more warlike measures. The Dutch bur-
ghers were seriously alarmed. For the first time
William of Orange saw a possibility of enlisting the
aid of his fearful and jealous countrymen in a crusade
of armed intervention in England to secure his
wife's inheritance. At that moment he learnt that
that inheritance was fatally threatened. The people

of England learnt it also. The Protestant succession to the throne, which had reconciled them to the present but temporary evil of a Catholic King, was in danger. The Queen was reported to be pregnant.[3]

It was William's chance and he knew it. Cold and unamiable, he had the essential element of greatness that seizes opportunity without flinching. If he could control England and turn her latent powers against France, he could straddle across Louis's march to world dominion. Beyond the waters of the North Sea the rough, boisterous, ruddy-faced people who had sent his grandfather to the scaffold and had twice exiled his father-in-law, were now looking to him as their only hope. Somehow, before Louis flung down the gauntlet to Europe and the armies of the great captains poured into the Netherlands, he must cross those waters.

In England a chill filled men's hearts. If a son was born to King James and lived, he would be brought up a Catholic and rule after his father. The Catholic prelates and the Jesuit Fathers who swarmed at Court, the papist lords who sat the Council Board, the papist officers who swaggered at the head of the regiments and companies of a standing army, would remain. Presently the talk of toleration would die away, what had happened in France would happen in England; religious liberty under a Catholic King would give place to priestly edicts, the jails of the inquisition and the shouts of Papist dragoons. The fires of Smithfield would be lit again.

This was the moment, while William's agent, Dyckvelt, was almost openly canvassing the malcontent magnates of England, that good King James chose to cross the *t*'s and dot the *i*'s of his religious policy. With a folly all his own he re-enacted his Declaration of Indulgence, suspending the penal laws and the oaths of admission to civil and military office, and commanded that it should be read in every Anglican pulpit. It was promulgated on April 27th; it was to be read on the last two Sundays of May and the first two of June. The pill of religious equality was to be forced down the throat of the Church of England once and for all. It was bitterly cold, with raging easterly winds prolonging winter throughout April. And all the while multitudes of flying French Huguenots, horror stricken and bereft of all they had, continued to pour into the country.[4]

The news from Holland grew more insistent: the ports were unusually busy. Even the King became suspicious. But with the facile optimism of an essentially weak man, he refused to let his mind dwell too much on the Dutch preparations. He gave orders, however, at the beginning of April that the Navy Office should prepare victuals for an extra thousand men against emergencies. Pepys himself saw to its execution. Yet on the day that the Declaration of Indulgence was promulgated the gravity of the news from Holland was such that he sent secret instructions to the acting Commander-in-Chief in the Downs written in his own hand. It looked to him, and for a moment his master too, as though the Dutch might be planning a sudden dive at his great ships at Chatham to rob him of all he had wrought so hard for during the past two years. They at all costs must be saved.[5]

Pepys acted with his usual energy and speed. On April 30th he instructed the Special Commissioners to hasten the despatch of the ships fitting out. On May 1st he sent them to Chatham to discuss with the chief officers of the Ordnance measures to secure the battle fleet. Finding the fortifications, which were the charge of the Ordnance Office, much neglected, they recommended that they should be at once repaired and a boom and chain got ready to close the

Medway at Upnor Castle. But they held that the most effective defence would be the immediate commissioning of all 3rd and 4th rates, manned by a force of 8000 men, to encounter the Dutch at sea.[6]

These resolutions Pepys laid next day before the King. They were received with little enthusiasm. To the royal mind, once more reassured by the false, beguiling Sunderland, too much alarm at Dutch preparations seemed to imply a distrust of his policy. After all they could scarcely be regarded as dangerous unless England herself were growing restive. This was exactly what James, protected as he was by God and the whole hierarchy of Heaven, was resolved not to believe. Besides, alarmist measures would be expensive and not only upset all the careful estimates which had been made for restoring and maintaining the Navy, but trench on other branches of the royal revenue. As it was the pay of the Yards was in arrears. There were many in the royal entourage of priests and backstair politicians who did not like Pepys and thought he served the King too well. They knew of better ways of spending his money than on ships and dockyards.[7]

James, however, did promise his old servant that he would himself visit Chatham in the following week and discuss with his principal officers of the Navy and Ordnance what might best be done to guard against accidents. On hearing the news Deane, always a little prone to extremes, became enthusiastic. "Happy the people of England", he wrote, "in a Prince so understanding matters of this nature as, of himself, to come to such resolutions as, in all human probability will be found the best and safest for securing his navy and justifying yourself hereafter should any accident happen thereto, which God forbid." Yet Pepys, though he would have been the last to admit it, may well have had his doubts.[8]

On the afternoon of Monday, May 7th, he and Hewer took coach for Chatham, with Samuel Atkins in attendance. For the next few days Atkins, probably at his chief's suggestion—for it was the kind of occasion in which Pepys, recalling the events of 1667, saw the need of vindicatory evidence—kept a diary. "We set out after 3", he wrote, "and arrived at Chatham Dock by 8, nothing passing that evening but walking about the Yard." The Navy Commissioners had already preceded them there.

Next morning at Sir Phineas Pett's house Pepys, formally presiding, asked Deane to explain the position to the rest of the Commissioners. It was their duty, they were informed, to secure the great ships in Chatham harbour and Gillingham Reach, but to remember that their sovereign did not wish to incur the expense of setting them to sea, since he did not believe the Dutch to have any hostile intent, "it being not their interest to exasperate either him or the people of England". While this official view of the situation was being debated, word was brought that his Majesty had arrived at Strood and was just taking barge for the Dockyard. After requesting Pepys, therefore, to open its proceedings in the royal presence, the meeting adjourned to dine while it still had the chance. As the recording Atkins put it, "we all went to the Hill House to eat a bit to be ready to wait on the King".

At one o'clock James landed at the Dockyard gate and at once went to Sir Phineas Pett's house. Here he mounted his horse and inspected a regiment of infantry which had been drawn up along the brick wall at the back. After viewing the new wharves and storehouses, he returned to the house, where, "hav-

ing eaten a bit standing and drunk a glass of wine",★
he repaired to the Banqueting House in the garden.
In these *alfresco* surroundings Pepys, in the presence
of the Prince of Denmark, Lord Dartmouth,
Deane, Berry, Tippetts, Hewer, Haddock, Booth,
Sotherne and Pett, reported the discussions of the
morning. But it proved too late to come to any
resolution that day, and when Pepys had finished his
speech, the King left to inspect the new batteries
down the river and spend the night in his yacht.

On the following day, Wednesday the 9th, the
King went over the yards and ships. He also
examined the famous New England tree, thirty-
nine inches in diameter, which was being made into a
mainmast for the *Royal Sovereign*. Afterwards in the
Banqueting House in Pett's garden, he announced
his decision to the assembled company, now
increased by the arrival of Sir Roger Strickland and
the young Duke of Grafton. He proposed to fit out
two more 3rd rates only and three 4th rates, to be
manned for economy's sake with the lowest complement of men practical. The remainder of the 3rd
rates would be moved above Upnor Castle. The 1st
and 2nd rates were to stay where they were.

His Majesty having made known these frugal
resolutions, nothing remained but to discuss the best
way of preserving the great ships in the circumstances. It was resolved to sheathe them with three or
four strakes of milled lead between wind and water,
the King pointing out that a bullet might pierce but
could not splinter such a protection. Deane stressed
the importance of guarding against any decay of
their timbers through lack of air. Pepys took the
opportunity to mention the business of flags, which

★ To save the Resident Commissioner expense he had thoughtfully
decided to take his meals on board his own yacht. *Pepysian MSS.,
Adm. Letters* xiv, 156–7.

was then occupying a good deal of his thoughts, and read "very distinctly over the table" (one suspects, looking straight at Strickland) a paper he had prepared on the subject. His Majesty graciously remarked that it would increase the honour of Admirals when it was clearly known who was Vice-Admiral and who Rear-Admiral. After that Pepys went on to speak about naval salutes and the extravagance they occasioned in wasting powder and needless drinking of healths, but was finally stopped by the King who remarked that it was late and adjourned further discussion to "a more solemn meeting in London". For news had reached him that the pregnant Queen had been taken ill.[9]

★   ★   ★

After the King's immediate departure for London, Pepys, Deane, and Hewer went down to Gillingham Reach to view the great ships. Here on board the *Britannia*, the finest of all the many ships they had given the Navy, they sat down to a treat of cold meats and a bowl of punch. Then they viewed Gillingham Fort, where they found only one man on duty and the state of the platforms and gun-carriages such, "as is better to be silent than to say anything as to their condition". Afterwards they walked back to Chatham through the woods. There was a touch of idyll in it—the three old friends, mirrored in Atkins's laconic journal, going home together in the calm of that May evening, their work, though they knew it not, almost done.[10]

It is the last time we shall see Pepys in his glory, before his world breaks in storm. His royal master's word was still law and his realm inviolate, and he the chosen and unchallenged ruler of the naval administration. At York Buildings all mankind stood before

him cap in hand. Even the King's son, Mr Fitz-
James,★ learning his trade as seaman with Captain
Lloyd of the *Sedgemoor* at distant Gibraltar, com-
plimented him with a gift. It was to Pepys that the
ambitious came when that spring Sir John Godwin's
death left a Naval Commissionership to be filled:
among others Sir Edward Dering, recalling that he
was still owed £8000 by the government for ancient
contracts, and Captain Vittles, "with moderate
hopes of having discharged myself in my trust
hitherto with a strict integrity and duty". The Service was learning at last to speak Pepys's language.[11]

It had reason to. His orders held. No longer could
a captain hope to trade for months at a stretch at the
King's expense: the jealous eye of the Admiralty
followed him in all places. Captain Killigrew of the
Dragon, commanding the squadron operating
against Sallee in Morocco, must have wondered that
the little autocrat of York Buildings should know
every movement of his ships. A commander who
dared to poke his nose unauthorised into Cadiz or
Lisbon was quickly apprised of his crime; the barren
rock of Gibraltar was the only harbour now allowed
to the captains of the once envied Straits squadron.
The naval age of gold had given place to one of iron.

An officer could not even drink like a gentleman;
when he did so he was tried by court-martial. "I did
believe myself", wrote one gallant captain who had
so offended, "(and have been taken notice of by
persons that inhabit both on shore and sea) to have
lived a very retired life, and sometimes in two
months together never was in a public house, and
then upon some occasion extraordinary. Yet I fall
into faults, although the original of this was the

★ Younger brother of the Duke of Berwick. *Pepysian MSS., Adm.
Letters* xiv, 16.

King's service (to my expense). If being a true penitent for my fault can make any atonement with his
Majesty for me, I am sure I am. And to demonstrate
that I am so, I shall avoid all manner of society where
wine, punch or other liquor may give cause of suspicion that a man may be in error of having drunk too
much. For I am resolved as long as I am in his
Majesty's service to avoid all sorts of strong drink,
either in public or private, for his Majesty's frown to
me is death."* He probably meant Mr Secretary
Pepys's. [12]

If Pepys could frown, he could also bless. The
widow and child of Captain Fowler, dead in the
performance of his duty, felt the effects of his kindness when they received a gratuity from the Crown
together with an additional £10 contributed out of
the Secretary of the Admiralty's own purse. A host
of poor and needy folk besieged York Buildings
with letters and more personal solicitations. Those
who were prepared to earn their living by honest
work, however humble, knew that Pepys would be
their friend. Some of them were his own kinsmen,
like young Samuel St Michel, whom he presented to
the King and for whom he secured a berth in a ship
of the line. But though he was his nephew and
godson, the boy had first to establish his worth by
serving a sixteen months' apprenticeship in navigation in the *Fubbs* yacht. Among other applicants
were two Pepyses who, though not of his kin, presumed on their names to ask his favour; proving
deserving of it, both received it. [13]

The young as we have seen were always sure of
his affectionate if severe interest. That July he got
Signor Verrio's son a place as volunteer on board the

* Capt. Sir William Jennens to S. P., Feb. 26th, 1688. *Rawl. MSS.
A.* 186, f. 8. See also *Pepysian MSS., Adm. Letters* xiv, 27, 37, 54, 93,
121.

Bonadventure; the same good offices were at the disposal of many other hopeful youths. He knew that
they could be formed for his stern, beneficent purposes and England's if the Service could have the
moulding of them while they were still pliable.
There were occasions, though, when he thought
them too young. "In friendship to you," he wrote to
an old acquaintance who had asked for a volunteer's
place for a son, "I can't omit to observe some
apprehension I have that the King will think 12
years, which you say is his age, as much too early for
a child to set out to sea as anything above 16 too
much." The King's thoughts, it should be remembered, were a time-honoured euphemism by which
Pepys indicated his own.[14]

*   *   *

That the King had other thoughts which were not
those of Pepys or of any other sound-headed Englishman was a misfortune that could not be helped. For
with his eyes shut to all that was happening both in
his own realm and the world outside, and his ears
closed to every counsel but that of the Palace priests,
that unhappy prince was rushing headlong to disaster. All his hopes were now set on securing the
election of a new Parliament in which the Cavalier
and Anglican party which had once been his mainstay should have no part. In every Corporation
Tories were being expelled and Dissenters and Papists put in their places. Judges, Lord Lieutenants and
the Archbishops were instructed to interrogate their
inferiors as to their willingness to comply with the
royal wishes at the forthcoming election. Those
who refused were to be punished.[15]

Unlike most of his countrymen Pepys had never
felt fear or dislike of the King's desire for religious

toleration. He did not even quarrel with his claim to suspend the Penal Laws. "Very fit it is", he wrote of his sovereign's breach of one of his own sacred regulations for the Service, "that the King should be at liberty to dispense with as well as to make his own rules." Yet he could not fail to feel alarmed at the way in which the most deep-rooted popular prejudices were being disregarded and the affections of the most loyal subjects recklessly alienated. At the end of March worthy Mr Loton, Chaplain of the Ordinary at Chatham, was threatened with summary dismissal because he had not shown himself sufficiently active in advocating the repeal of the Test Act and penal laws. John Loton, who had held his post with distinction for over a quarter of a century, was an old and honoured friend; many years before Pepys had presented him with a stone tablet of the Commandments for his church. He now intervened on his behalf, vouching for his loyalty and guaranteeing that, whatever his private views, Loton would support the royal candidate at Chatham in the event of a parliamentary election. But the order to read the Declaration of Indulgence in the pulpit was too much for Loton's overstrained conscience, as for many another clergyman's. His refusal to do so placed it beyond Pepys's power to help him further. Loton explained to him that it was founded on considerations that admitted of no further compromise. "I presume Mr Crewe will be glad of this opportunity to make a second attempt on the Navy, and I cannot reasonably expect your Honour's protection. God's will be done! I must choose suffering rather than sin, and will, by the grace of God, always walk by this rule; that popularity shall never corrupt my loyalty nor loyalty my conscience. I will first give to God the things that are God's, and then to Caesar the things that are

Caesar's." A little later, and in a more worldly but less popular cause, Pepys was to prove that the same rule was his.[16]

Clergymen far more important than Mr Loton found the royal instructions to read the Declaration too much for their consciences. The reading was ordered to take place on Sundays, May 20th and 27th in London and Westminster, and June 3rd and 10th in the country. It was almost everywhere disregarded. The lead in disobedience was given by the Bishops, formerly the most loyal of the King's subjects. On Friday the 18th of May seven, including Archbishop Sancroft and Pepys's friend, Dr Ken, now Bishop of Bath and Wells, met in Lambeth Palace and drew up a petition to the King begging him to withdraw his orders, since obedience to them must involve a breach of the Law. This document, signed by all, was taken the same evening by six of them to the Palace and presented to the indignant monarch, who could see in it nothing but downright mutiny. His view of it was confirmed by the simultaneous appearance of the offending petition in print. That same night it was sold in the streets and thrown broadcast on coffee-house tables. James felt, and not without justification, that the petition, so damaging to his credit and prerogative, was intended not so much for his own eyes as for those of his subjects.[17]

It was resolved therefore to prosecute the seven signatory Bishops for publishing a seditious libel. On the 8th of June they were summoned to the Council Chamber. Pepys was with the Lords of the Council who sat at that historic board. The proceedings were conducted by the King and Lord Chancellor Jeffreys. After many minutes of angry questioning the Archbishop and his colleagues admitted their signatures. They were then informed that a criminal

information would be exhibited against them in the
Court of King's Bench. When, like the true and
obstinate Englishmen that they were, they refused
to enter into recognisances, they were committed to
the Tower. Among those who were present at the
Council was Father Petre, the King's Confessor, the
most hated man in the kingdom. All down the river,
in Macaulay's classic phrase, from Whitehall to
London Bridge, the barge that bore the Bishops to
their gentle martyrdom passed between lines of
boats, while every roof was crowded with a multitude of sympathetic watchers.

The Law, in the hands of Jeffreys and the Judges,
had broken the power of English provincial self-
government; it would now, the King hoped, shatter
the resistance of the Church. Behind it lay the threat
of the army, encamped in its thousands on Hounslow Heath, armed with terrible and as yet untried
engines of destruction and reinforced daily by drafts
of what seemed to the English vile papist savages
from the bogs of Ireland. From all over the country
came tales, wildly exaggerated, of their excesses in
private houses or on the highway. The nation was
ready to believe any rumour against those who possessed the three supremely unpopular attributes of
being at once Irish, Catholics and soldiers. Nor
could all the King's careful orders for the strict
maintenance of military discipline reassure an
alarmed and outraged opinion.[18]

Pepys, playing his small part in this imbroglio,
appeared for a moment in the full limelight of
national publicity.* On June 29th the Bishops were
brought to trial in Westminster Hall. The Hall was

* So also did Will Hewer whose name appeared on the panel of the
Jury. *Ellis Correspondence* II, 2. But though his name did so, Hewer
himself did not. *Verney Memoirs* (1925) II, 457. Possibly Pepys got him
excused on the plea of naval urgency.

packed with the English aristocracy, now united by
the jealous national religion against their sovereign
and resolved to see their champions set free. Outside
a vast and noisy crowd waited in its turbulent
strength. It was like some great sporting contest
staged before the excited gaze of a nation.

From the first the government was seen to be
struggling against a force beyond its control, like
men in some frail skiff trying to weather an overwhelming sea. The Lord Chief Justice and his three
brethren, dependent servants of the Crown as they
were, made no pretence of their fearful deference to
the popular clamour. The Attorney- and Solicitor-
Generals spent many hours attempting to prove the
elementary and universally accepted facts of publication and delivery, and were forced, amid shouts of
laughter from the contemptuous nobility, to call official after official to prove what everybody in England knew. All the great men of the Bar were briefed
for the Bishops, led by Pepys's old chamber-fellow
of Cambridge days, Sir Robert Sawyer, the ex-
Attorney-General. They included a former Chief
Justice of the King's Bench, the same Pemberton
who had been so unsympathetic when Deane and
Pepys had appeared before him at the time of the
so-called Popish Plot of 1648–9. Against them the
newly appointed Attorney-General, Sir Thomas
Powis, and the Solicitor-General—the renegade
Whig, Sir William Williams—seemed men of straw.

To prove publication of the Bishops' petition in
Middlesex, the chief officials who had been present
at the Council meeting were called. The fantastic
legal quibble seemed likely to non-suit the Crown
even before the real case had begun to be argued.
For, though the Bishops' admission of their signatures was shown, publication in Middlesex was at
first made to depend on the production of a witness

able to swear that he had seen the original delivery of the petition. As no one had been present but the King himself, who could not be called, this was impossible. The Crown's only chance was to get someone who had attended the Council meeting to testify that on that occasion the Bishops had admitted that the petition before the Board was that which they had delivered to the King.

The three Clerks of the Council, Blathwayt, Bridgeman and Sir John Nicholas, were called in vain. None of them could recall an admission which had never been made for the simple reason that it had not been doubted for a moment by anyone. After the triumphant shout that followed the Crown's third failure, the Solicitor-General lost his temper and cried out, "Here's a wonderful great rejoicing that truth cannot prevail." Then, recovering himself, he added, "There's Mr Pepys, we'll examine him."

The little man, all straightforward dignity, was duly sworn. The Lord Chief Justice took personal charge of him, remarking, "Come, I'll ask the questions. Were you at the Council Board when my Lords the Bishops were committed?"

Mr Pepys. Yes, I was.

L.C.J. What were the questions that were asked either by the King or by my Lord Chancellor?

Mr Pepys. My Lord, I would remember as well as I could the very words; and the very words of the question were, I think, *My Lords, do you own this paper?* I do not remember anything was spoken about the delivering, but I believe it was understood by everybody at the table that that was the paper that they had delivered.

L.C.J. Well, have you done now? (The question was directed to the Attorney-General.) But to satisfy you I'll ask this question. Was this question asked, Was this the paper you delivered to the King?

Mr Pepys. No, my Lord.

Attorney-General. Pray, sir, do you remember whether the King himself asked the question?

Mr Pepys. You mean, I suppose, Mr Attorney, that these were the words, or something that imported their delivering it to the King.

Attorney-General. Yes, Sir.

Mr Pepys. Truly, I remember nothing of that.

Solicitor-General. Did you observe any discourse concerning their delivery of it to the King?

Mr Pepys. Indeed, Mr Solicitor, I did not.*

Unlike the other witnesses, Pepys made no attempt to evade the simple truth to win the good will of either King or nation. But like them he had to run the gauntlet of the mob as he came and went.[19]

Next morning, amid thunderous cheering, volleys of gunpowder and pealing bells, the excited populace took the acquitted Bishops to themselves. That night the Pope was burnt in effigy in the streets and many Catholics assaulted. On the same day the chiefs of the proud aristocracy who for the next century and a half were to rule England despatched to William of Orange, with whom they had long been in secret correspondence, their formal invitation to invade England at the head of a Dutch army. It was carried by the late Rear-Admiral of the kingdom, Arthur Herbert, disguised as a common seaman. Beneath the surface of national life revolution had begun.[20]

★   ★   ★

For nothing but a revolution could now do the business of Protestant England. William had no longer even the shadow of a right to intervene in his

* Cobbett and Howell, *State Trials* XII, 350, and F. Hargrave, *State Trials* IV, 363.

father-in-law's kingdom. Three weeks earlier his
wife had ceased to be heir presumptive to the throne.
In the early hours of Sunday, June 10th, a month
before her time, the Queen had given birth to a male
child. Pepys, announcing the great news to Sir
Roger Strickland shortly after two that morning,
wrote of the newcomer as being "in all the circumstances of health, full growth, and whatever may
encourage us to expect his long life as well as pray
for it". Less loyal souls felt differently. The fertility
of Mary of Modena had entailed a Catholic dynasty
on a militant Protestant nation. The Popish Terror
of a decade before was come again.

Fear and lies as ever went hand in hand. Though
the natal chamber of St James's had been crowded
with a numerous concourse of both sexes, many of
them were Papists, and few of those, who by virtue
of their constitutional station should have attended,
were present. The Archbishop of Canterbury was in
the Tower, the Princess Anne at Bath, the Princess
Mary in Holland, and most of the great Protestant
Lords in disgrace. It was at once bruited abroad, and
by some of the highest in the land, that the unwanted
child had entered the Palace in a warming pan. The
bawdy lie was soon the jest of every tavern and
coffee-house. The official celebrations of the birth,
though followed with interest in Rome, were
received by the English with little enthusiasm. At
Gloucester the Mayor was forced to commit the
churchwardens because they would not ring the
bells.[21]

But the Navy was still a law to itself. Pepys himself drafted the order for celebrating the Prince's
birth in the fleet. Here at least, whatever the attitude
of the fine gentlemen commanders, the personal
loyalty of the tarpaulins to their former Admiral
made the news sure of a welcome. Among the ships

of war in the Downs there was probably more goodwill to the Crown than anywhere else in the kingdom: even the army at Hounslow cheered the acquittal of the Bishops.[22]

The last days of May and the first of June, bringing new rumours of fleet movements in Holland, witnessed a further concentration of 4th and 5th rates in the Downs. On June 14th Strickland was reported to be in command of "more than 20 nimble frigates and fireships well appointed and daily expected to be joined by others of yet greater force from the River of Thames". To fit them out Pepys and Deane worked the clock round. "I am really weary," wrote the latter from Chatham on June 1st, "it being now 12 at night, having not been in bed . . . above five in twenty-four hours since my departure. Yet I shall think it no trouble if it content my great Master; otherwise no wealth would tempt a man to deal with so many vexations from ignorance, negligence and sloth." Other vessels were getting ready at Portsmouth; it was said that there would soon be 6500 sailors in pay, more than double the normal peacetime complement. In the meantime Strickland was ordered to shadow the Dutch fleet should it put to sea. On the 18th Pepys instructed him to send out relays of "small nimble frigates" in pairs to cruise "about the back of the Goodwin" and off Orfordness. They were "to speak with all ships passing those ways, and to gain what intelligence they could of the number, force and motion of the ships of any foreign Prince or State".[23]

But the battle fleet—the three score or so of great ships that in the last resort would have to do the King's business—remained in harbour. The men who should have manned them were scattered through the merchant marine, in foreign service or thronging the seaport steps and waterways where

the effects of the Service's discipline and tradition
never touched them and where they were subject to
all the impressions of popular rumour and opinion.
Herein lay the supreme lesson of seventeenth-
century naval history, that the silent pressure of sea
power could only be exercised when the Grand Fleet
was in being. Till a revolution in national finance
and opinion should make that possible, permanent
naval supremacy there could be none. Yet all else
requisite for that supremacy was already achieved.
The revolution alone was needed.

For, thanks to Pepys, Deane and Hewer, the work
of the Special Commission was almost finished. The
Navy was now sustained by discipline, wise rules
for every occasion and a growing tradition of service. And, lying silent at their moorings, were
fifty-nine ships of the line of battle, all but a dozen or
so of them with their repairs completed and ready to
be commissioned whenever order should be given
and men be found to man them. By June 20th Pepys
was able to present a plan, already discussed in the
spring with his royal master and Lord Godolphin,
for restoring the Navy to its old constitution of
Principal Officers and Commissioners, leaving the
invaluable Sir Anthony Deane as Inspector-General
of Works and Stores, and William Hewer of Accounts. It was resolved that the Special Commission, its purpose accomplished, should be dissolved before the end of the year.[24]

Meanwhile on the continent of Europe, as in England, the clouds grew more lowering. King Louis and
the Emperor were marching to war. In Rhineland
and Flanders, German and Frenchman, Protestant
and Catholic would soon be embattled in a conflict
that threatened to end in the universal hegemony of
the Lilies. The Dutch, knowing that they soon must
be embroiled and dreading an alliance between Eng-

land and France which James refused either to own or deny, were uniting behind their Stadtholder in his daring project of intervention. In England jealousy of the French and a deep-seated belief that the coming struggle would decide the future of Protestantism in the world were also drawing men nearer to Orange and further from the pro-French affinities of their King. The birth of the Prince of Wales and the invitation of the aristocratic chiefs in England decided William. "*Nunc aut nunquam*", now or never, he is said to have murmured. He was aware that his time had come.[25]

The strengthening of the English Channel Guard in June, itself the result of warlike movements in Holland, was attended by still greater activities on the part of the Dutch. But, faced by an increasingly complex situation, James only vacillated. At one moment he accepted King Louis's offer of a French fleet to co-operate with his own against the invaders; a few days later, fortified by official denials from the Dutch ambassador, he dismissed William's project as unthinkable and refused his cousin's offer with pride. The erratic movements of his ships indicated the changes in the royal mind. On the 2nd of July Strickland was ordered to Solebay. A few days later he was recalled to the Buoy of the Nore. On the 18th the King—according to some accounts to appease an incipient mutiny caused by the saying of mass on the flagship*—visited the fleet and took pains to ingratiate himself with the sailors, "behaving with great affability and taking notice of every particular officer". He did not know that certain of the gentlemen commanders, through the agency of Pepys's

---

* . . . "The true cause was to appease the seamen, who were ready to mutiny upon occasion of some sea captains using mass openly on board." (*Reresby*, 503.) There is no confirmation of this in Pepys's papers.

old enemy, Edward Russell, were already in secret
communication with William. On the 21st Strickland was again ordered to sea.[26]

About the same time came news of the loss of an
English admiral, who was neither a papist like
Strickland nor a traitor like Herbert or Russell,
though an attempt had been made about this time to
seduce him from his allegiance. Narbrough's expedition to the West Indies in search of treasure had
ended in sickness and death. Characteristically,
though stricken down by fever, he had refused to
sail for home until he had recovered a lost anchor.
Samuel Jackson, serving aboard his ship, described
the event in a letter of July 20th to his uncle Pepys.
The young man was plainly touched by his
Admiral's tragic end in that far place after his work
was done—"as though fate", he wrote, "had
decreed him to lie there". So was Pepys, who
mourned him, "not for private friendship's sake
only, (tho' that be very great) but for the sake of the
King and his Service, in which (without wrong to
anybody) I do not think there does survive one
superior, if any one equal (all qualifications considered), to Sir John Narbrough".*[27]

Narbrough's death was a real blow to the Navy,
which in the coming months was to have need of a
man of his resolution and experience in sea command. On the very day that the news of his death
reached London two of the most distinguished
officers of the Service, Sir John Berry and Sir William Booth, became involved in a most unseemly
broil while paying the Yard at Chatham. Pepys was
abroad with his cousin, Dr Gale, taking his Saturday
evening's recreation, when Berry in a sad heat
arrived at York Buildings to speak with him. Find-

* S. P. to Capt. Smith of the *Falcon*, July 19th, 1688. *Pepysian
MSS., Adm. Letters* XIV, 278.

ing him out he unwisely carried his angry tale to the
King, who ordered the Admiralty Secretary to make
an official investigation of the whole affair.

Pepys's task was the more unwelcome since both
Admirals were his personal friends. According to
Berry, Booth had pricked as absent from duty a
valued purser, on a false charge of Captain Vittles's
clerk—one "little better than a madman". When he
protested, he had been treated "with very scurrilous
language" before the clerks. Booth denied this. It
was, however, quite certain that the incident had not
ended before one Admiral had called the other a
"lump of flesh". At this Berry, who was notoriously
stout, had shouted, "Get out of the room, get out of
the room", and had finally left it himself in a fury,
threatening to appeal to the King.

Booth's version of course was different. He had
been presiding at the pay since seven in the
morning—without so much as a break for
dinner—when at four in the afternoon Berry, who
should have been there all the while, stumped into
the room and, turning his back on him, proceeded
without a word of apology or explanation to enquire
what was the matter with his purser. And, on being
informed, he had cried out that that was all nonsense
for he was an honest fellow, and without more ado
had directed the clerks to pay him. At which "extraordinary proceeding of Sir John Berry", Booth
declared, "I must confess I was provoked to an
unusual degree of passion and did flatly oppose Sir
John Berry, . . . peremptorily insisting (by virtue of
the place I was then in) upon the payment of the
mulct . . . I finally broke off the dispute and according to my duty in that place caused the defalcation to
be made. . . . Which done, and that being all which
Sir John Berry seemed concerned for, he withdrew,
leaving me to prosecute the remainder of the King's

business alone, which I did with the same quiet and satisfaction to all wherewith I had before done it." Booth admitted, however, that he had been "transported to such a degree of passion" that he had told his fellow admiral to hold his tongue. In the circumstances, Pepys, who took shorthand notes of the evidence, was forced to recommend that both officers should be temporarily relieved from duty.[28]

★   ★   ★

For a few weeks in the second half of the summer of 1688 there was a marked slackening in the tempo of public affairs, and warlike preparations were suspended. The infatuated King, who through all the alarms of the year had continued to correspond amicably with his son-in-law, again refused to believe the existence of the treacherous project now openly whispered in every coffee-house and market place. Instead he turned his gaze from the armaments of his neighbours to the morals of his subjects. A proclamation directed as much against the rich as the poor—a particularly injudicious exercise of tyrannical power—was issued against debauchery.★ The nation was to be made worthy of the divine blessing so recently and, as it seemed to James miraculously, vouchsafed it. On July 17th a magnificent celebration of fireworks was held on the Thames before a concourse of 100,000 spectators in honour of the Prince of Wales and his entry into a world which in seventy-seven rather weary years was to offer him few such courtesies.[29]

By the end of the month Strickland's fleet was

★ "It curbs even our loose houses and regulates our very sleeping; and the good wives are well-wishers to it, for that it obliges men and masters to keep good hours and go to bed betimes." *Ellis Correspondence* II, 14.

back in the Downs. On August 1st Pepys under orders from the Palace wrote that his sovereign would not require any greater force at sea that year. Money was tight, and there was some difficulty about paying the Yards. At Chatham Deane was industriously putting the finishing touches to the work of the Special Commission: "I can truly say", he wrote to Pepys, "that I never took more pains nor was more zealous to make a good issue than in this journey in all my life, and hope it will end well, it seeming a pleasure to rid the business offhand."[30]

It almost seemed at that hour as though the chief remaining naval business of the year would be to wind up the Commission, re-appoint old Sir Richard Haddock to the revived Comptrollership of the Navy and choose a new Victualling Comptroller in his place. Phineas Bowles, the former Storekeeper at Tangier, was seeking the post: his family, he explained, was a large and chargeable one, and, Pepys, on his frequent journeys between London and Windsor, was much solicited by this needy official. Sir William Warren was also after the job. The great timber merchant, who had first wooed Pepys with a silver dish and a cup a quarter of a century back, had now, what with "misfortune and losses by fires ashore and ships at sea", lost almost his entire estate. "Yet, Sir," as assured his ancient friend, "my spirits are not so low, nor my condition so bad, as to seek a place for the salary's sake. I have been bred in business at home and abroad, and always very painfully industrious therein for near 40 years. But now since my late misfortune by fire (which in a few hours consumed all I had) I am for want of business become as a fish out of water. And I should be the veriest fool in nature if I expected ease and rest in the place I offer at, having seen, for about 20 years together, your unwearied diligence day by day (and

most part of the night also) in all your stations, and
all under you, together with those you have chosen
out, as Sir Anthony Deane, Mr Hewer, Mr Hayter,
etc. who I hear have come into their employ as well
by your kindness as their own great merit."*[31]

But if the opening days of August 1688 seemed to
promise quiet, it was a promise quickly belied. The
hush was one of expectancy only, for the curtain was
ready to rise on the drama which had been preparing
for so long. All the protagonists were pursuing their
respective plans, and the clash between them could
no longer be delayed. Abroad Louis was preparing
to extend his boundaries. Europe was arming to
resist him, and William of Orange assembling his
ships and troops for his dash on England while there
was still time. If he were to wait till Louis turned his
legions towards Holland, he must needs wait for
ever. Meanwhile the Dutch ambassador continued
to deceive James, and James to deceive himself as to
his son-in-law's intentions.[32]

In England men waited breathlessly. All who had
any stake in the Protestant Reformation—the nobles
and gentry who held abbey lands, the clergy of the
threatened Established Church, the populace who
hated Rome—looked to William. The King looked
as resolutely away and pinned all his hopes on the
general election for which he had so long prepared
and which, he was assured, would secure him what
he so ardently desired—an anti-Anglican Parliament
to remove the stigma of the penal laws from the
statute book.[33]

Between these contending forces stood Pepys,
completing the last touches of his work of restoring,
consolidating and disciplining the Navy. Soon he
was to feel their shock and be drawn into the whirl-

* Sir W. Warren to S. P., Aug. 20th, 1688. *Rawl. MSS. A.* 179,
f. 68. See also *Rawl. MSS. A.* 189, ff. 100–1.

wind. In the second week of August he had a fore-
taste of what was to come, for Deane received warning from Harwich that there was a conspiracy
among their constituents to supplant them at the last
moment by others because they were believed to
have promised to vote for the repeal of the Test Act.
After all Pepys had done for Harwich, this was a
bitter pill to swallow.[34]

There was a worse shock in store, both for him and
his master. On August 16th, he left London at six in
the morning to attend the King at Windsor. That
day an account, too alarming to be ignored, arrived
from the English agent at the Hague of William's
preparations—of 23 ships of war at Amsterdam
already rigged with topmasts, 11 more at Helvoetsluys fitting out with all possible speed, and others in
the same advanced state of preparation elsewhere—
in all 90 ships, great and small. Pepys received
confirmation of this news from Captain Faseby and
from his old tutor, Joseph Hill, who in a letter
written from Rotterdam on August 19th, dwelt on
two mysteries, Mr Newton's *Principia*, "which is
understood by few but deservedly admired by all
that understand it", and the activity of the Dutch
fleet, whose purport seemed far more intelligible to
the lay mind.[35]

Chapter V
Invasion

"O, why does he stay so long behind?
Ho! by my shoul, 'tis a Protestant wind."
                              Lord Wharton, *Lilliburlero.*

The Admiralty could disregard the preparations on the other side of the North Sea no longer. On the night of August 17th Pepys countermanded the orders, issued in a calmer hour, for the fleet to sail westwards, and instructed Strickland to remain in the Downs "in the best readiness that may be for the execution of any orders". Three days later all leave was stopped and partial mobilisation ordered. All available frigates were to be concentrated in the Downs, six ships of the line fitted out for sea at once, and the 5th rates in harbour converted into fireships. All, as Pepys put it, was "to be dispatched as for life and death". Smacks were hastened down the river for scouting, frigates ordered to cruise off Orfordness and the Goodwins, and the *Mary* yacht sent scudding over to Holland to find the whereabout of the Dutch fleet.[1]

Pepys, dictating letters in the office at midnight, sitting with the King in Cabinet or hurrying between London and Windsor, was the nerve centre of the naval mobilisation. He was once more performing the task he had first essayed a quarter of a century before and had learnt to do better than anyone else in the world. By his side, as permanent chief of his London office, was Samuel Atkins, who during the Popish terror once had faced death for his sake.

103

Down the river his long-tried aides, Deane and Hewer, first chosen by him in the far days of his administrative youth, were doing all that masters of their profession could do. The latter, writing to him from the Admiralty at midnight on the 23rd, described how he had left Deane at Chatham at eight the previous evening, reaching town at four in the morning, and had since been drafting orders all day long for getting out the ships, paying a flying visit in the afternoon to Woolwich with Balty St Michel to hasten on the work there.

To Pepys it must have seemed as though all the doubts of the past twelve months had been suddenly resolved. Now that actual invasion was threatened there could no longer be any question of divided loyalties. His master was in danger and needed the services of all his subjects, "it being", he told a colleague, "the time in our whole lives wherein the same can be of most use and importance to him". It never even occurred to his simple loyalty that it would be possible to fail that test.[2]

Not every Englishman possessed his single-hearted faith. Many saw in William's threat a hope of deliverance; most did not know what to think. One well-informed and communicative gentleman, not altogether misreading his age and his fellow men, went so far as to disbelieve the whole story, asserting that the rumours of invasion were put abroad by the Army Secretary in order to pocket the fines of officers who ignored their recall from leave.[3]

Though even as late as mid-September James, still overpersuaded by Sunderland and the lying assurances of his son-in-law and the Dutch ambassador, could not bring himself to believe that William would dare to land at such a season, and though it was the fashion among the courtiers to make fun of such anxious patriots as Pepys, the possibility of invasion was at last beginning to be taken seriously. On Sunday, August 26th, an important conference was held in the royal closet at Windsor. In addition to the King and Mr Pepys, there were present Lord Dartmouth, Sir John Berry, Captain John Clements and three Elder Brethren of Trinity House, all experienced seamen. It was resolved to reject Sir Roger Strickland's advice to base his squadron on the Gunfleet on the grounds that it was an ill Road at such a season and that, if the wind should hang easterly, he would only be driven up the river by the Dutch. Instead he was to leave the Downs at the first opportunity and place himself between the North Sand Head and the Kentish Knock, there to continue under sail by day and to anchor by night. Should the Dutch slip by him down the Channel, he was to follow them as far as the Scillies and, at any attempt to land, "to proceed hostilely upon them". Should they bend their course into the Thames he was to follow them there also, endeavouring to get the wind of them. Only in the event of a westerly wind was he to return to the Downs.[4]

During the closing weeks of August and the first three of September mobilisation went forward by cululative steps, as the fears of the Ciyrt grew, waned and grew again. Down by the waterside and on Tower Hill the drums beat for volunteers, and at the ports the carpenters broke the Sabbath with hammering, and the press-gangs waited for incoming merchant ships. "The King our master", wrote Pepys on September 3rd to the Commander-in-Chief at Gibraltar, "has now for about fourteen or twenty days been greatly awakened, and indeed little less than surprised by a sudden and most extraordinary preparation in Holland for some immediate enterprise at sea by an endeavour of fitting forth all at once the greatest part of their biggest ships from all their provinces, and this with a degree of industry (by working day and night, even by candlelight) that has not been exceeded, if equalled, in the most pressing times of war, and this at a season of the year so unapt and unacquainted with preparations of this kind." Thanks, however, to the counter measures taken by the English naval administration, there was reason to hope that "by God Almighty's ordinary blessing, with the concurrence of the season, we may at last reckon ourselves safe against any extraordinary mischiefs that might be otherwise apprehended from so unusual a proceeding and insult from a neighbour in alliance".★ But he added that, though there might be no attempt at invasion for the moment, the complexion of affairs at home and abroad was such that there was little hope of being able to survive the next spring without a rupture.[5]

God Almighty's blessing, judging by the subsequent course of events, was less responsible for such safety as England enjoyed than Pepys's labours. These were attended by many difficulties of which the most serious were an almost universal shortage of men—intensified by the simultaneous recruitment of the army and James's reluctance to use the press-gang†—and inexplicable delays by those responsible for sending down guns and provisions. Lesser trials were the vagaries of the Post Office, which kept Pepys's midnight messengers hanging about for hours while its horses were being saddled. He met them all by cheerful and unflagging industry and by a serene loyalty that was an example to the whole Service.[6]

★ S. P. to Capt. Killigrew of the *Dragon*, Sept. 3rd 1688. *Pepysian MSS., Adm. Letters* XIV, 385–7.

† On Sept. 18th the fleet was reported to be 6000 seamen short of its complement, though this was probably an exaggeration. *Ellis Correspondence* II, 191.

In such a time of emergency there was no room for exclusions or for such peddling distinctions as had been depriving the public of good servants on the score of religion and politics. Sir Phineas Pett was permitted to remain at his post at Chatham, and his gout—a royal euphuism for unbending Protestantism—was conveniently forgotten. Booth and Berry returned to their Commissionerships and received commands at sea as well. Even Josiah Burchett was allowed to return to the Service, though not to the Holy of Holies above the Watergate which he had desecrated. Instead of an infinity of applications for a handful of places, there was a post henceforward for every qualified man. Yet Pepys's rules still held, for all who aspired to commissions had to show that they had been examined according to his regulations.[7]

Still, despite all the dangers which surrounded him, the King held to his perilous course. While time was yet left to him, his confessors and his conscience alike told him, he must do God's work, overthrow the Anglican monopoly, establish the freedom of the Roman Church in England and the lawful succession of a Catholic line. The non-conformist Parliament which was to secure these blessings was summoned to meet in November. Those who by their long loyalty to the Crown had earned the hatred of the "dissatisfied Party"—now rendered powerful by the King's favour—were those whose seats were hardest to hold. "I would be very glad to be serviceable to you and in you to the King in this affair as I could," Pepys wrote to Sir Phineas Pett who had appealed for his help at Rochester, "but am a little doubtful whether I can be able to attend you at the election, as having one of my own to look after, and at this time a very busy Office." He himself, his freehold at Harwich in danger, was forced to look

round for an alternative seat. He accordingly asked
his old friend Sir Robert Holmes, in the Isle of
Wight, to keep a "berth" for him there, where
Hewer also was to be provided for. Holmes replied
that he would gladly do so if he could, but begged
him to let the King know of the troubles in the island
itself. For here also the malcontents, encouraged by
the King's folly, were growing daily bolder: "I was
never so afraid as I am at present," he wrote, "for
fear of those devils falling upon me." In the meantime Pepys did his best to strengthen his hold on
Harwich by getting the Customs House removed to
that place from Ipswich. In the interstices of naval
business he even found time to spend some hours
closeted with the Customs' officials explaining to
them how much the removal would benefit the
trade of the country, not to mention the purses of
"the worthy gentlemen, our good friends of the
Corporation".[8]

*   *   *

Before the end of September even the King was
growing aware of the sinister nature of the forces
that were threatening him. Every day brought tales
of new defections to William. In the London streets
medals of the petitioning Bishops and prints of army
officers who had protested against the inflow of
papist recruits from Ireland were selling like hot
cakes. On the 20th James, who had been down the
river to Chatham and Sheerness to view the
fortifications and naval preparations, was brought
back post-haste to London by news from Holland
which it was no longer possible for him to disbelieve.* He is said to have turned white and speech-

----

* "He told me the Dutch were now coming to invade England in
good earnest. I presumed to ask if he really believed it. To which the
King replied with warmth, 'Do I see you, my Lord'?" Clarendon,
Diary, Sept. 24th, 1688.

less at the proofs of his son-in-law's treachery. Already, he was informed, the Dutch fleet was getting aboard the last requisites for an invasion—wheelbarrows, shovels, saddles and bridles. And, bold in the extreme as such a venture seemed at that season of the year, at any moment the invaders might appear off the English coast.★ Evelyn, arriving from the country, found the Court in such a panic as he could scarcely credit.[9]

These alarms were followed by new orders for mobilising the Navy and Army, and at last by a revolutionary change in the government's policy. To the bewilderment of the nation the ship of state was seen to put her helm about and go round to the opposite course. Frightened by the way events were shaping, entreated by the remaining Tories who still clung to him, and with even Sunderland and Jeffreys now counselling surrender, the unhappy King decided to reconcile himself with the great Party which had saved him in the past and which he had so rashly alienated. On September 21st, the day after the royal return from Chatham, a Proclamation was issued promising the exclusion of Catholics from the forthcoming Parliament. Yet even this spoke of the hated proposal to remove the penal laws. For it was not in James's nature to make a bold and shameless Elizabethan withdrawal. Instead he fell back, after the manner of his father, Charles I, step by step, and always a step too late.[10]

During the last days of September he interviewed the Bishops and restored Compton, already in the secret counsels of the invaders, to his see of London. On October 2nd he informed the Lord Mayor, Aldermen and Sheriffs that he would restore the

★ "We are all here in great hurry, and in hourly expectation of an invasion, upon what grounds nobody yet knows." W. Shaw to J. Ellis, Oct. 2nd, 1688. *Ellis Correspondence* ii, 230.

ancient Charter and privileges of the City, and ten days later made good the same promise to every borough in England. On the 5th the Ecclesiastical Commission was dissolved. A week later the Anglican President and Fellows of Magdalen College, Oxford, were re-instated. Pepys's learned friend, Dr Thomas Smith, stood with his fellow exiles at the College gate and afterwards marched with them in procession to the hall, where the Bishop of Winchester, in pursuance of the royal orders, solemnly struck the names of the upstart papist Fellows out of the buttery book. A shoal of dismissals of Roman Catholics from the Lord Lieutenancies and other key positions followed.

Yet the uneasiness and resentment in the public mind were now too deeply rooted to be removed by such belated measures, which most people were convinced were due to nothing but fear. Good and loyal Dr Smith, even while all the bells of Oxford rang with joy at his restoration, could not help suspecting from "some men's intolerable insolence", that an ill-use would be made of these astonishing changes. "Oh rare invasion," wrote one unregenerate malcontent, "to occasion so many gracious acts in restoring things to their legal foundation which hath been the work of many years past to unhinge!" So far from sharing the King's dread of an invasion a large section of the populace seemed now to want it passionately and prayed for an east wind to bring it to their shores. Half the nation was whistling *Lilliburlero*, the scurrilous anti-papist doggerel which the whig Lord Wharton—Swift's universal villain—had set to one of Purcell's irresistible airs. There must be a vengeance on Irishmen, Catholics and Palace politicians before the English would be content to be still again. And the one safety-valve that might have let off the national steam was denied: the writs for a Parliament were recalled on the grounds of the threatened invasion. In the shaken, veering counsels of the Palace the priests had won again. "The Virgin Mary", explained the profane Jeffreys, "is to do all!"[11]

As a matter of fact the devout King was not without hopes also of his Navy. So high were these, that sooner than offend the insular prejudices of his officers and seamen, he expressly refused an offer of French naval assistance. Though to set the battle fleet out to sea just as winter was falling was a feat unknown to the seventeenth century, a general mobilisation of all but the largest ships was ordered. On September 24th the senior officer in the Service, Lord Dartmouth—Pepys's old friend, George Legge—was appointed to the command, with Strickland as his Vice-Admiral and Berry Rear-Admiral. As Dartmouth was a firm Protestant, the measure was calculated not only to keep away the invaders but to appease the invaded. To give the appointment a still more Protestant complexion, Pepys invited Dr Peachell, the deprived Master of Magdalene, Cambridge, to accompany Dartmouth as his Chaplain: "judging", he wrote, "all the qualifications (piety, authority and learning) wished for therein meet abundantly in you". But not even Pepys's hint of a bishopric could persuade Peachell to accept. The good man had had enough of politics.[12]

On September 28th orders were given to such part of the fleet as could be manned and kept to sea in autumnal and winter storms to assemble at the Buoy of the Nore. Thither the squadron already at sea, under Strickland, now judged too light to encounter the impending attack, was ordered to fall back. Other ships were to proceed to the rendezvous as soon as they could be got ready, from Orfordness,

Yarmouth, Blackstakes, Chatham, the Hope, Long Reach, Deptford, Woolwich and Portsmouth. Even the Straits fleet at distant Gibraltar was laid under contribution. Nor were they to wait till they could be fully manned but to sail at the first opportunity before an easterly wind brought out the Dutch: if necessary they were to take soldiers aboard to make up their complements. On October 1st Fighting Instructions were issued to the Admiral.[13]

In their attitude to the invasion, which was then hourly expected, Pepys and his sovereign showed themselves in advance of the strategical conceptions of their time. While troops posted to the north where the main blow was expected to fall, sailors like Sir William Booth and Navy officials like Sir Phineas Pett talked of the importance of "putting the workmen of the Yards into military form and discipline". Theirs was the old fatal delusion that an island could be secured from invasion by purely defensive measures. "You in yours", Pepys wrote to the Commissioner at Chatham, "do say that you had his Majesty's warrant from me for putting the shipwrights and other workmen into a military posture, whereas the whole scope and purpose of the King's warrant is to oppose and suppress the proposition you and Sir William Booth had . . . made to the King for putting them into such a posture. So before anything can be done in demanding the supplies you desire of arms, powder, swords, etc., I am forced to desire you will consider the King's warrant again and what of that demand will be necessary to be made for enabling you to put in execution what the King's warrant does indeed desire, which is not the marshalling of the workmen and forming them into the same method and under the same discipline as soldiers are, but only distributing them and quartering them to the several posts (the particulars thereof the King does in a great measure reckon up to you in the said warrant) for the securing those their respective posts in case of any approaches of an enemy."[14]

But the bolder sea counsels of August 26th were superseded by a more cautious plan.* A Drake, a Blake, a Nelson, and perhaps, had he lived, a Narbrough might conceivably have dared all and met Orange's threat with a shock of frigates amid the Zeeland shoals while the battle fleet was making ready. Honest George Legge did not feel justified in taking so overwhelming a risk on a dead lee shore in a season of tempests. He preferred to keep his fleet in the Thames till he was able to meet the invader with equal or superior force. Recalling the limitations of seventeenth-century ships, it is hard to blame him. The technique of long cruising, and still more of close blockade in winter storms, had still to be learnt.

For the moment, therefore, the work of defending England depended mainly on Pepys and his subordinates in York Buildings and the river shipyards. And so long as the wind blew hard from the west and William's ships lay bound in their harbours, it might avail. But what if the wind should change before the work was complete? On that question the fate of England depended for five anxious weeks until it was decided, not by a daring Admiral with his guns blazing amid crowded transports, but by the winds of Heaven. In the formal Fighting Instructions which Pepys by orders of the Council drafted on October 1st, Dartmouth was empowered to "endeavour by all hostile means to sink, burn, take and otherwise destroy and disable"

* Mr Powley in his brilliant monograph on the *English Navy in the Revolution of 1688* seems to overlook the fact that the fatal decision to assemble the fleet at the Buoy of the Nore must almost certainly have been made on the advice of Lord Dartmouth, whose appointment to the command it closely followed.

the "armed force of foreigners and strangers", which a second William the Conqueror was preparing to launch against his country. Yet so long as Dartmouth remained in the Thames that was just what he could not do.[15]

The story of that fatal month which resolved the political destiny of unborn millions is to be found in the daily correspondence between the English Admiral and the Secretary of the Admiralty. It began on October 3rd when Pepys wrote to Dartmouth to congratulate him on his safe arrival at the Buoy of the Nore and to tell him of the steps he was taking, by moving buoys and lighthouses at Harwich and in the mouth of the River, to guard against a Dutch attack before the fleet was ready. It followed three themes—the transmission of news received from the Admiralty scouts, the measures for sending Dartmouth the ships, men, victuals, stores and guns he required, and Pepys's persistent attempts to coax his Lordship a little nearer the enemy. The last were conducted, both on his own and the King's account, with scrupulous deference to Dartmouth's proper freedom of action, his rights as a commander, and his feelings as a nobleman.[16]

The Admiral's constitutional reluctance to attack did not extend to epistolary operations against the Admiralty. As was his duty he engaged in these with considerable spirit and persistence. Always inclined to be despondent, and with much embittering experience behind him, Dartmouth in the isolation of his flagship could never rid his mind of the suspicion that the men on shore were denying him a fair deal. With his friend Pepys in command of the administration it was hard to say this in so many words, but the inevitable delays of a hasty mobilisation gave him plenty of matter for complaints. These he forwarded daily to Pepys, who passed them on to those concerned and answered them with forbearance. He admitted the delays in the victualling and apologised for them; that over-harassed department, he explained, had just had to take over the additional task of provisioning the military garrisons, which, "does occasion no small interruption". And his Majesty had in a single week haled the Victualling Commissioners three times into his presence to impress on them the urgency of his Lordship's needs.[17]

Dartmouth, anxious and weighed down with the responsibility of his position, was less patient in reply. "I here enclose you Mr Steventon (Agent to the Commissioners of the Victualling) his Memorial given me this day," he wrote on the 13th, "with my remarks thereon, which, after showing his Majesty, I desire you will transmit to the Victualling Office to prevent any further writing about it, or their saying the business is done, but that it may be really so." Neither then nor at any time in his life could Dartmouth, in ordinary relationships the most obliging and forbearing of men, resist the temptation of writing cutting letters. On at least one occasion Pepys was driven to complain of the injustice of his doing so, but the Admiral was inexorable. "Sir," he replied, "though I am very well assured you have assiduously performed your part as Secretary, yet other officers have not, as I have often repeated to you, and do once more most earnestly desire that all excuses may be laid aside and everything effectually done for his Majesty's service, the pressing necessities whereof oblige me to give you my opinion that a further delay may be of fatal consequence."*[18]

Pepys bore it all with patience, born of long service and understanding of Dartmouth's feelings.

* Lord Dartmouth to S. P., Oct. 13th, 1688. *Rawl. MSS. A.* 186, f. 353.

Yet it was not to be expected that the war at sea could be waged without that other and departmental war which always breaks out on such occasions on the home front. There was a sharp though decorous exchange of hostilities between the Secretary and the Admiral over the number of supernumeraries aboard the flagship. Fifty, Pepys explained, was the number allowed to the Lord High Admiral at sea, whereas an Admiral with the union flag at the maintop was only entitled to thirty. When Dartmouth replied with a broadside of historical arguments, Pepys returned his fire with extracts from his own Regulations. "What may have been done before the date of the last solemn Establishment in 1677 about the supernumerary allowance for flags I know not, or what has been done since, either abroad without order or by order from home, in the time of my absence from the Navy. And I do firmly believe it will never appear that fifty men were ever allowed to any flag but the standard since the date of that Establishment by any order that passed my hand." There was no shifting Pepys from his guns. [19]

Guns, indeed, were one of the causes of administrative battle. When Dartmouth complained of lack of men and victuals, Pepys, weary from long interviews with Watermen's Hall or the Victualling Commissioners, and confronted on his return to York Buildings with another of Dartmouth's angry letters, was sometimes driven to retaliate by allusions to the deficiences of the Ordnance Department, of which, inconveniently enough, Dartmouth was Master. "I persuade myself", he wrote of a complaint of lack of gunners' stores, "I need not trouble the officers of the Ordnance from hence with any intimations of what you observe relating to the wants some ships are still under, . . . as being well assured that it will be abundantly done by a

better hand, I mean your own." "How it has come
to pass", he added a little later, "I know not, . . . but
the King has understood from Captain Constable
that the *St Albans* had four ports on the quarterdeck
which the Establishment has provided no guns
for."[20]

Such exchanges were perhaps inevitable: under a
fierce strain of mind and body, even the noblest
tempers show the marks of human frailty. More
usually the tone of Pepys's correspondence with
Dartmouth was that of a brother in arms in a common service: "I pray God with all my heart to give
you the fruit of the pains which I am sure you are
taking for it."[21]

Far different was the spirit of some of the gentlemen commanders when confronted with the routine
requirements and restrictions of the Navy Board.
"Right Honourables," wrote Lord Berkeley in his
large, childish hand, "your letter of the 14th this
morning came to my hands, where you tell me you
have not power to add to my allowance of junk.
This for your Honours' sake I ought to keep to
myself, for should some sarcastical people know it, I
fear it would make a mighty jest. Indeed I did not
expect to have been denied so small a request, for
surely you do not think I should eat or sell the junk?
No, but he will suffer his boatswain to bobble him! I
should be sorry your Honours had so mean an opinion of my judgment as to think I would be put
upon, or of my affection to his Majesty's service to
see him cheated for the obliging of such a fellow as a
boatswain or carpenter." "We have received your
Lordship's answer of the 17th," the Navy Board
replied to this gentlemanly epistle, "the style of
which we know how to observe, though not to
imitate, intending to submit it with all humility to
the King to judge of the difference." Though the

reply was signed by Berry, Pett, Deane and Hewer, one suspects that the Admiralty Secretary may have had a hand in its drafting.[22]

Few of the gentlemen captains of the fleet came well out of the ordeal of mobilisation. Perhaps their hearts were with their elder brothers or cousins who plotted rebellion in their country houses and awaited their "deliverance" at the hands of Dutch William. Pepys told Dartmouth how it grieved him to the heart to hear how senior officers sauntered away their time when there was nobody at their backs: "I have this evening beseeched the King to lay his commands upon his sea captains that are still walking in Whitehall to repair to their charges, as some of them, to my astonishment as well as grief, to this day do." Here lay the root of all his difficulties. "My Lord," he replied to another of Dartmouth's complaints, "I observe what you say concerning the wants, or at least demands for supplies of stores, from your ships of the fleet. But it can be thought no new thing to anyone that has known the fitting forth of fleets so long as your Lordship and myself have done. For I hardly ever remember a ship that could not find something or other to ask within ten days after they went out. Nor do I ever expect to see it otherwise till commanders will think fit to observe their instructions more." It was for him the old, old story.[23]

Those admirable officials, the Special Commissioners, did their best. But they suffered from over-work and could not be everywhere at once: and Pepys had to warn Dartmouth early in October that he could not spare any more of them for the fleet since there were scarcely enough of them left in London to form a Board. On the 4th he found Deane "extremely indisposed, so as not to be able to stir out of doors, and poor Mr Hewer little better, through

the unintermitted succession of business to be dispatched from morning to night, and nobody at present to look after any part of it but them two". A
week later Deane was in bed: "considering", wrote
his loyal chief, "what has lain upon his hand and his
alone for a great while it is my wonder he has held up
so long". "I wish heartily your health," he wrote to
him on the 12th, "and were I at my liberty to stir
from this place would not have failed to visit you
long before now; and shall, I believe, very soon,
possibly at night if the Cabinet does not sit beyond 7
at night, that I may be with you and Mr Hewer
before 8; but after that hour don't expect me."*24

The mid-hour of mobilisation saw the execution
of the royal resolution of the previous spring to
restore the old administrative constitution of the
Navy. On October 12th the Special Commission
was formally dissolved and three days later the rule
of the Principal Officers revived. Lord Falkland
remained as Treasurer and Sir Richard Haddock was
recalled to the Comptrollership of the Navy Board,
Sir John Tippetts was re-appointed Surveyor, James
Sotherne Clerk of the Acts, and Sir Phineas Pett, Sir
Richard Beach and Balty St Michel Resident Commissioners at Chatham, Portsmouth and Deptford.
Sir John Berry and Sir William Booth, now both
flying their flags at sea, became Comptroller of Victualling and of Storekeeping Accounts respectively.
Deane and Hewer, the two pivot men of the Admiralty Special Commission, were retained as temporary Commissioners.25

The **work** of the Special Commission passed
almost unnoticed. In that crowded hour its very
success obliterated it. Contemporaries and posterity
were alike almost oblivious of it. Yet its achieve-

* S. P. to Sir A. Deane, Oct. 12th, 1688. *Pepysian MSS., Adm.
Letters* xv, 145–5.

ment was to remain a coping stone of the British imperial structure. In two and a half years, six months less than its estimated term, it had rebuilt almost wholly twenty ships, all of the line of battle, and repaired sixty-nine others. It had also built three new 4th rates and thirty-three storehouses, and laid down an eight months' reserve of sea stores for every ship—"such a treasure of stores", Pepys proudly claimed, "as England was never before mistress of". Nor, he might have added, of such a treasure of ships. Against the new naval strategy of the future the Special Commission provided Britain with a strength of fifty-nine capital ships of the first three rates. Henceforward the Grand Fleet was to be a permanent influence in the counsels of Europe and the world.

All this, including the ordinary charge of maintaining the Service, had been done at a cost of £307,000 p.a. or 22s. per man per month. Not a pennyworth of debt was left unpaid. And now during the closing weeks of its existence and at a time when navies were wont by immemorial custom to lay up for the winter, the Special Commission had on a sudden alarm prepared for sea no less than sixty-seven ships of war, including twelve 3rd rates of the line and twenty-eight 4th rates. No wonder Pepys was modestly pleased with his handiwork. "I cannot", he told the retiring Commissioners, "but with great satisfaction reflect upon the condition you will be remembered to have left the Navy of England in, when it shall appear that the last command you had to execute from the King was upon a warrant for fitting forth of ships presented him by me with blanks for the numbers to be filled at his pleasure with his own royal hand. God grant that this, which I take to be the first instance to be met with the kind since England had a Navy, may ever be within the power of your successors to follow you in.''[26]

★   ★   ★

Pepys by his life-work had taught his country how to equip, regulate and maintain a fleet. But he could not teach that fleet how to fight. That was still to be the lesson of her sea Admirals, grasped for a moment under the inspired tuition of such as Drake, Myngs and Blake, but awaiting the genius of the great captains of a later age to transform into a permanent habit and rule. Good honest gentleman that he was, Dartmouth was not such a teacher. The trident which Pepys had fashioned for him was for other hands to grasp.

Without a numerical superiority Dartmouth had no wish to risk his ships in battle with the Dutch. It seemed to him, as it seemed to another British Admiral under very different circumstances two centuries later, that the political issues were too great to be staked on the uncertain fate of a sea fight unless victory could be assured from the first. He had been entrusted with his country's fleet and it was his duty to keep it safe and intact. There are many who hold that by doing so he performed unconsciously the greatest service he could have done her, for it so survived unimpaired to fight a mightier enemy than the Dutch when the transient Stuart cause it failed to defend had vanished into smoke.

Be that as it may, Dartmouth from the start resisted every attempt to hustle his fleet out to sea, though strenuously protesting his desire to meet the enemy. While Pepys in the first week of October, ignoring all deficiencies that could not be remedied in such an emergency, despatched ship after ship to the Buoy of the Nore, telling the Admiral that it was

far better he should have them so than wait for their
full manning until the wind changed, that cautious
warrior contented himself with dictating letters
about the need for additional men and victuals. Had
he but these, he explained, he would not stay two
hours more at his anchorage. Pepys replied that the
administration did not wish to fetter him in any way
and left everything to his discretion. A letter of
October 5th from the King to the Admiral again
stressed the importance of getting his ships to sea
while he could: "I need not remind you to lose no
time to get out from among the sands as fast as
you can."[27]

But Dartmouth was not going to be hurried. On
the 4th one of his scouts had reported that there were
only seven Dutch ships of war riding off the Maas: if
the prevailing westerly gales continued he did not
doubt to be at sea before them. The gales continued:
as Pepys put it, "the wind (thanks be to God) sits".
Next day Dartmouth, commenting on some intelligence from Holland sent him from the Admiralty,
gave it as his opinion that the enemy's fleet would
try to engage him while the transports took a different direction to effect a landing. It never seemed to
occur to him that his best course might be to attack
the latter. In another letter he expressed his belief
that the transports would not come out at all so long
as his fleet remained in being. "I well know our
being beaten may prove a fatal consequence", was
the recurring motif of his correspondence. And he
dwelt sadly on his fears that he would be forced to
put to sea in the end "with few ships and those not in
the condition they ought to be" in a stormy, incle-
ment season of the year. It was the good, fearful,
gallant gentleman's nightmare.[28]

It is only when Dartmouth's unhappy position is
fully realised that his inadequacy as England's

Admiral at this juncture can be appreciated. It is
perfectly true that judged by purely technical considerations he was right not to venture his fleet on
the Dutch coast in mid-October. Seventeenth-
century ships were not made to stay at sea in autumnal gales. This was as true of the Dutch fleet as of the
English: it was even truer of their crowded transports. Had Dartmouth ventured to sea the English
fleet might well have been dashed to pieces on the
sands of Holland, though more probably it would
have been scattered and driven back piecemeal to its
own harbours. It was undermanned and still very
much under strength: every day it waited for reinforcements, Pepys's labours made it stronger. But,
however grateful posterity has cause to be to Dartmouth for keeping, all unconsciously, his fleet intact
to wage the wars of a new dynasty, it is only fair to
remember that that was not why he commanded it.
He was there to save his master's kingdom from
invasion. He was a Protestant, but he was also a
loyal gentleman who had eaten the King's bread.
Unlike others, he never intended to betray him
while drawing his pay.

Viewed in that light, Dartmouth's position was
simple. He had everything to gain by engaging William's transports and their escorts and scarcely anything to lose. For once the invader had landed, his
own carefully husbanded ships could do little
against them. They might cut off his supplies, but a
seventeenth-century army could live on the country, especially on so fat a one as England. And the
whole point of William's coming was that the
people, excited by anti-Catholic propaganda, might
rise in his support. Against that possibility was the
awkward fact that the would-be deliverer was coming at the head of a Dutch army and under cover of a
Dutch fleet, and that the English had no love for the

Dutch. For two generations they had been their rivals and antagonists. William of Orange's marriage with Mary of England had done much to quiet that antagonism and the fears of France and Catholicism felt by both peoples still more. Yet once let Dutchmen and Englishmen exchange blows, particularly on their ancient battlefield, the sea, and the fires of racial hatred would blaze up anew. William's hope was to avoid that clash at all costs. Dartmouth had it in his power to force it upon him should he venture to sea, though at the price of jeopardising his master's ships. But if they were not be jeopardised in so fatal a crisis of his own and his kingdom's fortunes, for what purpose had they been built?

His Majesty and the Secretary of the Admiralty were charmingly patient towards the loyal Admiral to whom they had entrusted their all. "Though all that are in the Hope should not be quite ready," wrote the former on October 8th, "consider well whether you should lose the opportunity of this westerly wind to get out from amongst the sands or venture to have the Dutch come and find you somewhere near the Buoy of the Oaze Edge amongst the sands. For you must expect they will come out and be looking for you with the first easterly wind." Dartmouth replied on the 12th that the King could not be more desirous to have him out of the sands than he was himself of leaving them, but that storms, lack of victuals and the non–arrival of the ships from Portsmouth prevented him. "I hope", he protested, "I am not blameable to get what I can together for so great a work as I have to do, with an enemy likely to be so much superior to me. And I judge it much more for your service to unite while we have time than to drop out in parcels with the hazard of being separated, especially knowing myself here in the best place to do my business while these winds continue. And be assured, Sir, I will be on sea upon the first alteration." The memory of the fatal division of the fleet before the Four Days' battle of 1666 still haunted the English memory. At almost any other time but this Dartmouth would have been right.[29]

In the same letter, however, the Admiral suggested that, as soon as the Portsmouth ships joined him and the wind moderated, he should show himself on the Dutch coast. He added, perhaps a little superflously, that he would be careful not to "peak himself" or do anything rash. Unfortunately this was the moment that the King, with true Stuart irresolution, chose to waver a little and to remind his Admiral of the season of the year and of "the blowing weather" to be expected. At any rate he must leave the decision to him, "being sure you will do what is best for my service, which you that are on the place are the only judges of, and must govern yourselves according to the enemy's motions and as wind and weather will permit". And, with ill-timed confidence, he pointed out that he had an army and enjoyed the peculiar protection of the Deity. "The Scots and Irish troops are marching as fast as they can to join me . . . I make no doubt but that God will protect me and prosper my arms both by land and sea."[30]

★　　★　　★

On that very day, October 14th, the wind shifted into the east. It was the anniversary of William the Conqueror's victory at Hastings. All England waited for invasion. But Dartmouth, though he had thirty-five fighting ships and fourteen fireships ready to sail, was now powerless. All he could do was to get his fleet as far as the Oaze Edge and there place himself in the best defensive posture he was able. But Pepys, thinking him on the eve of departure, wrote to him on the 16th to bid him Godspeed: "And now, my Lord, not knowing whether your stay may give me opportunity of writing to you before your leaving the river, I do most fervently beg of God Almighty to protect and guide you in your present undertaking so that you may return with the success and safety which all good men wish you." How often before had the little Secretary sent out English fleets with like wishes![31]

But an evil and treacherous inertia lay over the English naval action that fatal October. Pepys and his virtuous subordinates seemed like men running in a dream: they strove furiously yet saw all things motionless beside them. The victualling barges sent down the river in haste loitered for days before reaching the fleet, and the pressed seamen bound for the same destination flung the escorting musketeers overboard and swam ashore. And such was the conduct of the gentlemen captains that even Pepys began to despair. "Unless", he told Dartmouth on the 17th, "there be another spirit put into some of their commanders (I mean as to diligence and concernment for the Service and not making of it as a bye-business, annexed only as a convenience to their employments elsewhere), I shall bid goodnight to the expectations of any good to the Service from them, let you and myself make as much on't as we please. . . . But for ought I see gentlemen are got above being jealous of any censure, or else they would not appear to the King every day at Court complaining that their ships are not ready, while nothing is wanting towards making them ready but their own attendance on board."[32]

There was worse than slackness: there was black downright treachery by men in the King's pay. One

could not prove it, but one sensed it was there.
Dartmouth thanked God for the sea room at the
Oaze Edge that enabled him to keep his captains
aboard their own ships and thus incapable of caball-
ing. Which, he added, being both idle and English,
they might very well do, particularly with so many
pamphlets and newsletters about. On October 22nd
he warned the King of signs of dissatisfaction among
some of his younger commanders. "I am glad
Priestman is not amongst us, and I think he ought to
be a little watched for he sets up for a leading politician. The Duke of Grafton"—a bastard of the late
King and a Protestant—"was down here among
them a little after my coming, though he would not
let me know it. My Lord Berkeley I am told is very
pert, but I have taken him in the next ship to me and
shall know more of their tempers in a little time."
Yet the Admiral was still convinced that most of his
commanders were men of honour.[33]

For all the fears and jealousies of the nation there
were still many who were, and who felt, as one of
them put it, that an invader ought be opposed,
whatever his pretexts. "I trust", wrote honest
Charles Hatton on the 16th when the enemy were
expected hourly, "the nation in general will behave
themselves with loyalty to their prince and regard to
their country that the Dutch in 1688 will succeed no
better than the Spaniards in 1588." They were not
likely to if the English fleet could but meet their
transports on the high seas. But Dartmouth and his
ships were "hooked" among the sands at the Oaze
Edge and could not move.[34]

Pepys, who had warned Dartmouth from the first
of the danger of staying there too long, wrote to him
on the 17th of the royal fears that he would be
surprised by the Dutch taking advantage of the wind
that imprisoned him among the sands. Though

there were reports that they had suffered damage and delay by the storms their intentions no longer admitted of doubt. They were bringing, he reported, "an incredible number of coats and other clothing for the men they expect to raise here and small arms without stint, even to the making it a difficulty to buy a hand gun, pistol or sword in all the country, . . . and a vast quantity of lime, to what uses your Lordship is a much better judge that myself".[35]

Dartmouth also was well equipped. Victuals and men were now coming in fast and the Portsmouth ships had at last joined him. This he admitted in his letter to the King of the same day, "so that now we begin to look in earnest, and the fleet are all in as good heart as can be desired". And on October 20th, after nearly a week of suspense, the wind shifted back with gale force into the west. Every Catholic face shone. James was jubilant: it was plain, he told his Admiral, that God Almighty wished him well, "which will give you an opportunity to get out and hinder the enemy from coming over, and give you an opportunity of waiting on them when they shall come out".[36]

It was one that Dartmouth would not or could not seize. How far he was prevented from acting by the weather we cannot be certain. On the 20th he waited for a final store ship: on the 21st and 22nd for better weather. Pepys, struggling with tired workmen and recalcitrant captains, worked the clock round to get the last six ships down the river: "I do assure your Lordship", he told him, "I do with the same zeal continue to press the dispatch of the rest that are left behind that I would do for my victuals if I were hungry. And did it last night to the King at the Cabinet by observing to him in these very words, that these delays are no more than must be expected while gentlemen are allowed to hold ships at sea *in commendam* with troops and companies ashore, at a time when there is an equal necessity for their attendance upon both."[37]

One example of this kind of thing stuck long in Pepys's memory. Waiting in the Bedchamber for his royal master to leave the Closet for the evening meeting of the Cabinet, at a time when the whole future of England was hanging in the balance, he saw, to his anger and amazement, the captain of one of the new 3rd rates standing in the room. He resolved to expose him there and then in the royal presence, but was prevented by the King's arriving late. During the Cabinet meeting he sat simmering, and the moment the proceedings closed and before the King could rise, interposed, that though his Majesty had nothing further to add, he had something for which he was sorry. He then related what he had seen. "Upon which", he told Dartmouth, "the King with some surprise asked me what had brought him up from his ship. I answered I knew not, nor did he think fit upon his seeing me there to say anything of it to me or so much as to take notice of his being where I might not well have expected him. But I added that I took it (to make it at all supportable) that he had his Majesty's leave for it; though I observed to his Majesty that if leaves of that kind be signified to commanders by any hand than mine while I have the honour of serving him in my post, it would be to no purpose for me to pretend longer to give him the account I ought and he expected from me of his fleet."

But the King, it seemed, had granted no such leave nor had any idea what had brought the truant captain to town. "My lord," Pepys continued, "I do not think myself at liberty to mention anything said in that place on this occasion by any of my Lords.

But I think I may be bold here to say what passed between the King and myself only. . . . For (in one word) I will have all the world to know that, as considerable as it takes the profit of my employment to be, and indeed by the King's favour it is, it should not, were it ten times greater, purchase my staying in it one day longer than I can see his Service thrive as well as I. And that I am sure it never can, from the moment that such a violation as this in the discipline and honour of it passes uncensored."

Very different was the case of Captain Tennant of the *Tiger*, who in his eagerness to be gone had carried off the riggers from Chatham Dockyard much to everyone's inconvenience. "The truth is, Captain Tennant's zeal in getting his ship into condition to join your Lordship again was so laudable and indeed exemplary for others (if they would please to take notice of it) that it would almost have excused the carrying away a priest from the altar." There were times when even Pepys could approve a breach of his rules.[38]

★   ★   ★

Those waiting weeks at the end of October 1688 had something of the instability of a nightmare. The King fluctuated between blind confidence and active terror. On the 22nd the whole Palace was turned upside-down by a hastily-staged Presence at which he treated a great concourse of embarrassed noblemen and officials to the authentic tale of the royal delivery, presented with every circumstance of anatomical and womanly detail, even to the bloodstained linen, by a procession of mid-wives, nurses and ladies-in-waiting. Good Mrs Pearse, whom Elizabeth had once so unaccountably called wench, played a notable part in these matronly revelations.

They became, of course, the talk of the town, though not in the way the King had intended: "the men", wrote one outraged lady, "are grown very learned: it is shameful to hear what discourse is common amongst them, even to footmen and lackeys". Four days later, to everyone's astonishment and most people's joy, Lord Sunderland, whose double-dyed treachery had at last become clear even to his credulous master, was dismissed. Meanwhile the London mob burned a Popish chapel and waylaid such luckless Irish soldiers as were rash enough to stray from their quarters into the streets. Two of them taking a sabbath stroll were chased into St Michael's, Cornhill, where their frantic cries of "Mercy! Mercy!" were mistaken by the startled congregation for the first sounds of a massacre. On that sudden alarm, one Protestant leg at least was broken as its frightened owner leapt desperately out of a window.[39]

At the heart of a distressed kingdom Pepys pursued his business, looking neither to left nor right. "You must not wonder if at so busy a time as it has for divers weeks past been here to me in matters that would not admit of any interruption," he wrote as late as the 30th to old Sir Phineas Pett, "that I have no sooner answered your letter of the 22nd . . . upon the unseasonable difference . . . between yourself and Sir William Booth. I must confess divisions of that kind between gentlemen of the same commission must have too ill consequences to the King's service that they should be passed over without censure. It was my opinion so in what has not long before happened between Sir John Berry and Sir William Booth. And it is so in this. Nevertheless in a case like this of yours where one denies flatly what the other asserts, you affirming of his calling of you scoundrel, if not rascal, his saying that he cared not a turd for you, his giving your frequently the lie and challenging of you, while . . . he does not seem to own any particular of this, offering to prove upon oath by some of the standers-by that he did not treat you as you say he did, I find not myself able where to determine the right or the wrong to be." And he asked him to let him know the names of his witnesses.

In the same letter Pepys condoled with Pett on the ill-success of his election at Rochester, "concerning which I shall only say that tho' I was sorry for it, and I think you pretty hardly used in it by some that might (for the King's sake at least) have done otherwise than they did, though they would not for yours, yet I am far from wondering at it, since I verily persuade myself the greatest part of the Elections of England would have deceived expectations as much as this did yours for reasons out of yours and your friends' powers to have prevented. And therefore must as a Philosopher advise you to let it pass as a bad bargain of which few men in their lifetime escape without meeting of some."★ So true a philosopher had Pepys become, that in the midst of repelling an invasion, he even found time to write to the Bishop of London about the scandalous scarcity of chaplains in the Navy, praying the blessing of his Lordship's recommendation in so essential a pious a work: there were only eight, he pointed out, in a fleet of thirty-eight warships and twelve fireships. But the bishop was otherwise engaged, his strenuous if perjured piety providing the pivot on which the secret course of rebellion was turning. His thoughts were far away—with the invaders whom he had invited into England.[40]

★ S. P. to Sir P. Pett, Oct. 30th, 1688. *Pepysian MSS., Adm. Letters* xiv, 269–70.

But England's Admiral believed that the danger had passed. On the 24th he moved at last, sailing from the Nore in the morning and anchoring at noon in the Gunfleet. Its position among the Essex sands made it a perilous base at such juncture, as James had pointed out to Strickland eight months before. But Dartmouth seemed well content to be there, with as fine a winter squadron, he told the King, as England had ever set out. "Sir, we are now at sea before the Dutch after all their boasting, and I must confess I cannot see much sense in their attempt with the hazard of such a fleet and army at the latter end of October. . . . I wonder to hear by so many letters of the frights that are ashore, though I thank God they take no effects upon us here. . . . Your statesmen may take a nap and recover, the women sleep in their beds, and the cattle I think need not be drove from the shore." It was, as it were, an Admiral's lullaby to England.[41]

Across the North Sea command was held by men of a steelier temper. Two days later, in the evening of the 26th, Pepys was kept long from his bed by important news from the King's agent in Holland. A week before the Dutch, breaking every canon of naval warfare, had come out with 52 men-of-war and 500 transports from Helvoetsluys, as James, who knew his son-in-law's resolution, had warned Dartmouth they would do. But the sudden change of wind next day had given the King and his cautious champion-at-sea one last chance. The great gale of the week-end had driven back the laden transports and their escort of frigates in confusion to their moorings. Had it come a day later or had the English fleet, or even an outlying squadron of it, been there instead of lying cooped up in the Thames, their fate might well have been a terrible one. So it came to pass that one of the boldest feats of arms statesmen ever undertook★ escaped the destruction which in sober truth it seemed to merit and invite.[42]

In the course of the night that brought the news of the first Dutch attempt and the storm that defeated it, Pepys, writing at 2 a.m. on the 27th, urged on Dartmouth the advisability of appearing at once off the enemy's coast and taking advantage of their present confusion. Yet even in that vital hour, this model Secretary of the Admiralty was careful to assure him that under no circumstances would the King press on him any action contrary to his judgment, "in regard that you at sea keep better account of the courses of the wind, and more true, than we either do or can do here".[43]

Good subject and admirable seaman, the Admiral saw his fleet, not as a means for annihilating the enemy but as a sacred trust committed to his charge which it was his duty at all costs to keep intact. From on board his flagship, the ironically named *Resolution*, he wrote to Pepys on the 28th that he felt that this object was so essential to the nation's safety that, considering the time of year, it would be inadvisable to venture to the Dutch coast while the wind stayed in the west. This opinion he had placed before his commanders at a Council-of-War and received from them, with the one exception of Sir William Jennens ("in terms, I think, not very proper"),† their confirmation. The invader's design struck him as utterly desperate and ill-advised. "The whole proceeding at this season", he told his sovereign, "looks

---

★ D'Albeville reported in his letter of 20/30 Oct. that "Tromp refused to go". *Pepysian MSS., Adm. Letters* xv, 252.

† Burchett's view of Jennens' proposal, which he avers was backed by others, was that it carried "the greatest weight with it, had there been a real design of obstructing the Prince of Orange in his passage to England, but instead of that matters were so concerted and agreed among the commanders (who had frequently private meetings to

like the advice of land men, or at least men of desperate fortunes than men that know how to accomplish what they have undertaken." For his part he would not struggle too much against wind and weather but leave that to the Dutch. "Their growing mad shall not provoke me to follow their example." It was the attitude of the professional—careful, unimaginative and correct, and well suited to every occasion but that desperate hour.[44]

The councils of the invaders were moved by a different spirit. Orange, whose ignorance was bliss, had resolved to try again. Under his banner half the adventurers of Europe were gathered together. Of these none were more desperate than the English and Scottish exiles: "there is not in Hell a wickeder crew", the Marquis d'Albeville had written from the Hague. Such were the men who had planned treason with Shaftesbury and all but sent Pepys to the gallows in the roaring days of '79. Among them was Harbord who had bribed the false witnesses against him, and the old republican Wildman who had drunk and plotted with Scott. In their cups they spoke merrily of executing King James and of hanging the pretended Prince of Wales in his swaddling clothes. At their head was the dissolute, foul-tongued Herbert to whose desperate hands the great Liberator had entrusted the command of his fleet.

consider the circumstances of affairs) that had the Admiral come fairly up with the Dutch, it would not have been within his power to have done them much damage, although I have reason to believe that his Lordship and some of the captains would have exerted themselves to the utmost". Josiah Burchett, *A Complete History of the most Remarkable Transactions at Sea* (1720), 414.

The author of *George Byng, Lord Torrington's Memoirs*, takes the same view, that "though the great number of captains were steady in their principles for the King, yet the chiefest and most considerable of them were otherwise inclined and . . . brought over a majority of the council to think it was hazarding the fleet to lie on that dangerous coast at this time of the year".

By such rough instruments our liberties were made.[45]

Yet they did William's business, and all unknowing England's prudent Admiral gave them his aid. Some among them like Herbert and Russell had counted on dissatisfaction in the English Navy. But with Pepys to administer it and Dartmouth to command it, it was not in its loyalty that the country's first line of defence was to fail. "I hear", the Admiral wrote of his enemies, "they wear English colours and talk of treating with us. But pray, Sir, be assured I will suffer no language to be spoke to them but out of your guns." In his sober prudence he never gave himself a chance to use them.[46]

The divine favour was now offered to one more resolute. He did not refuse it. The final days of October saw the wind blowing again from the east. The anxious crowds who gazed up at the church vanes from the streets of English cities knew now that God was Protestant after all. On the 30th Dartmouth, unable to delude himself any longer as to the Dutch resolve and ability to sail, weighed anchor for the open sea. He was too late. The wind after its long westerly spell now stayed unwaveringly in the east. For more than three days he fought in vain to get clear of the sands off the mouth of the Thames. And on November 1st the Prince of Orange sailed once more from Helvoetsluys with the wind he had waited and prayed for in his sails. His and England's hour of destiny had come.[47]

Pepys, perhaps, knew it. "A pinch", he wrote on that fatal day as he waited for news from the fleet, "wherein the very being, as well as honour of his Crown and Government is at stake." Both that day and next listeners in the villages east of London fancied that they heard the sound of guns. But no

gun was fired. Steering first north-west towards the
Yorkshire coast, Orange's straggling Armada suddenly turned south-west towards the Channel while
Dartmouth and his men-of-war were still trying to
clear the Galloper Sand. On the morning of the 3rd
the invaders were sighted by the English frigates off
the Downs, and an hour after noon watchers on the
Dover cliffs saw them driving westwards before the
wind, their decks washed by great seas and so
numerous that there was no counting them. By
eleven that night the King and Pepys had learnt the
worst.[48]

   In that bitter hour of defeat no word of reproach to
the Admiral sullied Pepys's pen. In the letter that he
wrote to him in the early hours of the 4th there was
not so much as an expression even of regret. He
confined himself to recording the bare news and
how he had left the King in council with his generals
gallantly preparing orders for the despatch of his
army towards Portsmouth, now believed to be the
invaders' destination. Only long afterwards, and in
the secrecy of his private memoranda, did he commit to paper the sense of his own cruel disappointment at the memory of those wasted weeks—
wasted by the friend who had wielded the instrument he had so painfully and lovingly made. "What
a pother was heretofore made", he recorded recalling the silly charge that once had sent him to the
Tower, "about the pretended discovery of our
sands, etc., to strangers! While it now appears how
little use we were able to make of our supposed only
knowledge of them ourselves at so critical a juncture
as that was when my Lord Dartmouth could not tell
how to get his fleet out of them, though there by his
own choice and after all the cautions given him by
the King against the very evil he betrayed himself

and his unhappy master to by going thither." But whether Pepys was right or Dartmouth, no man now can say for certain.[49]

All next day and the day after news came to London as the invaders passed down the Channel. On November 4th there were reports that the Dutch had landed at Portsmouth, soon contradicted as their sails were sighted further and further to the west. On the 5th Pepys attended the council and dictated the usual routine letters from the office. It was not till the evening of the 6th, as the King was sitting to Kneller for a picture which Pepys had commissioned that artist to paint of him, that he learnt by letters from the little town of Dartmouth that the enemy were putting ashore in Torbay.[50]

Throughout these lamentable proceedings the English fleet, mobilised with such pains and hopes and now outwitted and out-manoeuvred, alternatively pursued its enemy or lay windbound among the sands. In London no one even knew for certain where it was, though on the morning of the 5th the Admiralty was informed that it had been seen passing Dover on the previous afternoon. Spartan in misfortune, Pepys wrote on the 6th to the Admiral at Portsmouth, where he hoped to find him, indicating rather than stating the extent of the blow that had befallen the kingdom. "Though all that know your Lordship, and above all the King, is abundantly assured that no part of your disappointment in relation to the Dutch fleet can be charged upon anything within your power to have prevented, yet the consequences of it in the said fleet's passing without the least interruption to the port they were bound for . . . are too visible and of too great moment to escape being lamented and, very certain I am, by none more than yourself. . . . Upon which I have nothing in command to say to your Lordship

by way of comment, saving that, since it has so
unhappily fallen out that the Dutch are in all probability at this hour peaceably putting on shore their
whole land force and baggage, so there is nothing
left within the power of your Lordship to obtain
from them in reference to the landing part, and that
consequently their men-of-war will now be at an
entire liberty to receive or attack you as they shall
think fit." It was the melancholy and inescapable
truth.[51]

Hardly had this letter been despatched but news
arrived from the unhappy Admiral, who was now
lying becalmed off Beachy Head. Not till daybreak
on Sunday the 4th had he managed to get his ships
clear from the sands in an E.S.E. gale. But it failed
him next day—that memorable 5th of November
when William landed in the west. "Thus", the poor
man ended his report to his sovereign, "I have given
your Majesty a true account of all my proceedings,
which are so far from the vain hopes I had that I take
myself for the most unfortunate man living, tho' I
know your Majesty is too just to expect more than
wind and weather will permit." In the meantime his
flag-officers and commanders were unanimously
opposed to attacking the Dutch fleet if a landing had
been effected. The only consolation was that the
Swallow frigate had captured a fly-boat with 200
men of one of the English regiments serving in
Holland whom William had pressed into his service.
The common soldiers, Dartmouth reported,
rejoiced when they were taken. They seemed to be
little in touch with the mood of their country.[52]

Pepys was the most magnanimous of men. Twice
again he reassured Dartmouth that he had nothing
with which to reproach himself and that he had done
all that a careful and prudent Admiral could do. The
King had commanded him to repeat his sense "of

your incapacity of doing more in that exigence for his service than you did, considering the place in which you were then hooked and the wind that then blew to the benefit of the Holland's fleet and disadvantage of yours''. It was rather a big consideration, particularly as the wind had blown in the opposite direction for so long. But of this Pepys said nothing.

Chapter VI
The Glorious Revolution

"The English confusion to Popery drink
Lilliburlero bullen a la!"

Lord Wharton, *Lilliburlero*.

Far down in the west country, the narrow lanes and
little steep hills that lie to the east of Torbay were
thronged with marching men. On Tuesday,
November 6th, the Dutch Prince's advance guard
had reached Newton Abbot, and in the market place
of that quiet town the Declaration of Liberation was
read to a gaping audience of farmers and graziers.
The gentry kept out of the way, the prudent remaining within doors and the more loyal taking horse for
London. On the 7th the march continued, eleven
thousand foot and four thousand horse, of whom at
least three parts were foreigners, passing Chudleigh
and the woods of Catholic Ugbrooke where,
unknown to all but the most faithful retainers of the
fallen Cliffords, the Secret Treaty of Dover—first
fatal parent of all that had now come to pass—lay
hidden.★

On the 8th watchers on the walls of Exeter saw
the glint of steel and heard the tramp of horses
coming out of the south-west. By nightfall the
western capital was a foreign camp. On Friday the
Prince of Orange rode down its twisted, cobbled

★ Two and a half centuries later, when the present writer stayed in
the house, it was brought in after dinner, according to family custom,
with the coffee and proudly displayed in its beautiful case by an
ancient butler.

streets under rocking steeples, while a large concourse—for it was Fair time and the city was full of country folk—gazed at the interminable procession of gentlemen of fortune and exiled adventurers attended by feathered and turbaned negroes, of furred and breast-plated horsemen from Sweden, of Brandenburgers and Swiss musketeers, of Dutch foot and cannon that had been dented in a hundred battles by Meuse and distant Danube, dragged by teams of innumerable cart-horses. By a strange irony that no one in England seemed to note, more than a quarter of them were Catholics. The fame of these alien warriors, their stature magnified a hundredfold by popular rumour and casting gigantic shadows across the winter sky, spread fast through the kingdom; an army of giants was about to expel the debased and stunted papists whom the King had recruited from the bogs of Ireland to enslave his people. A popular song, which recounted in innumerable verses the bawdy exploits of a tailor's wife with her spouse's apprentices, was reset to new and more stirring words by those who made it their business to give wings to rumour:

> Poor Berwick, how will thy dear joys
> Oppose this famed viaggio?
> Thy tallest sparks will be mere toys
> To Brandenburg and Swedish boys,
> Coraggio! coraggio!

Afterwards in the cathedral in the presence of empty stalls—for the Bishop and Dean had fled to London, and the Canons, hearing that the prayer for the infant Prince of Wales was to be omitted, had prudently absented themselves—the Liberator listened to Burnet thanking God in brazen tones for his fortunate voyage. And when that worthy instrument of the Lord's pleasure arose to read the Declaration, the very choir rose and scurried out in alarm.

For this, they reflected, was downright rebellion.[1]

Of all this Pepys as yet knew nothing. His place was in London among the Admiralty ledgers at York Buildings and in attendance on his master in closet and Council chamber. During those first days of the invasion he continued to work long into each night. He was above all things an Englishman—the very quintessence of that which we mean by English character—and it is the habitude of Englishmen in the hour of crisis and defeat to do the work that comes to their hands after their wonted manner. "My lord, it's late, and I have much to do to-night", is the phrase that ends Pepys's letters. He had suffered a crushing blow. He was not beaten, for he refused to accept it.

So he told Dartmouth in letters which followed one another in quick succession that he had moved the King at the Cabinet meeting to take up more merchantmen in the River and fit them out as fireships, that he was despatching more men and victuals, and that he could count on every support whenever he should feel himself able to attack the enemy. When Captain Rooth arrived on horseback—sore in the seat from the unwonted exercise—with papers taken from a captured Dutch fly-boat, it was Pepys's part to get them deciphered and pore over the figures and information they revealed. At two in the morning on Sunday, November 11th, he sat down to transmit the conclusions of his labours to Dartmouth: contrary to the Admiral's belief it appeared that the Dutch fleet guarding the transports at Torbay was no stronger in numbers than the English and weaker in quality.[2]

Pepys was again careful to assure Dartmouth that not the least blame attached to him for his failure to intercept the invaders. He knew well his old friend and chief's sensitive, fretting nature and wished to

fire, not depress, it. "I am yet under some fears", he
wrote on the 8th in a private letter—the second he
had sent him that day—"of your taking too much to
heart your late misfortune." For such, he added, he
was forced to call it. And he related how, after that
evening's Council meeting, he had asked the King
for a further assurance and received the comforting
answer that, however much foolish landsmen or
ill-willed seamen might take the liberty of censur-
ing, nothing could be more plain than the impossibility of his Admiral's serving him better than he had
done. "Therefore pray be fully at ease in this matter,
depending upon't that if I knew the least cause for
the contrary I would tell you of it. For so upon my
faith I would. Remember, too, how much worse
you were once used even where you were successful, I mean in the business of Tangier, and, withall,
how little you were the worse for it ten days after.
Once more, therefore, pray be at peace with yourself." Pepys never showed himself to better advantage than in this correspondence with this over-
anxious and irresolute sea-colleague. In his reply
Dartmouth told him that his kindness had eased his
heart: "I can never enough acknowledge your share
in my sufferings even from Tangier to the Long
Sands Head."[3]

On Saturday, November 10th, a week after the
Dutch fleet had passed down the Channel, Pepys
heard the King's artillery rumbling along the Strand
at the top of the street as it made its way under his old
friend, Sir Henry Shere, towards Piccadilly and the
Salisbury road. At that moment it still seemed possible that James might add William's head to Monmouth's. At Exeter the Prince of Orange seemed to
be waiting in vain for the gentry to join him. "As
yet", Pepys told Dartmouth, "we do not find one
man of quality that stirs, only a multitude of rabble

which signifies but little." The government hoped to concentrate the army on a line from the Dorset coast to the Bristol Channel and so hem in the invaders in the south-western peninsula, as Essex had been in '44 and Monmouth in '85. The corollary, which had sealed the fate of Monmouth, was a naval attack on the invader's transports. Successfully executed, the double plan must spell the Prince's ruin.[4]

Yet, though the Exchange remained thronged with merchants, and the royal troops marched on every road to the west in hopes that one good blow might end all for the best, there were secret forces at work of which the King and Pepys were unaware. So long as any regiments of the standing army were in their neighbourhood, the rustic magnates of northern and midland England remained discreetly in their country houses. But once the dusty backs of the red-coats had faded into the misty lanes of the south and west, the great lords who had invited William over plucked up their courage. And from Exeter and the printing presses of London, the Prince's Declaration circulated among the people, with its promise—so well attuned to anxious ears—of a free and legally constituted Parliament that would redress all grievances, resolve the legitimacy of the warming-pan Prince of Wales, settle the Succession and establish the lawful Protestant religion beyond challenge. And with the Declaration spread rumours which revived the worst fears of '78 and '41—of stores of knives, grid-irons and cauldrons hidden in papist cellars for massacring and roasting Protestants. Twice that week the Guards were forced to disperse riotous apprentices outside the monastery at Clerkenwell and other meeting-places of the hated Catholics.[5]

Nor could the Government, for all its momentary

superiority in military force, feel any certainty that new invaders might not arrive. As he sat in his customary place in St Martin's-in-the-Fields on the morning of Sunday, November 11th, Pepys was called back to the office by a messenger from the Postmaster-General. An express had just been received from Harwich that five thousand troops were waiting in transports at Rotterdam for a wind. Twice that day and in the Cabinet in the evening Pepys asked the King for definite orders. But in the end, as usual, all was left to Dartmouth's discretion.[6]

During the second week of November strenuous efforts were made by the Court and Admiralty to prepare the fleet for further action, the King sending his letters to Dartmouth unsealed and open for Pepys to approve and forward. While the Admiral aboard the *Resolution* in the Downs complained of the divisions of his captains, the want of victuals and stores, the state of his ships after the storms, and his fears that the Dutch forces were greater than had been estimated, Pepys continued to pour out letters to subordinates in the hope that something decisive would come at last of all his labours. To those whom he deemed in need of reproof he was more than usually severe, emphasising the need for speed and "good husbandry" and censoring mercilessly such iniquities as those of the Fishermen's Company, who instead of providing the statutory quota of seamen from among its own members used its press warrants to rake up all the unseaworthy scum of the town. No irregularity passed unnoticed by that eagle eye in the long panelled room above the Watergate. "However I have offended you by my ungovernable way of proceeding," pleaded Sir William Booth, "I am sure that nothing can make me want gratitude to put all your commands in execution, even to the last drop of my blood or shilling I have in the world. I cannot help your being angry with me now, but I do give you my word that I will never give you the least occasion as long as I have breath, for never man hath been so much mortified as I have been at your angry way of writing. I know you are Christian enough to forgive me." For Christian though he was, the great Secretary was apt to require a tooth for a tooth, and more, when crossed.[7]

To Dartmouth's reasons for delay he returned a courteous but firm iteration of the importance of closing with the Dutch fleet: after all, the enemy were presumably in the same plight. On the evening of November 12th the Council reviewed two reports of the number of ships of war with the Prince of Orange, the one from a Deal postmaster who had counted them as they passed through the Straits, the other from a Scottish lieutenant in the Dutch service who had deserted at Torbay. The latter, led before the Council, stated that the total force consisted of forty-four ships of war with twelve fireships, instead of the sixty hitherto supposed, and these but of moderate size, indifferently manned and victualled. He was sent off at once to the Downs with his report. "An ill horseman as most of us sailors are", he seems to have travelled but slowly.[8]

But though Pepys wrote cheerfully to the Admiral that on this new information "his Majesty with the advice of all my Lords this night at the Cabinet" had determined upon his being "authorised to proceed against this fleet", his own resolution was not matched by his master's, who wrote after the Council by the same mail such a letter as only a Stuart would have penned. "I think that the Buoy of the Nore ought not to be so much as thought on without you were much overpowered by the enemy. . . . You best know your own strength and whether you are in a condition to make use of this easterly wind to attempt anything upon them. At least I think there can be no danger of going to the Spithead, and I should think you are in more safety there when the wind should come westerly than in the Downs. T'would be of some reputation even your going but thither, but of much more if you thought yourself strong enough to look out for them. . . . And now that I have said this to you, I must leave all to your judgment who are on the place." Such sentiments would have been admirable in other circumstances or addressed to another man. With his kingdom at stake and with a bold blow needed to recover it, James could no longer afford them.[9]

For a day or two longer, it continued to seem, as one of the Clerks of the Council put it, "the quietest invasion that ever was". William remained in Exeter waiting for allies and causing little harm beyond an interruption of the mails. "Some of the scurf and meaner part run into them", it was reported, "as they would to see a show, but generally retreat the next day; most of our Western people having ever since Monmouth's time been much troubled with dreams of gibbets." The nightly sallies of the London 'prentices against the Catholic chapels in Lime Street, Bucklersbury and Clerkenwell were still dispersed without much difficulty: on the beat of drum and the appearance of a few militiamen, "the young mutineers" scampered away.[10]

So at least it seemed to the Court, where preparations for the forthcoming fight—another Sedgemoor, it was hoped—went on without any signs of unseemly haste. The King had originally intended to set out for the west on Thursday the 15th, but early in the week it became known that he would not leave till the week-end. His health was not good, and the royal train had to be furnished with a special supply of milch asses. Meanwhile it was confidently announced that "the army, 27,000 strong, will be able to offer battle by Tuesday next on Salisbury Plains and our Imperial monarch at the head of them".[11]

★   ★   ★

But already disquieting rumours were beginning to percolate. At first, for all the brave promises of aid offered Orange when he was still safely on the other side of the water, his only reported accessions of strength were a Devonshire hedge-squire and a few Buckinghamshire butchers and maltsters evading their creditors. But in the course of the second week of invasion, it was whispered in London that such whig grandees as the Earls of Shrewsbury and Macclesfield, Lord Mordaunt and Mr Sidney were on their way to the Prince's camp. Then on the evening of the 14th it was learnt by an express from Cirencester that the dissolute Lord Lovelace with a party of a hundred horse had been stopped by the local militia and only disarmed after serious loss of life.

Far worse followed next day. Shortly after noon, as the King was sitting down to dinner, an express arrived from the west. He read it, rose, left his dinner untasted and went into his Closet, leaving a buzz of conversation behind him. Soon all the Palace knew of the desertion on the previous day of the King's nephew by his first marriage, young Lord Cornbury, one of the chief officers of the Army, heir to the tory house of Hyde and grandson of the great Earl of Clarendon who had stood by the Stuarts in the darkest hour of their adversity. Riding out of the royal camp at Šalisbury at the head of three regiments of cavalry, he had attempted to lead them into the enemy's lines, and, on the discovery of his treachery, had himself gone over with his chief officers. The private soldiers would not go with him.[12]

In a single hour the bubble of confidence had been pricked. After that there was no trusting anyone in high place. The most tried loyalist was suspect: no one could be absent two days, a courtier wrote, but underwent censure. Other defections were spoken of, the most important being that of the west-country magnate, Edward Seymour, whose loyalty, apart from his Toryism, had always been of a limited nature, it being dubious whether a man so proud and imperious could feel that emotion consistently towards anyone but himself. The "turbulent mobile", following the lead of their betters, grew bolder: the Convent at Clerkenwell was uproariously pulled down, and by the end of the week terrified Catholics were moving their goods to the foreign embassies. News from the Continent fanned the rising fires of Protestant alarm: in the Palatinate and on the Rhine the armies of the most Catholic King were marching from strength to strength, the Germans being as much taken by surprise by their old tormentors' winter campaigning as James had been by Orange.* On the 16th France declared war on Holland, and all Europe was in the melting-pot. The Protestant English could not forget that Orange was the foe, and their own King the friend, of the French tyrant.[13]

On Saturday, November 17th, James prepared to leave the capital. Before he started for the front he called his officers together and, giving them the choice of laying down their commissions, begged

----

* ". . . it being sleeping time with the Germans who did not expect a campaign in the depths of the winter." *Ellis Correspondence* ii, 289.

them not to betray him by deserting his standard in
the field as Cornbury had done. Afterwards he asked
the Cabinet to witness his last will and testament.
Pepys's signature to this document appears immediately below the names of the Lords of the Council—Lord Chancellor Jeffreys, Melfort, Belasyse
and Arundell of Wardour, Preston, the Secretary
of State, and Godolphin—and above those of William Blathwayt, the Secretary-at-War, and William
Bridgeman, the Clerk of the Council. For all the
sorrow of the occasion it must have been a proud
moment for the son of a tailor who owed nothing to
birth and everything to his own efforts.[14]

Before the King set out, the Archbishops of Canterbury and York and a group of high tory peers and
bishops sought an audience. James showed no
pleasure at seeing them. They begged him to call a
speedy Parliament and steal the invader's thunder
rather than be forced to it by a general insurrection.
He refused, saying that he would hold no Parliament
while traitors were in arms in the kingdom. He
would answer them with steel of their own metal.[15]

At about two o'clock in the afternoon James left
for Windsor, taking his infant son with him. The
popular feeling about the Prince was such that he
dared not leave him in the capital: he felt it safer to
send him to Portsmouth. Pepys accompanied his
sovereign on the first stage of his journey as far as
Windsor. There that night he thought it advisable to
safeguard his own position against an adverse future
by a paper acknowledging the sums owing to him
on the count of his earlier services. This he got the
King to sign:

We do hereby graciously declare our continued sense of the
long and faithful services performed to our late dearest Brother
and our self by Mr. Pepys, our Secretary for the affairs of our
Admiralty of England, and that his long want of satisfaction to

his just pretensions attested by ourself when Duke of York and confirmed by our said dearest Brother in a statement thereof bearing date the second day of March 1678/9 shall be no impediment to his receiving the same from us; we hereby earnestly recommending him to the Lords Commissioners of the Treasury for their doing him full right on our behalf therein, and in what is further due to him in his account as late Treasurer for Tangier. Given at our Castle of Windsor on this 17th day of November 1688.

The sum at stake was in the neighbourhood of £28,000. If Pepys be judged as over-worldly for reminding his royal master of this ancient debt at such an hour, it should be remembered that he had refrained from doing so during the four and a half years of his second tenure of the Admiralty Secretaryship, when he could have obtained payment for it at almost any time. But he had felt that the Service he controlled had more need of the money than he. Only now, when the solid earth was quaking under his feet, did he ask that his debt on the community should be recorded. He was never paid.[16]

Next morning, Sunday the 18th, the King set out for Salisbury, sending the Prince of Wales towards Portsmouth. Pepys returned to London. He had much to cause him anxiety, for not only was his master's cause committed to an unknown battlefield in the west, but Dartmouth, spurred on by his exhortations, had at last resolved to attack the enemy. The fleet, after being becalmed for three days, had sailed from the Downs on the afternoon of Friday the 16th with a north-east wind, good weather and a settled hard sky. For a moment it seemed as though the long tide of ill fortune was about to turn. But on Sunday night, after Pepys got back to London, the clear frosty weather broke, the wind shifting into the south-west and rapidly increasing to gale intensity. So it continued for four days while Pepys, gazing out at grey, blowing sky and river, penned anxious and fruitless letters of enquiry. The tragedy for him—and it is hard to over-estimate the bitterness of it—was that had the wintry gales proper to that season commenced a fortnight earlier when the Prince's transports were at sea they might well have driven the invaders to as terrible an end as that which befell their predecessors in that other and greater '88 of a century before. "It is strange", Dartmouth had written to the King, "that such mad proceedings should have such success at this time of the year, but I hope God will bless your Majesty's forces at last." And now, when it might so have come to pass, the scales of fate were depressed still lower against a failing cause. For the long-expected tempest found the King's fleet at sea and the Dutch safe in an English anchorage.[17]

*   *   *

The week ending the 24th of November, the third of the invasion, was, for those in London, a time of waiting. The city remained strangely quiet: the sober and richer sort attending to their business and collecting their debts, while the noisier, "that gad about all day for coffee and news", contented themselves with whispering. Pepys watched the wind and drafted long letters of administrative detail against all contingencies. On Tuesday the 20th he wrote one of six crowded pages to the missing Admiral, and sent it to Portsmouth thinking it might perhaps catch him there. The Navy Office was busy getting six more fireships to drive the Dutch from their moorings, the *Roebuck* had sailed from Sheerness and the *Mermaid* would soon follow; the *Portland* was lying in Long Reach, "manned, victualled, and in all respects ready to sail excepting the wanting

of her guns". Concerning these Pepys left her commander, he told Dartmouth, "to make his own
moan to your Lordship as he has not spared to do to
me". "I do with great longings", he concluded, "to
hear of your Lordship and the fleet after the tempes-
tuous weather we have for some days past had."[18]

During that week of rumours—that the Dutch
fleet had been dispersed by the storm and had been
sighted in distress off Land's End, that the Prince of
Wales had been shipped to France, that a battle had
taken place in the west, that Kirke had been killed by
his own men on Salisbury Plain, and that fifty
thousand French had landed at Dover—Pepys was
made an unwilling party to a comic interlude
afforded by the childlike temper of his brother-in-
law Balty. On the evening of the 21st there arrived at
the Admiralty a long and passionate letter complaining of how on the previous day the *Phoenix*, long
delayed at Deptford by easterly winds, had been
prevented by the unaccountable absence of her captain from taking advantage of the sudden change to
the south-west. It seems that Balty, who was still
enjoying his brief heyday of prosperity as Commissioner at Deptford, had risen at half-past six to pursue his day's duties, and, on enquiring why the
Phoenix had not sailed with the morning tide, was
told by the Clerk of the Cheque that Captain Gifford
was in London. "On which", Balty explained, "my
zeal for his Majesty's service could not but move me
into some passion for such a neglect!" and he had
expressed himself with some freedom to the master.
After which he repaired to London for his customary Tuesday meeting with Sir Anthony Deane and
Mr Hewer "on his Majesty's affairs". Returning in
the evening, he found the wind still in the south-
west, and the captain of the *Phoenix* still away. He
therefore took it upon himself to order her lieuten-

ant to sail with the morning tide. Then, being very
weary, he went to bed.[19]

Yet scarcely had he begun his slumbers when
"rap, rap, at my door comes the 'Globe' boy bringing the enclosed note with express order to deliver it
to me presently. The contents when you see I leave
you to judge. . . . Oh! how soon", this virtuous
official commented, "will all government and rule
in the Navy be violated and trampled on if the Commissioners thereof may be thus used by every captain!" And he begged for the administration ("under
correction of your piercing judgment") of a gentle
reprimand to the erring commander. "Sir, this
comes from one who dares to do his duty and will
against all discouragements." He added that his
"well wishes for a fair wind and eager pressing" had
since had the desired effect, for the *Phoenix* had
sailed for Long Reach that morning.

Enclosed was Captain Gifford's note, ill-spelt,
ill-written but quite as passionate. After applying
"his piercing judgment" to this affecting correspondence Pepys seems to have administered a provisional rebuke both to the captain and to Balty,
notifying the former of the charge made against him
and enquiring of the latter whether his old fault of
hasty anger might not have led him into expressing
himself too freely. He was promptly rewarded by
indignant letters from both protagonists for whom
the war with the invaders had now become a minor
matter. From Long Reach Captain Gifford expressed in no uncertain terms his sense of outrage at a
landsman's interference, declaring it to be entirely
the pilot's fault that the *Phoenix* had not sailed on the
20th and complaining that Balty had insulted him
before his crew. As for his own absence, he had
never been away from his ship for more than a day
since he had taken command, and at the time com-

plained of was merely waiting for the pilot with a
runner in attendance to summon him the moment
he arrived. His diligence, he thought, merited praise
from the Commissioner rather than a complaint.

Balty's letter was worthy of his long mastery of
the epistolary art. He protested that though he must
ever and with all thankfulness acknowledge that his
brother-in-law's regard for him had been expressed
with tenderness, his own temper was certainly not
so overweening and soft as to make him take offence
without cause. What he had done had been due to
Captain Gifford's "ingentile, and I may well say
rough, if not rude, return to my zealous discharge of
the duty and trust incumbent on me for hastening to
sea all the additions of force possible at such a time as
this, when the King and kingdom are under the
highest dangers (probably) thro' a foreign invasion". No "personal disrespect or private pique" had
swayed him, nor had he used any "threatening or
unhandsome expressions". With "all openhearted-
ness, plainness and sincerity" he had told "the very
truth and nothing but the truth". It was his conviction that his was but another instance of the attempt
certain captains ("especially the Court-like finer sort
of 'um") were making to weaken the authority of
the Special Commission "by shooting these little
arrows through me (a member) at the whole
body".★

Next day when Balty waited on him, Pepys asked
him to answer, in writing and with brevity, certain
questions: the date of the Navy Board's order for
fitting out the *Phoenix*, the degree of experience of
the pilot, and the captain's state of sobriety at the
time of writing his note. He knew his Navy. Balty

★ B. St Michel to S. P., Nov. 23rd, 1688. *Rawl. MSS. A.* 186,
f. 212.

replied that he had enquired of the master of the *Globe* who had been drinking with Gifford: "he says he seemed to be sober, but I am apt to believe (the time of night considered) he might be somewhat warmed with wine." He may well have been, for it seemed that in the flurry of his departure the captain had impressed two Bailiff's officers, a butcher and a weed-cutter by vocation, and kept them forcibly under hatches—an illegality that brought upon him a warrant from the Lord Chief Justice and one of the Admiralty Secretary's sternest rebukes. The rest is silence. For the storm in a tea-cup roused by these lesser events was now submerged by a greater.[20]

Throughout the latter part of the week, while the gale continued unabated, tidings kept percolating to London of units of the fleet parted from their consorts and driven for shelter into southern habours. Then on the morning of Saturday the 24th definite news of Lord Dartmouth arrived from Portsmouth. "It is with an extraordinary degree of content", Pepys wrote to him at noon that day, "that I have just now received your Lordship's of yesterday from the Spithead . . . giving me ground of hoping that the loss his Majesty has sustained from the late tempests will prove much more tolerable than we have for many days lain under an apprehension it would have done." For he was able to add to the Admiral's account of the twenty-two ships which had returned with him to harbour—about half his battered fleet—news of another eleven; seven in the Downs, two in Portland Road, and two off the Isle of Wight. At nightfall he wrote again to inform him that a letter dated the 22nd, and opened by the King at Salisbury, had come in from Captain Churchill of the *Newcastle* at Plymouth. That officer, who had much to say about the condition of his ship, gave a graphic description of the leak which had caused his separation from his consorts. The real reason for his defection was to appear later.[21]

Pepys communicated his news to the Lords of the Council and sent an express to his master at Salisbury. But beyond his relief that his beloved fleet was safe, he had little cause to be pleased. The action on which he had pinned his own hopes and his country's had never taken place.

It was a sorry tale that Dartmouth had had to tell of "such variety of winds and storms as frustrated all my hopes and intentions for his Majesty's service". On the 19th, three days after he had sailed from the Downs, he had sighted the Dutch in Torbay. But by that time his own fleet was so divided and depleted that he had been forced to put back to St Helen's. "There is no resisting a storm in the Channel at this time of the year", he informed the King. "Their fortune hath been extravagant, for there hath been but three fair days since I came to sea, and they had two of them to land in, while I was becalmed off Beachy. But sure I shall have some luck at last, for I will struggle all I can and endure with patience till I can compass that service you expect from me. My business now shall be to get ready soon as possible, tho' the season of the year is intolerable, sixteen hours night to eight hours day with lee shores in the Channel is harder working than any battle. If it had pleased God to have continued the wind and weather, in all probability I could not have failed." The fact remained that he had done so.[22]

*   *   *

No battle took place on land either, and the power and dominion of England changed hands without a struggle. On Monday, November 19th, the King had reached Salisbury and next day the Prince of

Orange, leaving Seymour to govern the west, had started from Exeter to meet him. Somewhere on Salisbury Plain, it seemed, battle would be joined: men spoke of Stonehenge as the place where the fate of the realm would be decided. The advance guards met in skirmish at Wincanton, a troop of Sarsfield's horse falling back before Mackay's invading Scots. The King at the entreaty of Kirke and Churchill had proposed on the Wednesday to inspect his outposts at Warminster. But on the day before he set out, his health, undermined by early excesses and strained beyond endurance by the events of the past few weeks, failed him, and he was driven to his bed by a violent discharge of blood from the nose. During the next few days he remained at Salisbury in the hands of his doctors.[23]

Information of these events had come to the ears of those in authority in London, but public news remained scanty. Meanwhile rumour was busy: the sight of the King's officers in the Tower—Papists it was believed—planting mortars in the White Tower caused something of a panic in the City on Friday. That night news reached the capital from the north: the arch-rebel Delamere, with many "old Oliverians", was in arms in Cheshire. Worse followed next day; that the Earl of Danby, raising an alarm that papist soldiers were planning a massacre, had roused the local gentry and militia against the tiny garrison of York, seized the city, and declared for the Prince of Orange. Here was no "old Oliverian" but an eminent Cavalier whom less than ten years before the Whigs had threatened with a halter and sent to the Tower for his fidelity. Fired by such an example, alarmed by news of fresh triumphs across the water for the French King and with tales of an impending papist massacre, with no Parliament called and the Prince's Declaration in favour of one circulating everywhere, the country began to rise under the malcontent lords. The rabble came out in the towns and the honest gentry and freeholders, clad in their fathers' rusty armour, in the shires. At Nottingham, where the whig Earl of Devonshire declared for Orange on the 22nd, the local worthies announced themselves as "assembled together . . . for the defence of our laws, liberties, and properties (according to those free born liberties and privileges descended to us from our ancestors, the undoubted birthright of the subjects of this kingdom of England) . . . being by innumerable grievances made sensible that the very fundamentals of our liberty, religion and properties are about to be rooted out by our late Jesuitical Privy Council . . . and not being willing to deliver over our posterity to such conditions of Popery and slavery". What precise injury to their liberties as free-born Englishmen they had till now suffered, save a slight abrogation of their right to persecute those of another faith, they did not specify. But they would not, they said, be bugbeared by the "opprobrious term of rebels". "Such a riding and travelling about at such a rate as I never see in my life," wrote one onlooker, "they being resolved to subdue Popery." They were not disloyal, but merely, as was natural to Englishmen in a crisis, a little confused as to what was happening and intensely determined to do what all their neighbours were doing.[24]

Pepys had no share in their feelings. Though like other men he might be blind to the hidden stream of inevitable evolution of which all this turmoil was a part, he knew too much to be deceived by the propagandist cry that had brought out the honest militia of the East Riding. His heart was with the King who had stood beside him in his work of restoring the Navy. Others of his paid servants, fearing for their estates or places, might make their secret peace with the invader. It never occurred to Pepys to do anything so base.

Many did. On the evening of Saturday the 24th at Salisbury, ill in body and heart and feeling that his whole realm was crumbling behind him, James took the advice of his French generals, Feversham and de Duras, and resolved to fall back at once on London and the Thames. No sooner had the decision been taken, than the two leading English officers of the army, Lord Churchill and the King's nephew, the Duke of Grafton, who had long been in correspondence with the enemy, set out for William's lines. When on Sunday morning their absence became known, the camp broke up in confusion. Not since the last tragic hours of King John's reign had such a wholesale betrayal* been seen in England.

On the same afternoon a courier brought the news to London. All that evening the galleries of Whitehall were crowded with a vast, excited throng. Next morning those going to call the Princess Anne found that she had fled from the Palace in the night with Lord Churchill's wife. The rumour spread through the town that she had been murdered by Papists. But, as those who started it knew, she was already on the road to the north to join those in rebellion against her father, while Bishop Compton, who had sat with the inquisitors who tried to implicate Pepys back in '78, rode jackbooted and armed by her side.[25]

In that tragic hour a tried friend of Pepys and one

---

* Like the rest of the world I read with admiration Sir Winston Churchill's long and brilliant vindication of his great ancestor. His pages would, if it were possible, increase one's sense of gratitude to Marlborough for his services to his country, and one's admiration of his generosity, his charm and his genius. But nothing can alter the nature of his relationship to King James. It was the same as Pepys's, save that it was more intimate.

with as loyal a heart as his own defined the nature of the dilemma which confronted every good man in authority who still remained true to his trust. At Hartley Row, amid the cares of commanding the King's artillery on the retreat from Salisbury, Sir Henry Shere found time to write a letter to his old comrade and chief, Lord Dartmouth. He knew well, he told him, what a heavy burden of distress he must be under. "You have now a part to act, my Lord, which to my weak discerning is by much the most important of your life; which will appear plainer to you when I tell your Lordship that the King is almost quite deserted. You have heard of those who gave the first example, where my Lord Cornbury was the leader, my Lord Abingdon going in with him etc. Yesterday my Lord Churchill, the Duke of Grafton, and many with them besides two regiments, are gone to the Prince of Orange, and just now, while I am writing this, news is come (and I believe it true) that the Prince of Denmark, the Duke of Ormonde, my Lord Rochester and many others are likewise amongst the deserters. And every day will produce new accounts to add to the list and heap new calamities upon this poor unfortunate prince's head, who has been cursed with fools to his counsellors and knaves in his bosom, the one to advise him to his destruction, the other to desert him in his distress.

"The King is very ill, I fear, I may say dangerously so, at least in my opinion. He rests this night in the neighbouring village and tomorrow proceeds to London, whither we are moving as fast as our great body can march, and may expect tomorrow to have our quarters beaten up.

"Now my dear Lord, what will you do? I know you are a man of honour and I pray God keep you in that mind. You have therefore an insuperable task given you which nothing but divine inspiration can resolve how you will be able to go through with. While you remain firm in your obedience and faithful to your trust, you are sure to draw the envy, enmity and indignation of all those upon you who shall have forfeited that character, which has a fatal aspect on your fortune and future state, and, while you reflect on your family and circumstances, will not choose but cost you some sad reluctancies. And should you quite depart from your duty and allegiance in the high station wherein you now are, you will then be undone to yourself, for it would give you pangs of remorse that would haunt you to your grave.

"What then, is the temper between these extremes? If you contribute in any wise to the bringing in foreign force, you are undone without redemption. If you fight the Dutch fleet it will be as fatal, and little less if you give up your command so that the fleet should fall into hands that may render it useful to any of these ends which you might have prevented. Is it not possible for your Lordship to shun these rocks by artfully keeping the fleet for some days at sea (for this fermentation cannot last ten days) and by that means put it out of your power to obey or refuse? . . . But I am at my wits' end, and you will forgive me, my good Lord, while you know what an aching heart I have for you, and that out of the force of my love, gratitude and duty, I presume thus to interpose my poor opinion. God in his mercy and wisdom, bless and counsel your Lordship and send us a happy meeting."[26]

The King also wrote to Dartmouth on the same day, sending his letter by Lord Dover. This Catholic convert—the philandering Harry Jermyn of time past—was appointed to the command of the garrison at Portsmouth. He carried secret verbal instructions about the future of the Prince of Wales. At about four o'clock on Monday afternoon the unhappy monarch reached London to find that his second daughter as well as his first had betrayed him. Broken in spirit, he sat till late at night in council. As the only course now remaining, it was resolved to call the Lords Temporal and Spiritual, whose advice he had so summarily declined ten days before.[27]

When at eleven that night the Cabinet broke up, Pepys, who had been spending the day writing routine letters to the British Consuls in the Mediterranean, set down at the King's command for Dartmouth's benefit the circumstances of the Princess Anne's flight lest there should be any misconception about it in the fleet. He related how that morning Mrs Danvers and Sir Benjamin Bathurst had found her bed cold and her clothes of the previous day, even to her shoes and stockings, left behind, and how the Guard at the Cockpit door had seen a coach with six horses drive off in the night. The evilly disposed were now saying that the Papists had forced her away, whereas—so it seemed to Pepys—nothing could be thought more natural "than that the ladies should think it time to withdraw as soon as they had received tidings of their husbands having done the same".[28]

Next day, Tuesday the 27th, the Lords Temporal and Spiritual, or such of them as were in the capital and not with the rebels, met the King in the Dining Room of Whitehall. The Archbishop of Canterbury and James's brothers-in-law, the Earls of Clarendon and Rochester, were among them, with the Secretaries of State in attendance. They advised the King—some of them in language frank to the point of brutality—to call a free Parliament, issue an amnesty and appoint commissioners to open negotiations with the Prince of Orange. In an agony of reluctance the King agreed but asked for a further night to consider the last. The thought of any truck with traitors stuck in his throat.[29]

Perhaps it was the knowledge that a Parliament was certain to meet in the near future which caused Pepys to spare time that day from his official correspondence to write to his friends at Harwich. The proposal about re-opening the naval yard there, he told the Mayor and Corporation, had been approved by the King and would be set in hand so soon as the days began to lengthen. The Commissioners of Customs had agreed to the removal of the Customs House from Ipswich to Harwich, the only remaining impediment being the royal reluctance to injure old and deserving officials at the former place. "Not but that I shall firmly hope," Pepys explained, "cloudy as things at this day look, that Almighty God has it in his gracious purpose to support the King and his Government, and thoroughly to protect the Church of England both in its discipline and doctrine. But that hope not being entirely void of apprehensions that things may possibly end otherwise, I would be very glad, and so would Sir Anthony Deane, to do something while we may to the advantage of a place and society from which we have received so many obligations." And he asked Captain Langley to let him have an account of any expenses he might have been put to in removing the buoys in the river during the invasion, that he might get him reimbursed while still in a capacity for doing it. "For as matters stand," he added, "I know not how little awhile I may be so."[30]

Next day James agreed to all the proposals of the Lords Temporal and Spiritual. Pepys passed on the good news at once to Dartmouth, telling him that he had just come from attending the King at his

Cabinet where he had been graciously pleased to declare his royal purpose of calling a Parliament as speedily as the requisite time for issuing and returning the writs would admit. "But what pity it is", he observed, "that I could not bring this news without meeting something to abate some of the pleasure which the foregoing tidings must give to all good subjects, Mr Frowde"—the Postmaster—"stopping me in my way to tell me that my Lord of Bath had seized Plymouth for the Prince."[31]

Those Tories who wished for nothing more than a restoration of the old Cavalier and Church of England supremacy, were well pleased. The King had agreed to all they had asked. Nothing now remained but to make terms with Orange, render him thanks for his service and set the broken Constitution working again. The tory Nottingham, the trimmer Halifax, who eight years before had saved the legitimate succession by his speech in the Exclusion debate, and the inevitable Godolphin were appointed Commissioners to treat with the Prince. The Catholic Lieutenant of the Tower, Sir Edward Hales, was superseded by a Protestant. A free pardon was offered to all in rebellion. It was hoped that the Parliament which was to meet on January 13th would be as tory as that of 1685.[32]

But there were factors in the situation which the loyalist Tories had almost forgotten. There was Orange himself, who had not come to England purely for the spiritual good of that country and certainly not for that of the Cavalier Party. And there were Orange's friends. When Lord Clarendon, fresh from this eleventh-hour understanding with his royal master, hurried to make his peace at the Prince's camp at Salisbury, he was pained to encounter such old-time revolutionaries as Major Wildman and the preacher, Ferguson, very much at their ease and urgent for tory blood. Others both in London and the country appeared to share their hopes: the whig printing presses were never at rest, and lying rumours, disquieting in the extreme to loyal minds, spread like wildfire. The Tories might pay the piper, if they chose, but it was the Whigs who were calling the tune to which the nation was now dancing. And the tune was *Lilliburlero*. A false proclamation, accepted everywhere as genuine, called in the Prince's name on all Protestants to arrest and disarm the papist supporters of the King. And as those who remembered '78 recalled, a Protestant mob inspired by enthusiastic Whigs made little account of the difference between a Tory and a Papist.[33]

There was another factor which should have caused the jubilant Anglican loyalists some misgiving—the state of the King's mind. Of what was passing in it, Pepys perhaps knew more than any other Protestant about him. At the secret Cabinet after the royal return to London on the evening of the 25th, at which Pepys had been present, the question of sending the infant Prince of Wales out of England had been discussed. James's religious convictions being what they were, this was the essential condition on which the bewildered, defeated man would alone consent to call a Parliament whose first act, he knew, would be to insist on his son's education as a Protestant, if it did not—as the coarse libels now on every coffee-house table suggested—challenge his legitimacy. With the husband of the next heir invading the kingdom in arms, this last contingency indeed seemed almost inevitable. As a result of that mournful discussion Pepys next day prepared a secret warrant to Lord Dartmouth for the King's signature. He did so in his own hand, "as containing a matter which will not bear

being known to more than was at the debate of it till
we may be morally sure that no advice of it hence by
land could prevent the execution". The writing of
it must have caused him many an anxious thought.
It contained orders to aid Lord Dover in transporting the Prince of Wales to France.[34]

But for a few days the warrant and the royal letter
to Dartmouth which accompanied it were not
despatched. The rest after his travels may have given
the ailing King a last flicker of his old courage. He
still delayed committing himself to the fatal course
to which Father Petre was pressing him. Instead he
sent to Dartmouth on the 29th a brief letter, telling
him to preserve the fleet at all costs and asking him to
consider where best to dispose of his ships. "You
will have an account from Mr Pepys of what passes
here and the ill condition my affairs are in on shore,
so that I shall say nothing concerning them." Pepys
in his own letter—a long one—reported that as the
King did not anticipate any further opportunity of
venturing the fleet that winter, rigid economy and
retrenchment must now be the order of the day.
This was in reply to a somewhat querulous letter
from Dartmouth, asking for instructions. The long
sequence of failures was straining tempers: Pepys
himself became a little tart. "You are doing a very
good work in getting a strict account of the state of
your victuals. Pray be pleased to hasten it. For not-
withstanding all my pressing for the providing of
more, the Service may meet with disappointment
therein if the Commissioners of the Victualling here
go by one reckoning and the men eat by another."[35]

Yet on that very day the King, ill and surrounded
as he believed by a murderous populace, surren-
dered once more to his secret terrors. He sought out
the French ambassador and confided to him that his
negotiations with Orange were a mere feint to gain

time while he smuggled his wife and child to safety. He would never allow a Parliament to meet which would only force him to do what he was determined not to: to abandon his protection of his Catholic subjects and take arms against Louis. He would sooner entrust his sacred cause and dear ones to his French cousin. Once more he wrote to Dartmouth. "'Tis my son they aim at and 'tis my son I must endeavour to preserve whatsoever becomes of me. Therefore I conjure you to assist Lord Dover in getting him sent away in the yachts, as soon as wind and weather will permit, for the first port they can get to in France, and that with as much secrecy as may be." Next day, the last in November, Pepys transmitted orders to the captains of the *Anne* and *Isabella* yachts to fall down the river to Erith.[36]

At noon on December 1st Pepys wrote to Captain Macdonell of the *Assurance* frigate to fit his ship in readiness for any orders the King might give and to repair in person to town with the utmost diligence. On that day a warrant was also despatched to Portsmouth ordering Dover and Dartmouth to put their fatal instructions into execution. Two days later, on the 3rd, Pepys ordered the *Isabella* yacht to transport the Comte de Lauzun to France. From what followed we know that the Queen was intended to accompany him.[37]

Meanwhile Dartmouth at Porstmouth was at his wits' end. On every hand he was faced by demands for money. One of his captains complained that he had not two sixpences in the world and begged him to spare an old periwig to keep his bald head from the cold. The officers of the Ordnance, snowed under by simultaneous demands from fleet, army and garrisons, protested that they had not the wherewithal to furnish a single ship; and the dock-yard hands, denied by Lord Dover the cash which

Pepys had sent down to pay them, were on strike. The unhappy Admiral had therefore received the news of the calling of a Parliament with intense relief and despatched a humble Address, signed by himself and his captains, thanking the King for what he had done and beseeching him to open negotiations with Orange. This document, which reached Whitehall on the 2nd, plunged James into the deepest gloom. Coming from his own fleet, it was a terrible blow to his pride. Even Sir Roger Strickland, he noticed, was among the signatories. "The poor King is mightily broken", wrote a courtier, "a great heart can't so easily bend".[38]

In the course of the same day Dartmouth was confronted with his master's shattering instructions. His dilemma was a terrible one. If he sent the Prince overseas, he would give France a hostage and a perpetual temptation to invade England. He would also render himself guilty of treason. With what he described as the greatest grief of heart imaginable he sat down to reply, imploring James to remember how strict the laws were in this matter. "Pardon me, therefore, Sir, if on my bended knees I beg of you to apply yourself to other councils, for the doing this looks like nothing less than despair to the degree of not only giving your enemies encouragement but distrust of your friends and people, who I do not despair but will yet stand by you in the defence and right of your lawful successor." And he reminded the King how prophetically he had foretold his former misfortunes and advised him how to avoid them.[39]

Dartmouth prevailed with Dover to delay any further action until he had received a reply to his letter to the King. He was able to do so the more easily because certain of his captains, who were in secret communication with Orange, took it upon themselves to patrol the mouth of the harbour day and night. As the Commissioner of the Dockyard put it, nobody wanted a second Perkin Warbeck. So far as escape from Portsmouth was concerned the game was up, and the King knew it. Dartmouth's letter reached him on the evening of the 4th, and its contents were already common talk in the capital that night. On the morning of the 5th James replied bidding Dartmouth hold his hand until he had had time to consider the matter: in the evening he added a postscript ordering the infant Prince to be sent back to London by land or, if the roads were not safe, by sea to Margate under an escort. Three days later Pepys sent orders to Captain Fazeby of the *Mary* yacht, then at Porstmouth, to take the Prince of Wales and his retinue aboard and transport them to Greenwich. He need not have given himself the trouble, for Lord Dover, suspecting that the traitor captains were planning to seize his charge, had already slipped away with him at dead of night by coach for London.[40]

Here in the capital, the waves of popular feeling, fanned by the winds of rumour, were dashing with gale force against the King and those who stood by him. The hawkers bawled "A Hue and Cry after Father Petre" outside his now deserted Whitehall lodgings, houses and cellars were searched by the rabble for papist arms, and the magistrates were powerless. In the streets suspected Jesuits were hunted like dogs. The brave roaring days of '78 and '41 were come again. As Orange's army drew nearer, the prudent, fearing a siege, began to lay in provisions.

In the provinces also the malcontents found ready allies in the basest elements of society. At Newcastle, the roughs of the town, urged on by Lord Lumley, threw the King's statue into the Tyne. Hull,

Norwich, Chester, Shrewsbury and Worcester in turn went with the tide, the slender forces of order being submerged almost without a struggle in the fierce popular flood.★ At Cambridge priests' robes were burnt in the market place: a learned divine from one of the new Catholic colleges was forced to hide for his life in a "boghouse" and another made to dance naked in a ditch until he promised to change his religion. At Oxford the dissolute Lord Lovelace, released from Gloucester gaol by the mob, rode into the East Gate amid a blaze of orange ribands, the drums playing before him and a crowd of "rusty ruffians" surging after with drawn swords. Only in the Services did loyalty dare to raise its head; the private soldiers and the humbler sort of officers, who had no temptation to ape the treachery of their superiors, looked on with sullen faces. The desertions from the lower ranks of the Navy and Army were astonishingly few. Dartmouth wrote that now a Parliament had been called the seamen seemed perfectly satisfied and that the Prince of Orange would soon find things alter should he obstruct an honourable settlement.[41]

But Orange, who was as astute a politician as his uncle, Charles II, threw away no chances. Advancing slowly towards the capital, he maintained a passive silence and left the fury of his baser allies and the folly of the King to do his business. On Saturday, the 8th, after a judicious delay—for every fresh manifestation of private treachery and popular fanaticism would, as he well knew, shake his father-in-law's weak nerves—he received the Royal Commissioners at Hungerford. At the "Bear" inn, it was

★ "There was scarce an hour but his Majesty received, like Job, some message of some revolt or misfortune or other." *Sir John Reresby, Memoirs*, 536.

proposed that the invaders should halt pending the meeting of Parliament, that the royal troops should withdraw to a like distance the other side of London, and that all Catholic officers should be dismissed. These terms, so artfully contrived that they were too reasonable for loyal men to disapprove and too repugnant for James to accept, were put into writing on the 9th. "What if the King were to go away?" Halifax, dining with the Prince at Littlecote, asked Burnet. "There is nothing so much to be wished", was the reply.[42]

On the same day James, in London, his mind full of secret terrors, had come to a similar resolution. His Irish troops hooted in the streets, his priests in hiding and his child secretly conveyed back to London like a parcel of stolen goods, he took his fears once more to the sly and sympathetic Barillon. Many years before his father had warned him that for a King it was never far from the prison to the grave. He thought of himself as Richard II and of his son-in-law as another Bolingbroke. Many a King of England before him had fled and been restored, he told the Ambassador: he would preserve his rights to assert them on another occasion. There should be another year of Restoration, but not another '49. James in his blindness failed to see that the miracle of '60 had only come about because there had been a '49. He proposed to do what his father with all his mistakes had never done: to turn his back on his realm.[43]

In the storm and darkness of the night of December 9th the Queen and her infant son crossed the Thames in an open boat and, soaked in rain, took coach from Lambeth for Gravesend, where Lord Powis was waiting with a yacht to carry them to France. Next day, as soon as he learnt that they had

set sail, the King sent for the Lords and for the Lord
Mayor and Sheriffs and informed them of what he
had done, promising them that, however dark the
complexion of his affairs might look, he would not
abandon his post. He wrote to Dartmouth in the
same vein, acquainting Pepys with the contents of
his letter, which he gave to him to send.[44]

Yet there was still something which the King kept
even from his most faithful servants. In his heart, the
obstinate man had resolved to abandon neither his
prerogative of relieving his co-religionists nor his
alliance with Louis. Sooner than receive his Commissioners from Hungerford and the conditions
they brought, he would leave his unworthy subjects
to their fate. That night in the secrecy of his Closet
he burnt the unissued writs for summoning Parliament and sent for the Great Seal. Then he penned a
letter to Lord Feversham, ordering him to disband
the army, and another to Dartmouth telling him
what he was about to do. "My affairs", he wrote,
"are in so desperate a condition that I have been
obliged to send away the Queen and the Prince to
secure them at least, whatsoever becomes of me that
am resolved to venture all rather than consent to
anything in the least prejudicial to the crown or my
conscience. And having been basely deserted, . . . I
could no longer resolve to expose myself to no
purpose to what I might expect from the ambitious
Prince of Orange and the associated rebellious
Lords, and therefore have resolved to withdraw till
this violent storm is over, which will be in God's
good time, and hope that there will still remain in
this land seven thousand men that will not bow
down the knee to Baal and keep themselves free
from associations and such rebellious practices." It
had come right once before when times were as bad,

or worse: it might do so once again. He would escape from the reality he had been unable to master into the romance of his youth: exile, the odour and sanctity of martyrdom at the court of foreign princes, and above all hope—hope once again of that wonderful miraculous ending. The fleet could sail for Ireland and take service under Tyrconnel, that is if the captains would obey orders, and if not, "there is no remedy, and this I may say, never any Prince took more care of his sea and land men as I have done, and been so very ill repaid by them. I have not time to say more, being just a going to take horse."[45]

Pepys, knowing nothing of all this, had also written to Dartmouth. He instructed him that rigid economy must be enforced and pressing cease, the town and Exchange being full of complaints about the disorders of the press-gang: "and to say the truth," he added, "by all the despatch that I can observe made in the manning of the ships here, even with the help of pressing, it looks to me as if they would not be manned till March." And after a good deal of uninspired detail about victualling and the salaries of muster-masters, he gave the news. The rabble of Dover had taken the Castle, Dragoons had been worsted in a skirmish by the Prince of Orange's troops, a battalion of the Scots Guards at Maidenhead had gone over *en masse* to the invaders. In London the Roman Catholics were flying for their lives. "God (who only knows what is best) grant a quick and happy issue to that just indignation of his under which we are at this day fallen!" After which he expressed the two letters to Portsmouth and went to bed.[46]

He was awakened early in the morning by one of the King's French pages with a letter, sealed and addressed to Dartmouth in the royal hand. From him he learnt the shattering news that his master had left the Palace in the night, first commanding him to deliver two letters, one to the soldier, de Duras, and the other to Pepys to forward to Lord Dartmouth. This, without examining its contents, he sent off by express to Portsmouth.[47]

Chapter VII

The Interregnum

"I told him I was for a Parliament and the Protestant religion as well as they, but I was also for the King." *Sir J. Reresby*.

The King had gone. It soon appeared that he had taken the Great Seal with him or in some way disposed of it. The Lord Chancellor had also gone. So had the writs for assembling Parliament. And the army, it seemed, was going too, for Lord Feversham, true to his orders, was busy dissolving it unpaid. The kingdom had reverted to the state of nature.

It was this presumably that the King had intended—a just punishment on a stubborn, treacherous and stiff-necked people. They had denied the divine ordinance of kingly government: they should have a taste of the opposite—of anarchy, the "war of all against all". By his own withdrawal, his destruction of the writs, his removal of the Great Seal and his desperate orders to the heads of the armed forces, he had removed every recognised agency by which the business of government could be continued. And he had done it with dramatic and staggering suddenness.

It was an interesting situation, and of a kind to puzzle the ingenuity of the most learned political philosophers. But the English are not a race of abstract philosophers, and James never displayed a more remarkable incapacity to understand them and their institutions than in this fatal and final act. In

logic and law alike the government of the kingdom
had ceased. The leaders of the English proceeded to
act as though it had not ceased at all.

Within a couple of hours, in the midst of a prodigious uproar and confusion, a provisional government had been set up. The King's brother-in-
law, the high tory Lord Rochester, ordered the Captain of the Guard to muster his disbanded troop and
declare for the Prince of Orange. The leading
officers of the army resolved to do the same. The
Lords Temporal and Spiritual, or such of them as
were in London, assembled at the Guildhall under
the presidency of the Archbishop of Canterbury,
and constituted themselves a provisional government. They were mostly loyal Tories—for the great
whig lords and their less orthodox tory brethren
were elsewhere—but they chose a delegation to
invite the Prince of Orange to London, appointed a
new Governor of the Tower and drew up a Declaration deploring the non-performance of the royal
Proclamation to call a speedy Parliament. What was
more they announced their expectation that such a
Parliament would quickly be called with the Prince's
help.[1]

They sent for the Secretaries of State and they sent
for Mr Secretary Pepys of the Admiralty, requiring
his immediate attendance. At their command, he
wrote to Dartmouth recounting the events of that
day and instructing him to refrain from acts of hos-
tility against the Prince's fleet and to dismiss all
Catholic officers from his own. He added on his
own account that he had little thought when he
despatched the King's letter on the previous night that
he would so soon have had to send another after it.
In the light of what had happened since the bewildered awakening of that terrible morning, he must
have had misgivings as to what he had done. For by

so faithfully and promptly obeying his master's last orders, there was no saying what responsibilities he might have incurred.[2]

But like everyone else in London Pepys had more urgent and terrible anxieties. Roused from its squalid lairs in the outer liberties by the news that the King was fled and the army disbanded, the mob rose and took possession of the city. All that day the sound of its fury shook the windows of York Buildings. As in the days of the Medway disaster and Godfrey's murder, Pepys was faced with the loss of all he possessed. He was fortunate that his house in Buckingham Street stood in a kind of backwater. Those who lived in the Strand above were less fortunate, for here grimy patriots broke down the doors of all suspected of Popery or zeal for the King—at that moment accounted much the same thing—and burnt and plundered on pretext of seeking arms. The Catholic chapels went down in rubble and flame. Somehow Lord Dartmouth's regiment and the artillery train under Henry Shere managed to save the situation for the time being, fighting their way through the crowded streets to the Tower, "where there was so great a tumult", as Shere recorded, "that no one could have believed we could have escaped a man of us".

In the first hour of night the whole sky was ablaze, as the Mass house in Lincoln's Inn Fields was gutted and its contents piled by the howling rabble on to a bonfire. Then the fury of the populace turned against the foreign embassies, where the vanished papists were rumoured to have taken their goods for safety. Wild House, the stately residence of the Spanish Ambassador adjoining the Fields, was sacked, and an outraged grandee of Spain turned trembling and penniless into the night. The Legations of the Elector Palatine and the Grand Duke of Tuscany in the

Haymarket, where the captain of the Trained Bands on guard was shot dead, suffered likewise. Barillon's house in St James's Square was only saved by a strong detachment of the Horse Guards, hastily assembled by the Council and armed with ball. Afterwards the mob marched past the soldiers, holding aloft flickering gilt candlesticks in solemn mockery and plundered popish gewgaws, while thousands of hooligans, waving oranges on swords and staves, yelled joyously for the reign of Saturn so miraculously come again. "No law, no King", was the cry of the hour: next day the whole city should be looted. "A world", as one mournful Londoner wrote, "that is like to be very full of trouble!"

The wintry sun of December 12th rose on a ghastly spectacle. "The capital in many places presented the aspect of a city taken by storm. The Lords met at Whitehall and exerted themselves to restore tranquillity. The Trained Bands were ordered under arms. A body of cavalry was kept in readiness to disperse tumultuous assemblages."* The houseless Ronquillo, with every hasty honour that could be paid him, was lodged at Whitehall: "all sober people are extraordinarily concerned at this horrid violation of the law of nations". Pepys, shaken and ill, transmitted the orders of the Council of Peers to the ports that all outgoing vessels were to be searched and no one allowed to go down the river without a passport from the Lord Mayor. Meanwhile the Thames was infested with innumerable boats manned by roughs who searched and plundered every passer-by. To thousands of inoffensive, respectable men and women the state of nature described so often by the political theorists seemed to have arrived: "no King in Israel nor any face of government left us".[3]

During the day a circumstance occurred which

* Macaulay, *History of England* (1885 ed.) III, 302.

drew the mob eastwards and gave the authorities
time to take breath. A scrivener making his way
down a Wapping street saw peering out of an ale-
house window the coal-blackened, anguished, but
unmistakable face of Lord Chancellor Jeffreys. In a
few moments the wretched fugitive was driven
from his hiding place and surrounded. Pelted with
mud and stones he was dragged by the multitude
before the Lord Mayor, who was "so struck with
the terror of the rude populace and the disgrace of a
man who had made all people tremble before him"
that he fell weeping into a fit from which he never
recovered. Later, almost torn to pieces, Jeffreys was
smuggled into the Tower behind a forest of pikes
formed by two regiments of militia, while the
people surged after him yelling and holding out
halters. Poor Penn, the quaker, underwent a somewhat similar experience. As though to add to the
horror of that day it became known that Titus Oates
in his prison had once more put on his long-
discarded Doctor's robes.[4]

Evelyn from the quiet of Sayes Court, Deptford,
wrote anxiously to his old friend at York Buildings:

> I left you indisposed and send on purpose to learn how it is
> with you, and to know if in any sort I may serve you in this
> prodigious Revolution. You have many friends, but no man
> living who is more sincerely your servant or that has a greater
> value for you.
> We are here as yet (I thank God) unmolested; but this shak-
> ing menaces every corner, and the most philosophic breast
> cannot but be sensible of the motion. I am assured you need no
> precepts, nor I example so long as I have yours before me. And
> I would govern myself by your commands.

Methodically Pepys endorsed the letter: "Upon
the great Convulsion of State upon the King's withdrawing."[5]

A further convulsion was in store that night. The

evening began with an attack on Lord Powis's house in Lincoln's Inn Fields. But by now the authorities were ready. The mob was firmly met and driven off by the military. A period of comparative quiet followed. But those who wished for reasons of their own to destroy an ancient society had further resources. A little before midnight, a dreadful rumour, put about by men dressed as yokels, began to spread in the outer suburbs. Within half an hour the shout went up from every street: "Rise! Arm! Arm! The Irish are cutting throats!" Thousands of papist soldiers, it was reported, were advancing from Knightsbridge towards the centre of the city, setting fire to the houses and massacring man, woman and child. Amid affrighted crying the drums beat to arms. By one o'clock all the principal streets were barricaded and lined by the Trained Bands, while lighted candles blazed from every window. There was no more sleep that night. Not till dawn did the panic subside and the tired citizens withdraw to their houses.

*   *   *

By this time something like unanimity of feeling had been reached by the governing and well-to-do classes. Whatever their earlier differences of opinion, it was clear that only one thing could now save a distracted kingdom—the speedy arrival of the Prince of Orange. In that dark hour, Whig and Tory alike turned to him. Between their cowardly sovereign and the maddened mob, even the most loyal professors of non-resistance took the one road open. "I hope, dear," wrote Lady Dartmouth to her husband, "that you will be so wise to yourself and family as to do what becomes a reasonable man."[6]

Dartmouth had already done so. Confronted on the 12th by the news of the King's flight and an invitation from the Prince of Orange, long secreted in the rollers of Lieutenant Byng's breeches and now timely placed upon his dressing-table by his politically-minded captains, the Admiral felt at last that his course was clear. "Oh God!" he confided to Feversham, "what could make our master desert his kingdom and his friends?" And in the name of himself and of his captains he wrote to the Prince offering his services to help establish "the Protestant religion and liberties of England".[7]

Yet the tragic drama was not quite played out. During the past two days no one had had time to think of the King or speculate about his fate. But during the 13th rumours began to reach the capital that he had been captured by some Kentish fishermen—"a priest-codding" on the Thames— and brought captive to Faversham as a papist refugee. By the evening it was popularly believed that he had died as a result of the barbarous usage he had received. There well may have been many sad and loyal men who felt that it were best so.

But James was alive. He had survived even the indignity of having hands laid upon his person and his breeches rudely torn down while the scaly rabble searched for his jewels and money. The coronation ring, secreted in his pants, they failed to find. Then someone, suspecting the familiar lantern-jaw under his black periwig, had recognised him. Still denied liberty, he had been taken to a country inn and further insulted. Here, proudly defiant and tremblingly abject by turns, he awaited against his will the verdict of his heretic people.

As soon as the Council of Lords at the Guildhall was made aware of his plight, four of their members set out with a troop of Guards to his assistance. One of them, Pepys's friend the loyal Lord Ailesbury, hastened ahead of his companions and, galloping through a terrible night of wind and rain and a countryside insane with terror, reached Faversham by one o'clock next day. He found his sovereign trembling, unshaved and indignant. By quieting his fears and persuading him to return to his capital, this good, simple man almost changed the course of British history.[8]

To those who were not Tories, the unlooked-for news from Kent was not a little disconcerting. The continued presence of the King put a stop to the plans both of those who wanted to establish another Commonwealth and of those more numerous malcontents who wished to substitute William for James. English public opinion had stood for one royal decapitation but was not likely to stand for another; the halo of martyrdom invested the head of James's father and the echoes of that horrid act still sounded in men's ears. Yet from the provinces news continued to pour in of manifestations of the feeling, now released after long damming, against James's religious policy. Rumours of impending massacre by the disbanded and homeless Irish fanned the flames. At Oxford, the Princess Anne, still accompanied by the militant Bishop of London in blue cloak and breastplate, and escorted by eleven hundred horse, was received at the gate of Christ Church by the Chancellor, Vice-Chancellor and Doctors in their scarlet robes: over all this armed pageantry flew the device: *"Nolumus leges Angliae mutare."* And it followed that if the people of England were so passionately desirous of preserving their laws unchanged—particularly the more intolerant ones—they could not be inordinately anxious to retain a King who was as obstinately determined to change them.[9]

The Tories, who were less logical, wished to keep both their old laws and their old King, at least for so

long as he lived and so was King by Divine Right.
James's reluctant re-appearance reminded them of
both these inescapable facts. But during the past two
days in their dire necessity even the most loyal of
them had gone so far in ignoring his existence and
hailing his unhallowed rival and conqueror, that his
second coming put them into a quandary. Lord
Dartmouth, for instance, who during the interregnum had offered the fleet to the Prince of Orange,
hardly knew which way to turn when he heard the
news of his old master's return. "Your Majesty
knows", he wrote in desperation, "what condition
you left the fleet in, and me in the most unsupport-
able calamity of my life. What could I do but send to
the Prince of Orange when I found the whole nation
did? . . . But I hope all will end in your Majesty's
happy reestablishment. Mr Pepys will acquaint your
Majesty with the state of the fleet." On the whole
the best course seemed to be to lay the blame on
Pepys. The Admiral carefully endorsed the Secretary's hurried letter of the 11th that had brought him
the King's last fatal order: "Received the 14th by the
common post. Mr Pepys or whom this was committed to should be answerable for the delay, for this
letter came not till after the Council of War that sent
to the Prince upon the letter from the Lords at Guildhall." As Pepys expressly states that he sent it off
by express as soon as he received it on the dawn of
the 11th, its adventures during the intervening three
days of national anarchy must remain a mystery.[10]

Towards four o'clock on the afternoon of Sunday, December 16th, the King and his retinue
approached London. Fearful of his reception by the
populace, he meant to return as he had departed, by
the quiet southern bank and across the Lambeth
ferry. But one of those sudden waves of popular
reactionary feeling—so characteristic of England in

time of stress—had set it in his favour. Entering the cobbled streets of the Borough, James found himself as in the autumn of '79 on the crest of an unexpected surge of loyalty. Not fully understanding it, he was yet touched by the acclamations of the people; "though they hated his religion", he observed, "they did not despise his person". He resolved therefore to enter his capital openly. So it came to pass that he went through the Sabbath streets with a concourse of loyal lords and gentlemen riding before and a crowd following with loud huzzas, "to the great but short content", Pepys reported, "of all his subjects". And in the evening there were bonfires and the ringing of bells. Perhaps there flitted across James's tired, confused mind a memory of that dazzling day nearly thirty years before when he had ridden thus through the city beside his returning brother.[11]

Yet, for all the spontaneous, spasmodic sentimentality of England, the clock could not be put back. For a moment it looked as though a miracle had happened and that the Elizabethan, Clarendonian ideal—so dear to the tory heart—of a perfect union between the legitimate sovereign and the Anglican Church was about to be consummated again as in '60 and '85.★ Pepys, hurrying to the Palace with the Admiralty correspondence to welcome his old master, may perhaps have thought so: one suspects there were tears in his eyes as he went his familiar journey up the river that evening. But next day it became amply apparent even to eyes most blinded by loyalty and affection that the momentary vision was only a mirage. The world of fashion and power was with the rising sun in the west. And the King had learnt

★ ". . . All the clouds (as we thought) were vanishing, and a bright day again appearing." J. Evelyn to his son, Dec. 18th, 1688. *Diary and Correspondence of John Evelyn* (ed. H. B. Wheatley) III, 428.

nothing: he did not wish to learn. He attended Mass and rated his Cabinet and servants for their dealings with the usurping peers at the Guildhall during his absence. It was even said that the old concourse of papists and Jesuits filled the Bedchamber and ante-rooms as though the prodigious revolution of the past few weeks had never been. The only miracle was—if the rumour were true—how these devout gentlemen had so quickly reappeared from nowhere.[12]

"If the King had then prohibited all papists to refrain from coming near to him", thought Anthony Wood, "all had been well." Even so one doubts it. For Tories the course of inexorable time might be reversed. But there were others who did not mean to lose the advantage that James's flight had given them, and the soldier-politician, cold calculating Orange, least of all. He had taken his full measure now of his father-in-law, and he knew that whatever folly he had committed before, given the same circumstances, he would commit again. Fear could always make James do his business for him. He resolved therefore to give James cause to fear.

When the King's messenger, bearing tidings of his return and his readiness to confer with his son-in-law, reached Windsor, the Prince refused to see him and placed him under arrest. Instead he sent a Dutch official to inform James that he would not enter the capital in person until all the armed forces of the kingdom were placed under his command. It was the old Roundhead ultimatum of '42 in a new form. At a council of the Lords who supported William, held at the Castle on the afternoon of the 17th, it was determined that the King must withdraw from London. Three of their number, Halifax, Shrewsbury and the old rebel Delamere, were instructed to tell him so. The invading troops were ordered to advance immediately on the capital.

That evening they closed in from the west. Before dusk they were in occupation of the villages of Kensington and Chelsea. The King was undressing as the Dutch infantry under Count Solms, with fuses lighted for action, poured into the Mall. Old Lord Craven, who more than half a century before had fought for Gustavus Adolphus, begged his master to let him die at the head of the Coldstream Guard sooner than yield the Palace to the foreigner. James coldly refused and the invaders took possession of Whitehall.

Shortly after midnight the Prince's emissaries arrived from Windsor. They insisted that the King, deep in the sleep of weariness and despair, should be woken. They, who a brief while before had been his subjects, told him that he must leave early in the morning for Ham House. James, who had no other thought now but flight, pleaded to be sent instead to Rochester. A messenger was despatched back to William to obtain his permission. It was granted.

Towards midday on Tuesday, December 18th, the King went down the steps of Whitehall for the last time and entered his barge. It was raining. Evelyn, standing with Sir Charles Cottrell and Sir Stephen Fox at one of the windows of the New Buildings, saw him put out into the river with ten or twelve barges of Dutch soldiers following after to protect him, it was claimed, "from the insults of the mobile". But of such insults there was now no sign—only silence.[13]

In the pouring rain the victorious Prince of Orange, with General Schomberg sitting beside him in his carriage, drove down Piccadilly about four o'clock the same afternoon. The bells were rung, bonfires lit in the streets, and a crowd with slightly bedraggled favours cheered for the nation's Liber-

ator, though not as loudly, one onlooker noted,
as it had for James two days before.★ Perhaps the
presence of so many Dutch troops in their dingy
blue uniforms had a damping effect; perhaps it was
the rain. However inevitable and utilitarian, there
was something a little humiliating to national pride
in this revolution. The English, so jealous of foreigners as a rule, are sometimes strangely meek to some
particular species of foreigner momentarily in political fashion. They were now accorded their bellyful.
The streets round Westminster swarmed with ill-
favoured and ill-accoutred Dutchmen instead of the
gallant scarlet and gold of England: there were Hols-
teiners at Woolwich, Brandenburgers at Padding-
ton, "lousy" Scots at Lambeth, Birkenfeld's Germans at Kensington and other Teutons further afield
at Eltham, Kingston and Richmond. It was much
more, of course, than French papists and Irish cut-
throats. But the presence of all these armed
foreigners could not but remind the haughty English that, while it had on the whole been a bloodless
revolution, it had been a still more bloodless conquest. "The like was never or will be in a story,"
wrote one bewildered patriot, "a King with a great
army driven out of his kingdom by a lesser army
without fighting." "God damn Father Petre,"
grumbled Dixie, the King's old coachman, as he
drove sadly through the rain to Rochester, "damn
him! But for him, we had not been here." It was the
measure of poor King James's political ineptitude.[14]

★ ★ ★

★ "It is not to be imagined what a damp there was upon all sorts of
men throughout the town." Clarendon, *Diary*, Dec. 19th, 1688. "The
night was spent in ringing of bells, bonfires and other expressions of
joy by the rabble; but thinking men of the City seemed displeased at
the King's being forced to withdraw a second time." Sir J. Reresby,
Memoirs, 541.

The professional placeholders and all those who were great or would be great now went to acclaim the Prince. Evelyn saw him holding levee in the midst of them at St James's, "very stately, serious and reserved". He seemed more interested in affairs of State than ceremony. Pepys, sadly doing business, one suspects automatically like a man in a dream,— there is a shorthand copy of a note of his of that day in response to a request of one of Charles II's daughters, Lady Sussex, to carry her goods to France— received Orange's orders for transmission to Dartmouth at Spithead. The fleet was to be brought with all speed to the Buoy of the Nore. He himself was ordered to attend the Prince next day.[15]

The master who for more than twenty years had watched over Pepys's service, who had learnt to recognise it for what it was and had made him virtual ruler of the Navy, was now fallen beyond hope of recovery. The instrument of power which Pepys had made it his life's work to create had failed utterly to save the cause on which his own fortunes and his sovereign's had depended. His enemies, William Harbord, Arthur Herbert and Edward Russell, stood at the Prince of Orange's right hand, high in his favour and gratitude. He could look now for little more in life but oblivion, disgrace and perhaps proscription.

On the morning of Wednesday, December 19th, the day set for his audience of the Prince, the weather changed suddenly to intense cold and frost. Seldom can Pepys have looked out on the river beneath his windows with sadder thoughts. What happened at that audience we do not know. Yet it cannot have been altogether unfavourable, for the Prince desired him to remain for the present at his post and Pepys consented. When he got home he found a letter awaiting him that reminded him that there are

things in this world more precious than the favours
of fortune and the smiles of the great. It came from
William Hewer who had been his confidant for
twenty-eight years, who once had been beaten by
him for staying out late at night, and who had risen
in the world in his service and now was richer than
he. Couched in the seeming cold and formal convention of the day, it was the kind of letter which might
conceivably have caused the creator of mankind to
be not wholly displeased with his handiwork. After
wishing that the evening's audience would prove to
Pepys's satisfaction, Hewer went on: "If not, I know
you will cheerfully acquiesce in whatever circumstance God Almighty shall think most proper for
you, which I hope may prove more to your satisfaction than you can imagine. You may rest assured
that I am wholly yours, and that you shall never
want the utmost of my constant, faithful and personal service, the utmost I can do being inconsider-
able to what your kindness and favour to me has and
does oblige me to. And therefore, as all I have proceeded from you, so all I have and am is and shall be
at your service." "A letter of great tenderness at a
time of difficulty", was Pepys's endorsement.[16]

For the present, however, Pepys remained at his
post. He had done nothing to save himself which his
own conscience or any man could construe as a
betrayal of his master. But he was still that which he
had been in the far days before the Stuart monarchy
was restored, an Englishman with a sense of his duty
to his country. To him as to the great nobleman,
Halifax, who through dark and devious ways had
done so much to guide the course of that revolution,
the earth of England, though inferior perhaps to that
of many places abroad, had something of divinity in
it: he was one who "would die rather than see a spire
of English grass trampled down by a foreign tres-

passer". At that hour she was on the verge of war
with a great military power. The fleet he had built
and reclaimed and tended, and which had failed,
through no fault of his, to serve the King, was still
needed to serve England. A newsletter of December
25th has a significant note:

Some few days since Secretary Peepes received a letter from
an ingenious gentleman in France, who gives an account that
the French are setting out 50 sail of men-of-war in their yards in
Brittany, and that great numbers of landsmen were drawing
down towards the coasts.

Pepys showed the letter at once to the Prince.[17]

On Friday, December 21st, the new ruler of the
country gave an audience to some sixty of the temporal and spiritual peers at St James's. He would not,
he declared, seize the Crown or declare himself, as
some about him suggested, a conqueror. He had
come at their invitation to enable Englishmen to
reassert their laws and liberties in a free and legally
constituted Parliament: he had no intention of going
back on his declared word. He would continue to conduct the military affairs of the nation,
but he would leave the settling of the civil government in their hands.[18]

The implied promise simplified Pepys's position.
The constitution of the kingdom to whose
sovereign he had sworn his allegiance remained as
before; meanwhile as the administrative officer
responsible for the first defensive Service of the
realm, it was his plain duty to assist the chief military
administrator now accepted as such by King and
nation. For the purposes of his work he was now the
Prince's man, just as he had been James's when the
latter was Duke of York and Lord High Admiral.

His task was not, of course, easy. The Prince was
cold, aloof and difficult of access to all but his Dutch

confidants, and advising him in naval affairs were men in whose judgment, and still less in whose goodwill, Pepys would not confide. Both Edward Russell and Arthur Herbert in their earlier days as gentlemen captains had felt the lash of the great Secretary's whip. The first, as Harbord's brother-in-law, had recklessly plotted nine years before to take his life and honour, while the other's name was a byword for indiscipline and corruption. But both men now represented something greater than themselves, and Pepys knew what belonged to his place. The correctness of his official attitude revealed the perfected technique of a lifetime. On the 22nd, in reply to a letter of Edward Russell's enclosing a copy of the Prince's orders for bringing the fleet to the mouth of the river, he expressed himself with immaculate and courteous rectitude:

Sir,

I acknowledge, with many thanks, the favour of yours this morning; and do no less readily subscribe to you for the form than the matter of the enclosed papers.

I shall endeavour to kiss your hand some time this day if your indisposition, which I am sorry for, will permit it, in order to the discoursing some particulars against the fleet's coming in. Remaining, with very great respect, your faithful and most humble servant,

S. Pepys.

In matters of politics Russell and Herbert might far have outdistanced the dry-as-dust Secretary among his ledgers, but when it came to the niceties of battle by administrative correspondence, he was their master every time. More than any other man he evolved the gentle art of bureaucratic defence and offence. It is not the least of his claims to fame that he was the father of the Civil Service and of a system which, for all the challenge of ignorant mobs and authoritarian tanks and bayonets, still survives in many parts of the world to-day. It adds still more to this unassuming Englishman's stature that that system was supported and carried across the oceans by the same instrument of sea power which Pepys spent his administrative life in creating.[19]

*   *   *

The Christmas season of 1688—*Anno Mirabili* as Evelyn dated it—came in with frozen skies. It brought further political changes. On Saturday, December 22nd, the Lords met in their own House to debate the manner of calling the forthcoming Parliament. The majority, led by Archbishop Sancroft, held that to avoid a constitutional break and too great a strain on good men's loyalty, the writs should be issued in the King's name. It was hoped to get the royal consent to this next day, and a delegation was despatched to Rochester to procure it. But on Sunday news reached London that James, blind to the last, had fled secretly in the night and taken ship for France. What William had hoped for had come to pass; no royal ruler but he was left in England and, by his rival's flight into the arms of Louis, the nation was committed to war with France and dependence on himself and his Grand Alliance.[20]

To the Tories it was the end of their hard-won, brief and chequered spell of prosperity. That union between anointed King, national Church and people for which they had fought so obstinately was now broken beyond hope of mending. "Our poor master", wrote Francis Gwynn to Dartmouth, "is once again gone from Rochester, . . . and hath so entirely given up all there that there will be no ceremony, I doubt, used towards him or the child, which is the word he is now called by. He chose as ill a time now as he did before, for tomorrow the Lords are to meet

concerning a Parliament, and I wish he had stayed to
hear what their method had been." The King's flight
meant that an actual revolution must now be followed by what to an ordinary Englishman was far
worse, a legal one. "What", asked Lord Rochester,
"can the most loyal and dutiful body in the world do
without a head?" The Whigs were jubilant, for the
very ground on which their adversaries stood had
opened under their feet. The "tantivies" had no
choice left them but apostasy to their own principles
or proscription. It has frequently been the lot of the
tory party in England to be betrayed by its own
leaders. In the long run this has not harmed it, for the
English are a conservative people. But at the time
the betrayal has always been paid for by the exclusion from public life of the noblest among the
Tories.[21]

The Prince of Orange followed up his victory
quickly. On the day the King departed he ordered
the French ambassador to leave England and summoned all available members of Charles II's last
House of Commons, together with the Lord
Mayor, Aldermen and leading Common Council-
lors of London, to meet him on the day after
Christmas. He thus publicly severed all means of
communication with the fugitive King and ensured
the support of a body which was certain to be predominantly whig and therefore opposed to any
reconciliation with him. Elected in the final flood-
tide of the Popish Terror, Charles's last Parliament
had been fanatically exclusionist. On Christmas Eve
the Lords met under the presidency of Halifax and
accepted the *fait accompli*; the Archbishop refrained
from attending. Next day they presented an Address
begging the Prince to issue circular letters in his
name to the electoral bodies to return members to a
national Convention, and in the meantime to

assume the provisional government of the country. On Boxing Day the assembled Commoners and city fathers, sitting in St Stephen's Chapel under the chairmanship of the exclusionist, Henry Powle, agreed to a like resolution. A tory motion of Sir Robert Sawyer's, intended to limit the Prince's potential claims by giving him the formal title of Administrator, was easily talked out. "The poor King not considered or mentioned", Lady Dartmouth reported to her absent husband; "the door shut upon him as if he had never been." At the time that monarch, accompanied by his priests, was travelling thankfully from Ambleteuse to the Palace of Saint Germain, where Louis the Magnificent was waiting to receive him.[22]

Pepys spent the festive season in the performance of his administrative duties. On Christmas Eve he sat in "a solemn conference" with Sir Richard Haddock and the other Victualling Commissioners at the Navy Office, wrestling with the dual problem of how to get provisions down the river to a starving fleet in the teeth of an easterly gale, and how to pay for them with cash payments from the Treasury three weeks in arrears. This was the kind of conundrum with which he had formerly been long familiar: "we are under the last degree of thoughtfulness", he told Dartmouth in a letter written on Christmas Day, "what possible way is there to remedy this". With hostilities against France likely to begin at any moment, he had plenty to occupy him. Warned by the Admiral that Guernsey, if not hastily secured, might become a thorn in the flesh of England, he obtained authority from the Prince on Christmas Day to prepare orders for sending frigates there. At the same time he made provision for protecting the Holland packet boats from French privateers.[23]

Pepys's next letter to Dartmouth was written on Boxing Day. It had an unwonted chill about it. For the Admiral, like all the rest of the great world, had taken the not unnatural step of applying to the fount of honour direct, and instead of corresponding as to the disposition of the fleet through the normal medium of the Admiralty, had despatched his private secretary, Phineas Bowles, to London to wait on the Prince and Edward Russell. But neither received him with any enthusiasm, and the Prince subsequently summoned Pepys and handed him Dartmouth's letter. He instructed him to send for Bowles and obtain from him the account of the fleet, "in order", as Pepys observed in his letter with a certain frigid satisfaction, "to my reporting the result thereof to him".

For Pepys was furious. He felt that Dartmouth had not only been unfriendly to him personally but had insulted his office. Only a few months before Bowles had been petitioning him for employment in a most abject manner: he naturally regarded him as one of his own creatures. That he should now be used to approach the Prince behind his back struck him as outrageous. He showed his displeasure in characteristic fashion. "Your Lordship judges very rightly of Mr Pepys not being pleased with my coming up to the Prince without application to him," wrote the discomfited Bowles, "and this day he has given me a taste of his displeasure on my desiring to know what orders were gone to your Lordship, telling me that they were sent, and that I, bringing nothing to him, he did not think it material to communicate to me, so that he will have me in the dark in the matter. . . . I find him much altered since my being with him the first night, but possibly it's more out of personal dislike to me than to your Lordship's proceedings." For Pepys had now another cause of anger with Dartmouth. "He is pleased", Bowles continued, "to call your commissioning Captain Collins for the *Fubbs* yacht a double irregularity, first on the score of Captain Sanders being (as he says) still living, and then next of her not being under your Lordship's command." For Pepys, as his frowning picture by Kneller reveals, could present a very stern and unforgiving front to those who had done wrong. Nor, in his just indignation, did he make much account of whom he offended.[24]

He even found time at this troubled season for an inter-departmental duel with his *vis-à-vis* of the Army. It was conducted by both sides with scrupulous official politeness. Writing on December 28th to Mr Blathwayt, the Secretary-at-War, about the embarkation of the reinforcements for the Channel Islands, Pepys had occasion to refer to a serious infringement, doubtless accidental, by the military forces, of one of the most sacred rights of the Navy:

There was another particular wherein, upon application expressly made to me this morning by Sir Richard Haddock in the name of himself and the Board, I was necessitated to move his Highness, namely that notice being brought to the Commissioners of the Navy at Deptford of a regiment of the Prince's Foot ordered to be quartered in the town of Deptford, and the Quarter Master's resorting to the said Commissioner with his desire that he may have liberty to quarter some of the officers of the said regiment in the Officers' houses within the Dock and Store-yards there, the Commissioner according to his duty desired and obtained time this day to communicate the same to the Navy Board, who immediately dispatched one of their number (Sir Richard Haddock) in all their names, pressing me to acquaint his Highness with it as a proposal that in no age appears to have been made before, nor can now be admitted without infinite inconveniences and particularly that of exposing his Majesty's ships to fire (as well them in the wet as dry dock) and his Magazines (most of which are combustible) both on float and in the Store houses, not only to fire but to embezzlement. And that too not wholly from what is to be suspected of the soldiers, but even from the King's Officers and workmen themselves when they shall have such a justification ready as the laying it upon the soldiers to the bereaving the Navy Board of the means they now have of challenging a very strict account from the Store-keepers, Watchmen and others charged with the safe custody of them, from the pretence they will raise from this accident of being rendered incapable of answering for their security.

His Highness, upon my opening this to him, was pleased to seem fully satisfied in the Navy Board's reasoning herein, directing me to notify the same to you for your preparing, and doing what is necessary for the Navy Board's satisfaction in it. I very well know how little necessary it is to press them in anything, but the Commissioners of the Navy telling me that they have but this day allowed them for preventing what the Quarter-Master tells them will otherwise be put in execution tomorrow, I leave it to you to give it what dispatch you see reasonable. I am most respectfully

Your humble servant,
S. Pepys.*

For in this as in other matters Pepys was the Navy's watchdog. In whose name he still regarded himself as being such, his reference to the King's ships makes plain.[25]

The old year closed and the new year came in with Pepys still performing the familiar routine, waiting on the Prince at St James's and Whitehall for orders and for warrants to be signed, sending men and ships to the Channel Islands and transporting poor disbanded Irish soldiers for internment in the Isle of Wight, allotting frigates to escort the packet boats from Harwich to Holland, and transmitting instructions to Dartmouth. Every care had to be taken to reduce expense, for the outgoings of the past three months had been enormous and scarcely anything

* S. P. to Mr Blathwayt, Dec. 28th, 1688. *Royal Society MSS.*, III, 129.

was coming in. Eighteen ships were to be left at Spithead for laying up at Portsmouth, and the rest of the fleet was to make for the River as soon as the unlucky Admiral could get a wind to bring it. But although Pepys wrote almost daily to hasten matters the weather for the last twelve days of December and the first eight of January remained adverse. The cold was so intense that the very Thames began to be frozen over. At the turn of the year Dartmouth managed to get as far as the Downs, but dared come no further for fear of his ships becoming ice-bound. [26]

The quarrel between Pepys and his old friend and colleague was short-lived. On December 28th, after receiving Pepys's protest, Dartmouth penned a letter of apology explaining that the only reason he had sent Bowles up to London was the absence of letters from the Admiralty and his grief and distraction for his royal master. Situated far from the centre of affairs, he had been utterly in the dark as to what was happening. "I should be very ungrateful if I were capable of making any unkind return to you", he added. "Pray deny me not your private and friendly advice, by which I shall be glad to govern myself; and I hope we may yet be helpful to one another. I am sure all things shall be done on my part as becomes your obliged and affectionate friend." [27]

Though the explanation was not wholly satisfactory, Pepys accepted it. "I thank you with all my heart", he replied on January 2nd, "for your last, under your own hand, of the 28th December, for, I must own it, I thought your usage of me in the particular you mention somewhat unnatural, especially at a juncture so little needing it from one's friends. But, my Lord, you have done both yourself and me right in the trouble you have given yourself for my satisfaction about it. And I assure you, nothing on't shall longer stick with me, but, on the contrary, a desire of rendering your Lordship all the faithful services that (during the little remainder of my abode here) I shall be able to pay you." For, though he still had his duty to do, Pepys regarded his career as finished. "It will be matter of great content to me if I may be able by any means to be of use to your Lordship, though I have given over even the thinking on't for myself." Dartmouth returned his thanks in a letter of genuine affection. "It is no small part of friendship, in this age," he wrote, "to forgive the mistakes even of a friend, which mine really were and no other. Whatever becomes of me or you, I will always own and covet your friendship."[28]

During the first week of the new year the naval situation changed rapidly. The arrest of English merchants in France and the seizure of their ships had already created a state of virtual war. At the same time news from Ireland showed that that country was on the verge of rebellion. The focus of national interest passed from the armies which had held the stage during the Revolution to the Navy which had stood by watching. Only a few days before the administration had been working out plans for laying up the fleet, "the Prince intending", as Pepys told Dartmouth, "with all speed he conveniently can to retrench the present charge of the Navy". As so often before in the history of seventeenth-century England, the want of money had been the predominant consideration. Even as late as January 3rd orders were given on the Prince's instructions for discharging forty-nine ships. But a successful appeal made on New Year's Day to the City of London for a loan brought about an immediate change in the situation.[29]

Its effects were felt as early as January 4th. On that

day Pepys received orders, first from Captain Russell by letter and later from the Prince in person, that the ships under Dartmouth, instead of going to their respective ports to lay up, should remain together at the Buoy of the Nore. At the same time two frigates were ordered to cruise off the coasts of Ireland.

Dartmouth was anxious to leave the fleet in the Downs, on account of the continued frost, and come up to London to pay his court to the Prince. But on the 8th the wind shifted, and the frost, which had continued since December 19th, broke.

Pepys, who visited St James's that day to lay Dartmouth's petition before the Prince, has left us a description of the scene. "For so soon as the Prince . . . had read your Lordship's letter to him and heard your other to me, he was pleased presently to observe that your Lordship's advice touching the ships and desires concerning yourself being founded all along upon a supposed continuance of the frost and N.E. wind that blew, he did believe that the whole of those measures were now at an end, the wind being come about the S.E. and the frost broke with a great and continued rain, then just before his eyes as we stood in the garden windows; adding that he thought it would be much better that your Lordship should come about (as was before determined) to see the fleet safe brought in, and the rather (to give it you in your own words) because when you are gone there will be nobody to heed it, Sir John Berry being at Portsmouth." In another and more personal letter of the same date Pepys expressed his regret that he could not send the Admiral a reply more acceptable to his wishes. "The truth is," he assured him, "the sudden and extraordinary change of weather all this day did naturally administer to his Highness matter for the answer he was pleased to give. Which he gave with so much earnestness, yet with no disregard towards your Lordship, that I thought it of more moment to you to forbear pressing it further."

Yet Pepys was well aware that, if the frost on the Thames had broken, another had set in that boded ill for Dartmouth and himself and showed little sign of thawing. He gave the Admiral a hint of it in his letter, telling him that he concurred with him in his desire to tighten the laws against neglectful masters and pilots—"and if it ever comes in my way to do aught towards the remedying of it, I am sure I shall. But it must be done in Parliament, and how many things now before must of preference be given them there for the consideration of any matter so remote as that at this day is, is hard to judge."[30]

Chapter VIII
Defeat

"Good God! where is loyalty and Christian charity?"
Lord Clarendon, *Diary*, Dec. 29th, 1688.

If Dartmouth had lost his sense of proportion, Pepys had not. The Convention Parliament had been summoned to Westminster on January 22nd and writs had gone out in the Prince's name to the electoral bodies. These had been accompanied by a flood of whig pamphlets and broadsheets, blackening everything that had been done in King James's reign and all who had been his servants. There were plenty of simple folk who expected the forthcoming assembly to effect some wonderful change for the better in the affairs of men; and there was a more than adequate supply of knaves who, for their own ends, encouraged them in that belief. But Pepys had been through too many arbitrary changes and revolutions to be under any further delusions as to what must happen to honest men in the course of them. He was a moderate, if loyal, Tory, which is only another name for a man who wishes to see the world better but is quite certain that it cannot be made so by violence and injustice. His wise old friend, John Evelyn, who was another, forecast what was likely to take place in a letter to his son. "By what I collect, the ambitious and covetous will be canvassing for places of honour and rich employment. . . . If none of this happen, and that success do not quite alter the principles of men in power, we are to suspect *Astrea* upon earth again.

204

But, as I have often told you, I look for no mighty improvement of mankind in this declining age and catalysis. A Parliament (legally called) of brave and worthy patriots, not influenced by faction nor terrified by power or corrupted by self-interest, would produce a kind of new creation amongst us. But it will grow old, and dissolve to chaos again, unless the same stupendous Providence (which has put this opportunity into men's hands to make us happy) dispose them to do just and righteous things, and to use their empire with moderation, justice, piety and for the public good. Upon the whole matter, those who seek employment before the grandees are served may suspend their solicitation." Pepys would doubtless have concurred with Evelyn.[1]

His own constituency provided a case in point. On January 1st he wrote to his friends at Harwich offering himself for election to the Convention. But Pepys as head of the naval administration was a very different person from Pepys in his present precarious situation. Excuses began to pour in, even from his most faithful adherents. The alteration in the size of the Corporation by the resumption of the old Charter had made a strange change; the Town Clerk, Daniel Smith, was offended because Pepys had not written to him sufficiently often; the question of the local Lights—Pepys until recently had been Master of Trinity House—prejudiced interested persons. Hints were dropped that he and Deane ought to visit the town if they were to make headway against the two whig candidates who were being put up against them. Mr Sandford wrote on the 5th to let Pepys know that both the Town Clerk and his old correspondent Mr Langley, the Mayor, were secretly working against him: "Sir, it wounds us to observe such a parcel of ungrateful men."

Pepys refrained from vain recriminations and replied courteously to them all. "As to myself," he wrote to Mr Seaman on the 8th, "if they shall think fit to chose me I shall with all respect accept of the same and own myself obliged to 'um by it. But if they have any other in their eye that they do really conceive of better capacity and interest than I, God forbid I should repine at the choice of him."

A week before the poll a few loyal supporters were still hopeful: "as yet", one of them reported on the 8th, "I have no reason to suspect but that your Honour will carry it". Two days later Pepys was warned that, though Deane had now withdrawn in his favour, hoping to leave the representation of the Borough to him and Sir Thomas Middleton—"a very worthy gentleman agreed upon by all parties"—the electors were showing a preference for John Eldred, the whig candidate. On receipt of this blow on the 12th Pepys did for a moment allow himself a modest expression of vexation: had he foreseen such disappointments at Harwich, he told Simon Sandford, he could easily have provided for himself elsewhere. "But as I have slipped my time, and so it is become too late to talk of any such thing now, so would it make me appear more solicitious for the thing than I really am. . . . It happens to be a very busy post tonight with me", he added.★

In a letter of the same date to the Mayor he wrote at greater length:

What it is that has wrought a change, I neither know nor think decent for me to enquire into. . . . I am very loath to believe what I have on this occasion had suggested to me, that

★ *Rawl. MSS. A.* 179, f. 163. Curiously enough there are no entries in the Admiralty Letter Book from Jan. 11th to 13th inclusive. *Pepysian MSS., Adm. Letters* xv, 525. But in *Rawl. MSS. A.* 186, ff. 122 *et seq.* will be found detailed orders, dated Jan. 12th, for despatching squadrons to the Mediterranean, the Channel and Ireland.

there are not wanting some to whom my professions on behalf of the Church of England are made matter of offence. But if that be so, I am contented on that score to be rejected both from Parliament and everything else all the days of my life rather than be once admitted thereto on any other. . . .

For your advice about my coming down I have had no answer from the Corporation to my late letter encouraging me thereto. And having never heretofore wanted their invitation (nor is it long since the last Mayor brought both Sir Anthony Deane and me a very kind one) I am loath now to go uninvited. . . . Nor indeed could I at this day (were my encouragements greater), except the Prince's dispensing with my present attendance here, the fleet being but just now brought by my Lord Dartmouth into the river in order to its being part laid up and part set immediately out again in several squadrons for the security of commerce against the insults apprehended from the French.

But as I have heretofore, so I do again pray you not to let my friends want anything of the respect that would be paid them (by way of entertainment) were I myself there. Which I shall with a most ready thankfulness reimburse you for, either here or at Harwich upon demand, whatsoever be the issue of the Corporation's pleasure towards me. Nor shall it be long before I make them a visit in acknowledgment of their old favours, whether they give me any new ones to thank them for on this occasion or no.

The tide, he knew, was too strong against him: for, as he was warned, men's minds, honesty and manners had altered of late.[2]

*　　*　　*

Though his enemies were in the gate and at any moment his unyielding vigilance at his post might be visited by a repetition of the fate he had suffered in '79, Pepys abated nothing of his disciplinary zeal or of his precision. At the end of December he reported to the Prince that he had seen more commanders and officers of the fleet in town—without any leave that he knew of from the Admiral—than he ever remembered, "and this", as he told Dartmouth, "at a time when nobody can forsee what occasions may arise for the service of their ships". A fortnight later, in the midst of mobilisation, he wrote to his old acquaintance, Captain Graydon of the *Saudadoes*, that he had heard that he had left his command and come to London, "without any leave that I know of from his Highness, while his Highness was at the time calling upon me once or twice a day to know whether the ships he had ordered to Harwich were gone or no. I told him further that it was an instance of such a piece of liberty as I had never before met with in near 30 years' service and that I believe would not now be adventured upon by any commander in the fleet from the Admiral downwards but yourself, and that for discipline's sake an account ought to be given of it to a court-martial. And when the Service will admit, it shall be no fault of mine if it be not. And this I have the rather done, and do the more frankly tell it you, because I take you for an ingenious man and one that for that reason (though I could have been glad to have been more successful in it) both have and am known to have at all times heretofore endeavoured to do good offices to the King, and should for the same reason (were I to continue in the Navy) very willingly do towards you with his Highness. But at the same time where such an irregularity as this appears, be it in friend or foe, tending to the immediate subversion of all good order in the Navy, it shall never want its full observation from me as long as I have any place in it."★3

Nor did the Secretary in the hour of his decline fear the frown of the great. When the powerful Lord Berkeley, now in high favour with the triumphant

★ S. P. to Capt. Graydon of the *Saudadoes*, Jan. 14th, 1689. *Pepysian MSS., Adm. Letters* xv, 525–6. Graydon came to a bad end in the West Indies fifteen years later.

party, asked for leave to abandon his squadron in the Downs and come up to London on grounds of pretended ill-health, Pepys, who well knew that his request would be granted, apprised him of the fact but made his displeasure clear. His letter of application arrived too late, he told him—it was past nine at night—to ask the Prince's pleasure on it that day, but he would not fail to do so on the morrow, "not doubting, your health being concerned in it, but it will be to your satisfaction. Otherwise I could not have encouraged your Lordship to expect it, his Highness having no longer ago than yesterday refused the same request from my Lord Dartmouth, as being unwilling to dispense with a Flag before it had well discharged itself of the body of the ships it was to bring about to the Nore." To this expression of his disapproval, Pepys added a more direct rebuke for Berkeley's casual attitude towards a disgraceful accident that had befallen one of the 3rd rates under his command. "It seems a very deplorable story which your Lordship is pleased to give me of the loss of such a ship as the *Sedgemoor*. . . . It is what I hope will not be suffered to pass without full justice done upon it, if the persons upon whom the miscarriage is chargeable are, or can be laid hold on." A week later Pepys had occasion again to complain of Berkeley, this time in a letter to the Navy Board:

Gentlemen. I cannot but give it you (hoping that it may not yet be too late) as my opinion that my Lord Berkeley has gone a great deal too fast in his ordering the body of the *Sedgemoor* to be broken up before he has authority from the Lord Admiral, . . . as being a matter that even the Lord High Admiral himself would be thought to do an extraordinary thing even in his adventuring to order it to be done without the opinion of the Navy Board for it leading him thereto and the approbation of the Prince confirming the same.

For though, where such great men were concerned, Pepys might now be quite powerless, he was deter-

mined that while he remained at his post no irregularity should pass unrebuked, lest the rule of law he
had created should be handed down impaired by an
ill precedent to his successors.[4]

★   ★   ★

Sea changes beyond Pepys's capacity to control
were happening fast. On January 10th he transmitted orders to Dartmouth to hand over the fleet on its
arrival at the Nore to his second-in-command and
report at St James's. Two days later, on Saturday
12th, he was received in an audience with Admiral
Herbert—now restored to all and more than all his
old authority—at which the Prince announced his
decision of continuing 10,000 men in sea pay during
the remainder of the winter. Twelve ships were to
proceed at once to the Mediterranean under Sir John
Berry, another eight to Ireland and six to patrol the
Channel, while another eighteen, unassigned, were
left to be laid up. On Pepys representing the growing financial straits of the Navy Board and the Victualling Commissioners, the Prince promised to lay
the matter immediately before the Commissioners
of the Treasury.★ During the following week, until
cash was forthcoming, Pepys for the last time faced
the task of allaying a mutiny among the unpaid
seamen. On the 16th he drafted a proclamation to
the fleet, denying "groundless reports of late industriously spread among the seamen touching the
uncertainty of their receiving wages due to them",
and promising that all arrears should be paid
"according to the known methods of the Navy". At
that moment the men of at least one of the ships in
the Downs were in open mutiny.[5]

★ "His Highness was pleased to be very sensible of the matter."
S. P. to Navy Victuallers, Jan. 14th, 1689. *Pepysian MSS., Adm.
Letters* xv, 527.

Such poor simple folk were easily frightened, and happily as easily appeased. They received their arrears of pay, and the great men proceeded with their task of liquidating the Revolution they had made. The Convention on which so many hopes rested, and so many fears, was due to meet on the 22nd. A week before Evelyn at a meeting at Lambeth Palace found the Church of England Tories sadly divided: some, including most of the bishops, were for a Regency, some for making the Princess Mary Queen, and a few for calling back the King on conditions. Such tory considerations took little account of the dominant trends of opinion in the country—of the ambitions and fears of the whig peers and politic tory lords, now committed by their own past to undying enmity towards James, of the catchwords of the gullible multitude, of the attitude of the all-powerful Prince himself. It was said in the coffee-houses that Oates had been received at Court and graciously treated, that James was about to put himself at the head of the Papists in Ireland, that King Louis was preparing an army to invade England and restore the exile to his throne. A rumour that the Convention would recall the King sent prices tumbling in remote country market places; the pamphleteers and the mobmasters, marshalled once more by such cunning contrivers as Pepys's old persecutor, Wildman, knew their business.[6]

On the 17th Pepys issued an order to the captain of the *Fubbs* yacht to sail at once for Holland with Arthur Herbert on board, and another to Sir John Berry to despatch a squadron to Goree to escort Herbert and the Princess of Orange back to England. It was more than ten years since he had transmitted similar orders to carry her from her native land as a young bride. Next day he learnt from Harwich that he had lost his election. A certain

Captain Ridley, it appeared, had spread a tale in the town that Pepys was a Papist and went to Mass, and that he had frequently seen him in the King's Chapel. The Dissenters, and even "a kind of Quaker", though disqualified by law from doing so, insisted on recording their votes, and the Mayor's attempts to stop them were "over-ruled by noise and tumult". Thereupon in the most arbitrary way Mr Smith, the Town Clerk, had declared Pepys's opponent chosen. Middleton and Eldred carried the two seats and Pepys was left at the bottom of the poll. "By which", reported Hippolitus de Luzancy, Vicar of Harwich and himself a former convert from Catholicism, "you may easily be made sensible how we are overrun with pride, heat and faction, and unjust to ourselves to that prodigious degree as to deprive ourselves of the greatest honour and advantage which we could ever attain to in the choice of so great and so good a man as you are. Had reason had the least place amongst, us, or any love for ourselves, we had certainly carried it for you." After the declaration of the poll, he told Pepys, whilst the victorious members of the Corporation were chairing Eldred up and down the street, a fellow had raised the cry of "No Tower men! No men out of the Tower!" But no one joined in, the majority of the freemen, who under the ancient and now restored constitution had no votes, declaring roundly that, had they had their rights, they would have chosen Pepys. The seamen were particularly friendly towards him.[7]

Pepys took his defeat well. He wrote next day to the Mayor acknowledging his letter. "If what the Corporation has done gives them but as much content as it do me, I can assure you neither of us have any cause of being dissatisfied with it; nor shall anything that has passed herein lessen the desires I have ever had and shall always have of doing the Corporation and every member of it all the services and good offices I am able whenever they shall give me any opportunity for it. And this even to Mr Smith himself; though I must needs say he has used me a little hardly if his proceedings in this matter towards me have had no better ground than that which he mentioned to you about my preventing the Corporation's obtaining the reversion of the Harwich Lights; the reversion of all Lights having been granted by King Charles the Second, by a Declaration thereof at the Council Table, to the poor of the Trinity House, and myself being also a member (under oath) of that body long before I had any relation to the Corporation of Harwich.

"True it is I am very sorry for the trouble which you and the rest of my friends have sustained for my sake on this occasion, that being (upon my faith) the only uneasiness that falls to my share in this matter. But as I hope both they and you will in your kindness excuse it, so I pray you and them to depend upon it that I shall always remember and thankfully acknowledge it.

"And for what at my desire you have disbursed in the entertainments of my friends on this occasion, pray do me the favour to lay out as much for me (whatever it is) with them in a glass of wine to the Corporation's health, and your own, and their's, and the gentlemen's your new burgesses." A few days later he paid a modest bill for £8. 5s. 6d., £5. 12s. 6d. of which was for wine, £1. 10s. 6d. for meat and £1. 2s. 6d. for beer, bread, oysters, fire and tobacco. The privilege of representing one's fellow citizens cost no less in the seventeenth century than it does to-day. It was twenty-one years since Pepys had first contemplated the idea of putting himself forward as a Parliament man should he "continue in the Navy", and more than fifteen since he had become one. He was little likely now to continue in the Navy, and his absence from a place where he had suffered so much can hardly have caused him much grief.[8]

★   ★   ★

Thus it came about that the Convention, when it assembled at Westminster on January 22nd, 1689 to do its business, met without Pepys. He would have been uncomfortable there from the start, for the Commons, elected by the old, close, exclusionist Corporations, at once chose Henry Powle, one of his tormentors of earlier days, to be their Speaker. They then agreed on an address of thanks to the Prince of Orange, appointed a day of Public Thanksgiving for his having been made the instrument of the kingdom's deliverance from Popery and arbitrary government and adjourned till the 28th. Among much other hopeful business lying before them was a petition from Dr Titus Oates, setting forth the sad condition he had long lain under and how unjustly he had been used. The only consolation for an old-fashioned Tory who remembered '79 was that Major Wildman was said to be very ill.[9]

Pepys awaited the issue in quiet. He continued to transact the business of the Admiralty from his house in York Buildings, relinquishing nothing of his former severity and refusing leave left and right. He told his friend, Sir William Booth, that the Prince had informed him that "there were too many already here . . . at a juncture like this when their absence from their duties could be very ill dispensed with". Meanwhile he pursued in such leisure as he had the dignified and learned tastes which with the

years had become increasingly dear to him. On the
day before the Convention met again to consider the
state of the nation and dispose of its ancient throne
and constitution, he entertained John Evelyn to dinner at the Admiralty, providing as a virtuoso's
diversion an infant prodigy, son to one of his other
guests. After dinner Pepys and Evelyn put to this
child of less than twelve years old many questions
which he answered in a most extraordinary manner,
so readily and pertly and covering so wide a range of
subjects that they decided that his surprising knowledge could never be explained as a mere freak of
memory. "There was not anything", Evelyn afterwards recorded, "in Chronology, History, Geogra-
phy, the several systems of Astronomy, courses of
the stars, longitude, latitude, doctrine of the
spheres, courses and sources of rivers, creeks, harbours, eminent cities, boundaries and bearing of
countries, not only in Europe but in any other part
of the earth, which he did not readily resolve and
demonstrate his knowledge of, readily drawing out
with a pen anything he would describe. He was able
not only to repeat the most famous things which are
left us in any of the Greek or Roman histories,
monarchies, republics, wars, colonies, exploits by
sea and land, but all the sacred stories of the Old and
New Testament; the succession of all the monarchies, Babylonian, Persian, Greek, Roman with all
the lower Emperors, Popes, Heresiarchs and Councils, what they were called about, what they determined of in the controversy about Easter, the tenets
of the Gnostics, Sabellians, Arians, Nestorians, the
difference between St Cyprian and Stephen about
rebaptisation, the Schisms. We leaped from that to
other things totally different, to Olympic years and
Synochronisms; we asked him questions which
could not be resolved without considerable medita-

tion and judgment, nay of some particulars of the Civil Laws, of the Digest and Code. He gave a stupendous account of both natural and moral philosophy, and even in metaphysics.

"Having thus exhausted ourselves rather than this wonderful child, or angel rather, for he was as beautiful and lovely in countenance as in knowledge, we concluded in asking him if in all he had read or heard of, he had ever met with anything which was like this expedition of the Prince of Orange, with so small a force to obtain three great kingdoms without any contest. After a little thought he told us that he knew of nothing which did more resemble it than the coming of Constantine the Great out of Great Britain through France and Italy, so tedious a march, to meet Maxentius, whom he overthrew at Pons Milvius with very little conflict, and at the very gates of Rome, which he entered and was received with triumph, and obtained the Empire, not of three kingdoms only, but of all the then known world. He was perfect in the Latin authors, spake French naturally, and gave us a description of France, Italy, Savoy, Spain, ancient and modernly divided; as also of ancient Greece, Scythia and northern countries and tracts. We left questioning further. He did this without any set or formal repetitions, as one who had learned things without book, but as if he minded other things, going about the room, and toying with a parrot there, and as he was at dinner (*tanquam aliud agens*; as it were) seeming to be full of play, of a lively, sprightly temper, always smiling and exceeding pleasant, without the least levity, rudeness or childishness." One is grateful to Evelyn for the mention of the parrot—brought back, no doubt, by some sailor—that the Admiralty Secretary kept in his hospitable house. With its many opportunities, it must surely have excelled all other fowls of its kind in the wisdom and distinction of its conversation.

Next day, Monday, being the 28th January, the Commons resolved themselves into a committee of the whole House to consider the state of the nation. The general expectation was that the Prince and Princess of Orange would be raised to the throne. But it was first necessary to dispose of its present occupant. The spokesman of those who wished to preserve the old constitution unimpaired was Sir Christopher Musgrave, Pepys's companion on his journey through the North in '82, and son to the great Westmorland squire Sir Philip, than whom, as one of his contemporaries wrote, a worthier Englishman was never found. He asked the assembled lawyers whether any Parliament had a right to depose the King. The whig challenge to the Tories, crystallised after half a century of restatement and struggle, was formulated by one with whom Pepys had crossed swords more than once. "I have heard", said Sir Robert Howard, "that the King has his crown by a divine right; but we, the people, have a divine right too." All government was grounded upon a compact with the people. The King had broken it.

It was left to the tory lawyers, who had defended the seven bishops against the exercise of arbitrary monarchical power, to point out how much more delicate a structure an ancient government was than the whig argument supposed. The social compact was a fiction: the conception of government, so unnatural to the self-seeking animal, man, had grown gradually out of elemental barbarism and anarchy, and could only be preserved from the ever-threatening and destructive forces of individual selfishness by the acceptance of its essential parts as sacred and unalterable. The ancient Estates of the Realm, of which the Crown was one and the Commons another, could not be undermined without grave injury to the whole community, not only in the present generation but in those to come: secured and limited by the rule of known law, they were for all time and of divine ordinance. Sir Robert Sawyer—Pepys's chamber-fellow or "chum" of Cambridge days—maintained that the Commons had no right to exercise authority over its fellow Estate, the Crown. Nor could it speak for the people as a whole, since it only represented "the freeholders and the class possessed of property, by no means the nation; perhaps not the fourth part of the nation". According to a brother lawyer, Sawyer was a proud, affected and poor-spirited man with his eye ever upon prosperity and success. But he acquitted himself courageously that day. He was followed by Sir Heneage Finch, the ex-Solicitor-General, who warned the House against appealing to the hypothetical state of nature "for in that case where would be the right of property that everybody possessed?" As for the proposal to dispose of the Crown, however badly King James might have governed, he could not forfeit more than he had possessed—the personal exercise of the regal powers. He could not forfeit what was not his to forfeit, the hereditary Crown itself.

But such speakers were few. And their opponents were in no mood to listen. They had suffered a prolonged political eclipse and many of them persecution: they were now in an overwhelming majority. Few of them were philosophers; they were practical and mostly not over-scrupulous men to whom power had come suddenly. One of them put their policy, if not their case, in a nutshell by a brusque "We found the throne vacant and are to supply the defect. I say we represent the more valuable part and

all those who deserve a share in the Government."
And the brazen-faced, bullying apostate, Sir William Williams, the Welsh lawyer who had taken the chief part in the prosecution of the seven bishops, now declared roundly, "We come to supply what the King has taken from us."

It was moved that James II having endeavoured to subvert the constitution by breaking the original contract between King and people, and by the advice of Jesuits and other wicked persons violated the laws and withdrawn himself from the kingdom, had abdicated the government and that the throne had thereby become vacant. At the instance of Colonel Birch, the bluff old Puritan Boanerges against whom Pepys had so often contended, it was also resolved that experience had shown it to be inconsistent with the safety and welfare of a Protestant kingdom to be governed by a popish Prince.

These resolutions were at once carried to the Lords. Here the Tories were stronger, and Rochester and Nottingham, contending vigorously for respecting the integrity of the Constitution and the conscience of all those office-holders in Church and State who had taken the Oath of Allegiance to King James, only failed by two votes to carry the day in favour of a Regency. It took another week of wrangling and the sight and sound of the London rabble in Palace Yard before the Lords were ready to agree with the Commons that the throne was vacant. During that time the mobmasters wasted no opportunity of fanning the popular fear of popery and a papist King. At Oxford, on the day habitually set apart for mourning the martyrdom of Charles I, a horrible looking instrument was exhibited at the "Red Lion" with the device, "Invented, as they say, by a Popish bishop to screw Protestants to death by degrees: something to put into the mouth that they shall make no noises."★10

★   ★   ★

Pepys was not an hereditary aristocrat nor a great landed magnate. He was a man of the people, who had risen from the ranks in the service of the Crown, administering England for the benefit not of a class but of the people as a whole. He believed in regal government and a strong executive because in his own limited sphere he had had to fight for years against those who sought to turn national interests to class and sectarian ends: for tarpaulins against ignorant gentlemen commanders, for honest administration against graft and corrupt contractors, for rule, industry and integrity in the management of the public service against the arbitrary will of privileged and irresponsible individuals. That his royal master had made tragic mistakes he knew as well as any man. But there is little virtue in loyalty if it is to be dispensed with at the first sign of any flaw in the human object of that loyalty. And it is when there is a weak or a bad king that the principle of hereditary monarchy would seem to depend most on the loyalty of those who subscribe to it. Pepys may have been wrong: it is easy to argue that he was. But it cannot be denied that he behaved like a brave and honest man. Once before he had staked his all and faced Tower, mob and scaffold sooner than submit to what he knew to be wrong. Though he had been no supporter of the King's arbitrary courses, still less of his folly, he knew him for one who had tried to do his duty after his own lights and had been shamefully traduced and misrepresented by those who pretended to public motives which in

★ "This to make papists odious." *Anthony Wood, Life and Times* (ed. Clarke, 1894) III, 297.

many cases they were far from feeling. He had eaten his bread and sworn him allegiance.

Looking back over the course of our subsequent history, we believe the Revolution of 1688 to have been a necessary and perhaps inevitable step in the evolution of our country, though it may be argued that, by weakening the authority of the central executive unduly, it exposed the English people to that unchecked greed and exploitation of the poor by the strong which accompanied the industrialisation of the next century. Samuel Pepys is not to be blamed because he could not think of the Revolution as anything glorious. The magnates who made it might coin noble phrases about the laws and liberties of their country, but they were mostly men who had broken their oaths and who cut a shabbier figure in the eyes of their own contemporaries than they do in ours. And lurking behind the Revolution were the very men—Harbord, Wildman, Aaron Smith— who a few years before had stooped to the lowest depths of perjury and violence in order to destroy both Pepys and his royal master. He could not see them as patriots, even if we now believe that their machinations served the ultimate good of their country. An ignorant porter from Wapping or a bumpkin dazzled by a lace coat and an orange favour might consider such hellrake lords as Lovelace, Wharton and Macclesfield high-spirited tribunes of the people. They did not seem so to Pepys. To Roger North,* who knew them well, the strangest

---

* Roger North has often been traduced by later historians, notably by Macaulay. A collation of his writings with contemporary documents does not support the partisan charge of inaccuracy. His account of Samuel Atkins's cross-examination in 1678, for instance, tested by Atkins's manuscript narrative, is remarkably conscientious. Pepys's friend, Lord Clarendon (*Diary*, Jan. 16th, 1689), thought him one of the only two honest lawyers he had met. A well edited edition of his writings has long been needed.

phenomenon of the Revolution was that the reformers of the age were "the most vicious, lewd and scandalous of all mankind, and the sober and judicious part were those borne hard upon. . . . And for whoring, drunkenness and professed atheism they had not their fellows. Impetuous, injurious and cruel, and yet the cause of religion and property was in their hands, and supported by them as they had the good or ill luck to persuade the world."

While the Lords were still debating whether the Crown was vacant, the question was being resolved elsewhere to whom it should be granted and on what terms. The Tories who had been defeated in their hopes of a Regency fell back on yet another expedient: the vesting of the Crown in James's eldest Protestant child, Mary of Orange, who was at least in the line of legal succession. "I must confess any government is better than none," pleaded Nottingham in the Lords, "but I earnestly desire we may enjoy our ancient constitution."

William saw to it that this proposal had short shrift: he would not, he let it be known, be his wife's subject. But a hope that he might be raised to the throne alone, with the virtual abandonment of all pretence of legality, was felt to savour too much of republicanism and of another military Commonwealth. On Wednesday, February 6th, the Lords in conference with the Commons agreed that the Crown should be offered jointly to William and Mary and the exercise of its powers be vested in William alone. Meanwhile the chief legal experts of the Commons, under the chairmanship of a young whig lawyer of genius named Somers, drew up the heads of the nation's grievances in a formal Declaration of Rights which was to accompany the offer.

The Revolution was now complete. Early on February 12th the yacht that brought the Princess of

Orange from Holland dropped anchor off Greenwich. That afternoon she took possession of her fallen father's palace at Whitehall. Next day—Ash Wednesday—in the Banqueting Hall, whence their common grandfather had stepped on to the scaffold in vindication of the ancient laws and constitution of the kingdom, William and Mary accepted King James's throne from the Convention which had declared it vacant. A vast crowd thronged the wet roadway below the Palace all the way to Charing Cross. It is possible that Pepys, who as a boy of fifteen had seen the axe fall in the very place where now Garter-King-at-Arms proclaimed the new sovereigns, was a mute spectator of yet another momentous scene in the history of his country. It is more probable that he remained in his house by the river, hearing only the distant kettle-drums and trumpets and the sound of the acclaiming multitude as the Heralds' procession passed down the Strand towards Temple Bar. His evening mail, read while the sky above the City reflected the glare of a hundred bonfires, struck a note of gentle irony. For good Mr Langley, the Mayor of Harwich, was seeking the advice of his former representative as to how to behave towards an inn-keeper who had been "so rude as to call his Highness, the Prince of Orange, son of a Flemish bitch!" History does not relate whether the offending publican was a Jacobite or only the more extreme kind of Whig.[11]

There was nothing now left for Pepys but to lay down his office and go. The last test of loyalty is a man's readiness to sacrifice what he desires for the sake of what he loves. Pepys was one who all his life, though perhaps in a lesser degree as he grew older, had coveted wealth, place and public repute: he was by nature a worldling. But he had been brought up in a school that sets spiritual values above those of this world, however desirable, and through all the changes of life he had remained true at heart to the ideals of his youth. He did not now fail them, nor they him.

Whether the new King, so silent, serious and reserved to all the changing throng about him, would have retained the services of the great Admiralty Secretary against the wishes of such powerful gentlemen of the sea Service as Edward Russell who had invited him to England and Arthur Herbert who had carried him there, one cannot tell. It is possible, for William, however brought over, had not come to England to be the King of the Whigs or even of renegade Tories. When the new government was announced it was found to contain the names of honourable and moderate men like Nottingham and Godolphin. But Pepys left William no option. He acknowledged him as King, and, after his acceptance of the Crown, wrote of him as such in his official letters. But he had sworn oaths of lifelong fealty to another and he would not forswear them. By the standards of either a Christian or a gentleman it is hard to blame him.*[12]

So Pepys, in Evelyn's classic phrase, laid down his office and would serve no more. He did so with courtesy and without haste. William had accompanied his acceptance of the throne with a Proclamation retaining, until his further pleasure should be known, all Protestant office-holders who occupied their present places on the 1st of December. So long

* For the evidence that Pepys voluntarily laid down his office see the title-page of a bundle of papers in the Bodleian Library, entitled "A Copy of the Entries of all the Acts of His Royal Highness the Prince of Orange, prepared by Mr Pepys, relating to the Admiralty and Navy from the time of his coming to Whitehall and entrance upon the government to that of Mr Pepys's voluntary ceasing to act further therein". *Rawl. MSS. A*. 186, ff. 112 *et seq*. See also the famous passage in Evelyn's *Diary* after Pepys's death.

as this general suspension of offices continued Pepys was prepared to carry out his familiar duties; he knew it would not be for long, for the rooms of Whitehall were filled with eager seekers after emoluments and power. He arranged for the transport of the Queen-Dowager's servants and good to Calais, sent out frigates for the last time to deal with the Dunkirk privateers and procured leave for Admiral Berry to wind up his affairs in London before sailing for the Straits. He also did a few last small kindnesses for some old and deserving subordinates: wrote to Sir Phineas Pett asking him to prevent an injustice to James Pearse, purser of the *Britannia* and son of his old friend, the Surgeon-General,★ and forwarded Bagwell's name to the Navy Office as the first of three candidates for a vacancy as second assistant at Chatham. Did he, one wonders, recall for a second that remote passionate day when he had strained the forefinger of his right hand struggling with Bagwell's reluctant, dubious, yielding wife?[13]

A week after his succession William issued a further order for a "public cessation" of all offices until their beneficiaries were authorised to act by fresh powers. It was the signal for Pepys to withdraw. On February 20th he wrote on points of official detail to the Commanders-in-Chief at Portsmouth and the Medway, to the Navy Office about laying up a ship, to Lord Dartmouth as Master-General of the Ordnance about the disposal of her guns, to the captain of the *Defiance* about receiving a chaplain on board and to three of the yacht commanders to afford closer protection to the Harwich packet boats. He also drafted a letter—it cannot have

★ S. P. to Sir P. Pett, Feb. 22nd, 1689. *Rawl. MSS. A.* 179, f. 262. The request, one is glad to know, was granted. P. Pett to S. P., March 9th *Rawl. MSS. A.* 170, f. 79.

been a very congenial task—to Captain Gifford of the *Phoenix*, ordering him to sail for the Brill to fetch over Mrs Harbord with her "company, baggage and servants" and another in French to the Duchesse de Bouillon—left behind in the suddenness of Queen Mary of Modena's departure—informing her that the King, on whom he had just waited, had reluctantly decided that he could not spare the *Fubbs* yacht to carry her to Dieppe.[14]

According to Pepys's own account given in the following July to a Parliamentary Committee, February 20th was the last day on which he acted as Secretary to the Admiralty. But his Admiralty Letter Book—in which copies of all his correspondence were entered and which, despite many applications, remained in his hands after his resignation—reveals that he continued to dictate official letters for two more days. On February 22nd—the day before his 56th birthday—he wrote to the Navy Board urging that every ship in the Yards should be got ready against the King's need. On the same day he acknowledged the good wishes of several captains of the fleet, assured them of his good will so long as it lay in his power to do them any service and wished them good fortune. Their various queries, he explained, he could not answer owing to the general cessation of offices. He hoped, however, that his Majesty would shortly come to a determination about the affairs of the Admiralty.[15]

To one sea captain, an old acquaintance to whom he had formerly entrusted the training of his own nephew, Pepys wrote more implicitly. Though by virtue of the public cessation, he told Tyrrell of the *Mordaunt*, he could not send him any official order, he was privately of opinion that it was the right of the senior captain alone "to wear the distinction pendant and perform the duty of Commander-in-

Chief. Therefore, unless you take yourself to be an older captain than Captain Shovell (which does not appear in any of the Records here), I cannot but think that it will be well taken by the King and those to whom he shall commit the administration of the Admiralty, that you should forbear, . . . as being that I hold best to suit with the good order and discipline of the Navy, and what may prevent several inconveniences which may otherwise happen thereto. Which having said out of my friendship to you and the goodwill which I shall always bear towards the prosperity of the Navy, I leave it with you to make use of as you shall think fit." With this graceful farewell, Pepys took his leave of the Service.[16]

★   ★   ★

During the ten days which elapsed between his retirement and the appointment of his successor, three more letters were entered in Pepys's Admiralty Letter Book. All were addressed to Admiral Herbert. The first, dated the 26th of February, dealt with the administrative records of his office. "I am very sorry for my not being in the way of waiting on your at your calling here this morning. The list you desired and now enquired after, has been a good while in readiness for you, and as perfect as by any information I can make it." On March 1st Pepys wrote again, enclosing much invaluable information about such matters as the pay of pilots, protections to masters and crews of packet boats, the completion of the musters taken by the Navy Office and the return of the officers of the Sheerness Yard to their dwellings lately occupied by the military. "The following particulars are what you will give me leave (in addition to those I troubled you with last

night) to mention now to you as matters that seem
to call for some speedy orders." No personal differences marred Pepys's farewell to his office. In the
closing act of his career he was too great for petty
jealousy or spite.[17]

On March 5th the King formally appointed Herbert head of the new Admiralty Commission, joining with him such old political adversaries of Pepys's
as Sir Thomas Lee and William Sacheverell and one
"Orange" Tory, Sir John Lowther. On the same
day Pepys, still writing from the comely house in
York Buildings which he had made the Admiralty
of England, forwarded to Herbert a batch of letters
from foreign stations with a brief covering note:

Sir,
    The enclosed letters coming to hand since my last, you will
excuse the trouble of having them transmitted (for the King's
service) to you from

                        Your most humble servant,
                                Samuel Pepys.

After that there are no further entries in the
Admiralty Letter Book. But one other letter of
Pepys's of that day was preserved among the
unsorted papers which long after his death found
their way into the Bodleian Library with the Rawlinson Manuscripts. It was written to his old friend
and fellow civil servant, Richard Cooling, who had
helped to put him wise to the opportunities of office
on his first entering the King's service nearly thirty
years before.★ The good man had just been resworn
as a Clerk of the Privy Council:

    It is at the suit of the bearer, Mr Stedwell, rather than from
any reason I have to think that at this time of day my interces-

    ★ "He told me how he had a project for all us secretaries to join
together and get money by bringing all business into our hands."
Diary July 5th, 1660.

sion can be of any avail to him, that I take upon me to be his
solicitor to you; though I am persuaded he wont fare the worse
with my friend, Mr Cooling, that he uses my name, or that I
tell you he was a servant of my Lord Sandwich's and of both
our Royal Masters, and has acquitted himself very well for
many years together under my observation in the Navy. If any
of these considerations, and one more, namely that he married
a very good servant of mine, may stand him in any stead in the
matter before you, wherein he is recommended, and that I shall
acknowledge very thankfully the favour to him, pray let him
have your help.

To anyone acquainted with all that Pepys had been,
and done, there is something very moving in this
last gentle and persuasive letter.[18]

On assuming office as First Lord of the Admiralty, Herbert appointed Phineas Bowles as Secretary
of the new Admiralty Commission. But the office
which Pepys had held remained vacant, for with his
passing it ceased to exist. Bowles was a senior clerk,
dismissable at pleasure and wholly subordinate to a
Board of politicians and sea officers—the hired servant and never the administrative ruler of the Navy.
His successors, one of whom, Josiah Burchett,
Pepys's former clerk, was already working in the
office, were for all practical purposes permanent
civil servants. But Pepys had been something more:
the administrator-in-chief of the Service and at the
same time the equivalent of a modern First Lord of
the Admiralty, planning and presenting estimates to
Treasury and Parliament and representing the Navy
in the eyes of the country. During the last four years
he had been responsible to the King only. No other
subject but he had held any authority in the Admiralty. His remuneration had been that of a high
officer of State and four times greater than that of his
successor. In all but name he had been Secretary of
State for Marine Affairs, like his great contemporary
across the water, Jean Baptiste Colbert, Marquis de

Seignelay. Had it not been for the Revolution, as has been recently suggested, Pepys might well have been rewarded by the recognition of such an office. He had begun his official career forty years before in an age when rank and birth counted infinitely more than they do to-day, as a subordinate clerk, ignorant of the first rudiments of his profession. He had attained to a unique mastery of its every aspect. When he ended his work the tonnage of the Navy was 101,032 tons as compared with 62,594 when he began it. Yet, as the sequel was to show, this had been the least part of his achievement.[19]

Epilogue

The three years which had seen the culmination of
Pepys's work for the Navy had ended in revolution,
the deposition and usurpation of the Crown he had
served, and the nemesis and ruin of his world. The
Court of the Stuarts, the political ideals which had
prevailed there, and his honoured place in it, had
vanished as though they had never been. The men he
had hated, who had plotted against his life, who had
broken—as he imagined, though wrongly—the
work to which he had given his all, now inherited
the power and the glory. And, lucky to escape in
peace, Pepys withdrew into the shades.

Yet, as so often in England, the twilight proved
the pleasantest part of the day. In the Indian summer
of his closing decade, in the little paradise he had
created overlooking the river above Inigo Jones's
Watergate—and from which the new Commissioners of the Admiralty tried in vain to dislodge him—
Pepys learnt to sublimate defeat and grow old grace-
fully. Here, ambition laid aside and passion spent, he
enjoyed the, for him, incomparable solace of music,
cultivated the society of learned friends and the most
famous virtuosos of the age—among them Newton,
Wren, Dryden, Kneller, Purcell, the scholars Wallis,
Wanley and Bentley, and John Evelyn—and, amas-
sing materials for a history of the Navy he never
lived to complete, perfected the exquisite library of
three thousand beautifully bound books with its
unique collection of manuscripts, which he

231

bequeathed with the twelve presses he had specially designed for them, to his old Cambridge college, Magdalene.

Nor did his fidelity to his royal master, or the Revolution and triumph of his enemies, undo, as he had feared, his life's work for the Navy. His hard-won administrative rules and the battle-fleet he had built and repaired assured for his country, even during his lifetime, that primacy in the world's seas which she was never wholly to lose until she relinquished it in our own day. Despite some initial attempts by his political opponents and persecutors to molest him, by the time of his death in 1703—the year before the Navy captured the great Mediterranean strategic prize of Gibraltar—Pepys was everywhere recognised and esteemed as the great and beneficent public servant he had been. "To your praises, Sir," declared the Orator of the University of Oxford in a Latin Diploma presented to him in the closing years of his life, "the whole ocean bears witness; you have truly encompassed Britain with wooden walls!"

He left his country three legacies—his work for the Admiralty and Navy, the Pepys Library and, unknown to his comtemporaries, on the shelves of the latter the six tell-tale shorthand diaries which he had compiled in the days of his early manhood and marriage, and which, first published nearly a century and a quarter after his death, are today recognised as the greatest of all diaries and one of the world's immortal books.

It was left to his friend and fellow diarist, John Evelyn, to epitomise his life. "This day," he wrote in his journal, "died Mr Sam Pepys, a very worthy, industrious, curious person, none in England exceeding him in knowledge of the Navy, in which he had passed thro' all the most considerable offices,

Clerk of the Acts and Secretary of the Admiralty, all of which he performed with great integrity. When James II went out of England he laid down his office and would serve no more, but, withdrawing himself from all public affairs, he lived at Clapham with his partner, Mr Hewer, formerly his clerk, in a very noble and sweet place, where he enjoyed the fruits of his labours in great prosperity. He was universally loved, hospitable, generous, learned in many things, skilled in music, a very great cherisher of learned men of whom he had the conversation."

ABBREVIATIONS USED
FOR ADDITIONAL READING
BIBLIOGRAPHICAL NOTES
INDEX

ABBREVIATIONS USED

Manuscript Sources

Pepysian MSS. In the Pepys Library, Magdalene College, Cambridge.

   Adm. Letters. Admiralty Letters.

   Misc. Miscellanies.

   Mornamont. "My Two Volumes of Mornamont", Pepysian MSS. No. 2881–2.

Bodl. Bodleian Library, Oxford.

Rawl. MSS. Rawlinson Manuscripts, Bodleian Library.

B.M. British Museum, London.

P.R.O. Public Record Office, London.

S.P. State Papers, Public Record Office.

Tanner and Wheatley MSS. Manuscript notes collected by the late Mr H. B. Wheatley and the late Dr J. R. Tanner, in the possession of the author.

Printed Sources

Ailesbury. Memoirs of Thomas, Earl of Ailesbury. Roxburghe Club. 1890.

Ashley, Maurice. The Glorious Revolution of 1688. 1966.

Bramston. The Autobiography of Sir John Bramston. Camden Society. 1845.

Braybrooke IV. Vol. IV of Diary and Correspondence of Samuel Pepys. Ed. Lord Braybrooke. 1898.

Burchett. J. Burchett. A Complete History of the most remarkable Transactions at Sea. 1720.

Burnet. Bishop Burnet. History of his own Time. 1833.

Cartwright. Dr Thomas Cartwright, Diary. Camden Society. 1843.

C.J. Commons' Journals.

Churchill. Winston Churchill. Marlborough, his Life and Times. 1933.

Clarendon. The State Letters of Henry Earl of Clarendon. Ed. S. W. Singer. 1828.

Clarke. Life of James II. Ed. J. S. Clarke. 1816.

C.P. MSS. A Descriptive Catalogue of the Naval Manuscripts in the Pepysian Library. Ed. J. R. Tanner. 1903–23.

C.S.P.D. Calendar of State Papers, Domestic series.

D. Diary of Samuel Pepys. Ed. H. B. Wheatley. 1893–6.

Dalrymple. J. Dalrymple, Memoirs of Great Britain and Ireland (4th ed.). 1773.

Davey. S. J. Davey, Catalogue. 1889.

D'Orleans. F. J. D'Orleans, The History of the Revolutions in England (2nd ed.). 1722.

Echard. L. Echard, History of England (3rd ed.). 1720.

E.H.R. English Historical Review.

Ehrman, John. The Navy in the War of William III. 1953.

Ellis. The Ellis Correspondence. Ed. G. J. W. Agar-Ellis. 1829.

Evelyn. J. Evelyn, The Diary of. Ed. A. Dobson. 1908.

Feiling. K. Feiling, A History of the Tory Party, 1640–1714. 1924.

Fox. C. J. Fox, A History of the Early Part of the Reign of James the Second. 1808.

Grey. A. Grey, Debates of the House of Commons. 1769.

Hatton. Correspondence of the Family of Hatton. Camden Society. 1876.

H.M.C. Historical Manuscripts Commission Reports.

Howarth. Letters and the Second Diary of Samuel Pepys. Ed. R. G. Howarth. 1932.

Kenyon, J. P. The Nobility in the Revolution of 1688. 1963.

L.C.C. Survey. London County Council Survey of London. Vol. xviii, The Strand (The Parish of St Martin's-in-the-Fields, Part II). 1937.

Lediard. T. Lediard, The Naval History of England. 1735.

L.J. Lords' Journals.

Luttrell. N. Luttrell, A Brief Historical Relation of State Affairs. 1857.

Macaulay. Lord Macaulay, History of England (Albany ed.). 1898.

Mackintosh. Sir James Mackintosh, History of the Revolution in England. 1834.

Macpherson. Original Papers . . . arranged by James Macpherson. 1775.

Mazure. F. A. J. Mazure, Histoire de la Révolution de 1688 en Angleterre. 1825.

Memoires. Pepys's Memoires of the Royal Navy, 1679–1688. Ed. J. R. Tanner. 1906.

Naval Minutes. Samuel Pepys's Naval Minutes. Ed. J. R. Tanner. 1926.

North. Roger North, Lives of the Norths. 1890 ed.

Ogg, David. England in the Reigns of James II and William III. 1955.

Parlt. Hist. The Parliamentary History of England. Ed. W. Cobbett. 1806–20.

Petty-Southwell Corr. The Marquis of Lansdowne, The Petty-Southwell Correspondence 1676–1687. 1928.

Powley. E. B. Powley, The English Navy in the Revolution of 1688. 1928.

Prideaux. Letters of Humphrey Prideaux. Ed. E. M. Thompson. Camden Society. 1875.

Ranke. L. von Ranke, A History of England principally in the seventeenth century. 1875.

Reresby. Memoirs of Sir John Reresby. Ed. Andrew Browning. 1936.

Routh. E. M. G. Routh, Tangier, England's lost Atlantic Outpost. 1912.

Smith. The Life, Journals and Correspondence of Samuel Pepys. Ed. Rev. J. Smith. 1841.

Tangier Papers. The Tangier Papers of Samuel Pepys. Ed. E. Chappell. Navy Records Society. 1935.

Tanner, Corr. Private Correspondence and Miscellaneous Papers of Samuel Pepys, 1679–1703. Ed. J. R. Tanner. 1926.

Torrington. Memoirs relating to the Lord Torrington. Ed. J. K. Laughton. Camden Society. 1889.

Trevelyan, G. M. The English Revolution. 1938.

Verney Memoirs. Memoirs of the Verney Family. 1925 ed.

Welwood. J. Welwood, Memoirs of the Most Material Transactions in England for the last Hundred Years (6th ed.). 1718.

Whitear. W. W. Whitear, More Pepysiana. 1927.

Wood. The Life and Times of Anthony Wood. Ed. A. Clark. 1891.

BIBLIOGRAPHICAL NOTES

CHAPTER I.
THE GREAT SECRETARY

[1] *Ranke* IV, 280; *D'Orleans* 284–5; *Ellis* I, 7, 20, 55, 60 et seq.; *Ailesbury* I, 150, 162–4; *Welwood* 156; *Evelyn* 3 Nov., 4 Dec. 1685; 19, 24, 30 Jan. 1686; *Luttrell* I, 358, 360, 368–71, 376–7; *Mackintosh* 56 et seq.; *Burnet* III, 75, 79–82; *Bramston* 228 et seq.; *Reresby* 399–400, 416–17; *Ailesbury* I, 103–4, 127–8, 146.

[2] *Pepysian MSS.*, No. 1490, pp. 58–60, 66–71; *Adm. Letters* XII, 66; *Rawl. MSS. A.* 177, f. 134; *Memoires* 47–9; *Ellis* I, 119; *C.P. MSS.* 1, 86–7.

[3] *Pepysian MSS.*, No. 1490, p. 71; *Adm. Letters* XII, 96–7, 105, 107, 123, 215; *Naval Minutes* 250–1; *Rawl. MSS. A.* 177, f. 134; *A.* 189, f. 8; *Luttrell* I, 384.

[4] *Pepysian MSS., Adm. Letters* XII, 58, 283, 293–6; *Memoires* 38–45, 47–9.

[5] *Memoires* 55–68; *C.P. MSS.* I, 210–12; *Rawl. MSS. A.* 451, f. 32; *Pepysian MS.* No. 2867, Naval Precedents 186, 245.

[6] *Pepysian MSS., Adm. Letters* XII, 248, XIII, 1–2.

[7] *Pepysian MS.* No. 2867, Naval Precedents 156 et seq.; *C.P. MSS.* 1, 213–15.

[8] *C.P. MSS.* 1, 216; *Pepysian MSS.,* No. 2867, Naval Precedents 639 et seq.; *Adm. Letters* XII, 252–3; *Rawl. MSS. A.* 189, ff. 275–8.

[9] *H.M.C. Rutland* II, 109–10; *Ellis* I, 127–8, 137, 143; *Pepysian MSS., Adm. Letters* XII, 147, 165, 192, 274–5, 285; *Rawl. MSS. A.* 189, f. 205.

[10] *Rawl. MSS. A.* 171, ff. 26, 98; *Pepysian MSS., Adm. Letters* XII, 85; *Naval Minutes* 250.

[11] *H.M.C. Rep.* VII (Graham 379); *Pepysian MSS.,* No. 1490, pp. 58–60; *Adm. Letters* XII, 96–7, 107, 209, 231, 331, 337, 381, 414; *Rawl. MSS. A.* 185, f. 243; *A.* 189, ff. 39–48, 53–9, 60.

[12] *Pepysian MSS., Adm. Letters* XIII, 24, 69, 120–1; *Rawl. MSS. A.* 189, ff. 131, 154; *Howarth* 178–9; *H.M.C. Rep.* VI (Gordon-Cumming 687).

[13] *Rawl. MSS. A.* 189, ff. 308–11, 401; *C.P. MSS.* 1, 72, 91; *Pepysian MSS.* No. 1490, p. 257; *Naval Minutes* 277–8; *Ellis* I, 195, 197.

[14] *Ranke* IV, 281–302; *Luttrell* I, 376–84; *Ailesbury* I, 125; *Reresby* 420–4; *Burnet* III, 97–100; *Bramston* 225, 234, 238–50; *Evelyn* 25 June, 8 Sept. 1686; *Welwood* 171–5; *H.M.C. Portland* III, 397; *Mackintosh* 56–99; *Ellis* I, 104, 118–19, 122–3, 126–7, 144–50, 172–3.

[15] *H.M.C. Rep.* VII (*Verney* 500); *Pepysian MSS., Adm. Letters* XII, 180–1, 406–7; *Davey* Item 2884; *Ellis* I, 271; *Rawl. MSS. A.* 189, f. 218; *Howarth* 173–4; *Luttrell* I, 383.

[16] *Pepysian MSS., Adm. Letters* XII, 244, 257–8, 351; *Davey* Item 2885.

[17] *Rawl. MSS. A.* 189, ff. 218, 268, 279–80, 329; *Pepysian MSS., Adm. Letters* X, 73–4, 81; XII, 448; *C.P. MSS.* I, 220–1; *Howarth* 171–4.

[18] *Pepysian MSS., Adm. Letters* XII, 448; *H.M.C. Rep.* V (*Magdalene College* 484); *Howarth* 176–7; *Rawl. MSS. A.* 189, ff. 145, 294–5, 298, 300–3, 318.

[19] *Howarth* 173; *Rawl. MSS. A.* 189, ff. 233, 331.

[20] *Ranke* IV, 300–11; *Luttrell* I, 383, 391; *Ailesbury* I, 152; *Mackintosh* 130 et seq.; *Reresby* 426, 440–2; *Bramston* 251–4, 259; *Evelyn* 29 Dec. 1686; 17 Jan. 1687.

CHAPTER II.
HIS ORDERS HOLD

[1] *Ellis* I, 83–4, 89, 111.

[2] *Ranke* IV, 309–13; *D'Orleans* 290; *Burnet* III, 102; *Mackintosh* 185; *Bramston* 268–70; *Reresby* 444–5, 447–51; *Pepysian MSS., Adm. Letters* XII, 382, 386–7; *Rawl. MSS. A.* 189, ff. 220, 222, 229, 231, 259; *Smith* II, 51–6.

[3] *Ranke* IV, 334–6; *G. N. Clark, The Later Stuarts* 119; *Burnet* III, 149–55; *Mackintosh* 134–9; *Bramston* 274–7, 301; *Rawl. MSS. A.* 189, f. 318; *Howarth* 176–7.

[4] *Rawl. MSS. A.* 179, f. 6; *A.* 189, f. 145; *Braybrooke* IV, (1898 ed.), 239.

[5] *Rawl. MSS. A.* 177, ff. 140–1; *A.* 189, f. 145; *Ranke* IV, 311–12; *Luttrell* I, 396; *Mackintosh* 154; *Burnet* III, 100–1, 274; *Bramston* 270.

[6] *Tanner, Corr.* I, 286; *Pepysian MS.* No. 2141, Letter of 19 March 1682; *Rawl. MSS. A.* 189, ff. 296–7; *C.* 859, f. 151v; *Howarth* 178; *Smith* II, 91–5; *H.M.C. Hodgkin* 180–1; *Mackintosh* 371.

[7] *Cartwright* 54.

[8] *Pepysian MSS., Adm. Letters* xII, 243; *Rawl. MSS. A.* 189, f. 226; *Howarth* 172–7.

[9] *Rawl. MSS. A.* 189, ff. 78; 224–5; *Pepysian MSS., Adm. Letters* xIII, 445.

[10] *Rawl. MSS. A.* 189, ff. 312, 314, 316; *Howarth* 174–5.

[11] *Howarth* 175–6; *Rawl. MSS. A.* 189, ff. 319, 321–2; *Luttrell* I, 396.

[12] *Rawl. MSS. A.* 179, ff. 98, 100; *A.* 189, f. 313; *Howarth* 184, 188, 190–3.

[13] *Pepysian MSS., Adm. Letters* xII, 457; *Rawl. MSS. A.* 171, ff. 26–7, 29, 36; *A.* 189 ff. 29, 31; *Smith* II, 75–6, 113–16, 124; *Howarth* 179.

[14] *Rawl. MSS. A.* 179, ff. 30, 113; *A.* 189, ff. 17, 19, 49–52, 85, 135, 198, 318; *Howarth* 176–7, 180, 187; *Smith* II, 74–5, 90–1, 124–5; *Davey* Item 2886.

[15] *Smith* II, 82–4; *Wheatley and Tanner MSS.; Pepysian MS.* No. 1825; *J. R. Tanner, Mr Pepys* 263; *Rawl. MSS. A.* 189, f. 23.

[16] *Rawl. MSS. A.* 171, f. 89, *A.* 189, ff. 261–3.

[17] *Pepysian MSS., Adm. Letters* xIII, 1–2, 237–8; xIV, 12; *Rawl. MSS. A.* 171, f. 116.

[18] *Rawl. MSS. A.* 171, f. 63; *Pepysian MSS., Adm. Letters* xIII, 243; xIV, 2, 10, 27, 53.

[19] *Pepysian MSS., Adm. Letters* xI, 555; xIII, 6, 203.

[20] *Pepysian MSS. Adm. Letters* xIII, 179, 183, 274–9.

[21] *Pepysian MSS., Adm. Letters* xIII, 1, 235, 247.

[22] *Pepysian MSS., Adm. Letters* xIII, 205; *Howarth* 181–5; *Rawl. MSS. A.* 179, ff. 18, 20–1; *A.* 189, ff. 1, 3, 8, 11, 16.

[23] *Pepysian MSS., Adm. Letters* xIII, 2, 8–9, 11, 16, 18, 25, 28–9, 32 et seq.; *Rawl. MSS. A.* 171, f. 161; *A.* 177, ff. 1–76; *A.* 179, f. 226.

[24] *Pepysian MSS., Adm. Letters* xIII, 116–17, 122, 125–7, 128–9, 136–8, 151–2; *Rawl. MSS. A.* 189, ff. 83, 115, 125; *Smith* II, 77–81.

[25] *Pepysian MSS., Adm. Letters* xIII, 175–6, 179, 183, 238, 292, 308–9, 339; *H.M.C. Portland* III, 401; *Naval Minutes* 104; *Luttrell* I, 399, 407, 409.

[26] *Luttrell* I, 397, 407, 413; *Hatton* II, 67–9; *H.M.C. Rep.* vII (*Verney* 482); *Bramston* 282–3; *Rawl. MSS. A.* 189, ff. 370–8; *Pepysian MSS., Adm. Letters* xIII, 175–6, 255–6, 292; xIV, 25–6; E. F. Ward, *Christopher Monck, Duke of Albemarle* (1915) 243–7

[27] *Bramston* 300; *Rawl. MSS. A.* 189, ff. 15–16; *D.* 1486, f. 15; *Ellis* I, 325; *Smith* II, 58–9, 60–3; *Pepysian MSS., Adm. Letters* xIII, 198–9.

[28] *Pepysian MSS., Adm. Letters* xii, 422–3; xiii, 154; *Misc.* xi, 18, 20; *Ailesbury* i, 107; *C.P. MSS.* i, 111, 298–9; *Ellis* i, 197; *Rawl. MSS. A.* 186, ff. 239, 263–4.

CHAPTER III.
PLEASURES OF A VIRTUOSO

[1] *Evelyn* 2 June 1686; 10 March; 10 April; 12 May 1687; *Luttrell* i, 383, 392–3, 395, 411; *Hatton* ii, 69; *Burnet* iii, 102–3, 161–7, 184–7, 193–5; *Ellis* i, 226–8, 235–6, 255–6, 260 272–3, 312–13, 338–9; *Ranke* iv, 310–41; *Macaulay; D'Orleans* 292; *Reresby* 452, 456, 581–2; *Mackintosh* 145–97; *Bramston* 270–2, 280–1, 283–97, 304.

[2] *Luttrell* i, 411; *Bramston* 298; *Mackintosh* 201–2; *Burnet* iii, 189–90; *Reresby* 469–70; *Pepysian MSS., Adm. Letters* xiii, 241–2, 253–4, 291, 294; *Ellis* i, 336–7; *Hatton* ii, 70–1; *H.M.C. Portland* iii, 399–404; *Rawl. MSS. A.* 186, f. 233; *A.* 189, f. 35.

[3] *Rawl. MSS. A.* 186, f. 233; *A.* 189, f. 21; *H.M.C. Portland* iii, 400; *Pepysian MSS., Adm. Letters* xiii, 254–5; *A. Wood, Athenae Oxonienses* (1721 ed.) ii, 949; *H.M.C. Hodgkin* 181.

[4] *Rawl. MSS. A.* 179, f. 8; *A.* 186, f. 233; *Pepysian MSS., Adm. Letters* xiii, 9, 15; No. 2879, Miscellanies xi, 161; *Howarth* 186.

[5] *Rawl. MSS. A.* 171, f. 7; *A.* 179, f. 119; *A.* 186, f. 233; *Nichols, Literary Anecdotes* i, 423; iii, 613; *Smith* ii, 103–4; *Wheatley and Tanner MSS.; Howarth* 189

[6] *Braybrooke* (1898 ed.) iv, 238; *Rawl. MSS. A.* 171, f. 4.

[7] *H.M.C. Hodgkin* 169; *Rawl. MSS. A.* 171, ff. 137–8; *A.* 177, ff. 126–7, 134; *A.* 189, f. 8; *Smith* ii, 215; *Reresby* 401.

[8] *L.C.C. Survey of London* xviii (Strand); *Mariner's Mirror* xxiv, No. 2 (April 1938), *D. Bonner-Smith, Samuel Pepys and York Buildings; Rawl. MSS. A.* 179, f. 78.

[9] *Smith* ii, 214–15.

[10] *Smith* ii, 110–11; *Rawl. MSS. A.* 179, f. 4; *Hodgkin Autograph Letters* (App. 1914), Lot 239; *Rawl. MSS. A.* 171, f. 17; *A.* 179, f. 4; *A.* 186, ff. 4–5; *A.* 193 (title-page).

[11] *Rawl. MSS. A.* 189, f. 35; *Smith* ii, 219; *Davey* Item 2889; *Smith* ii, 219/20; *Pepysian MSS., Adm. Letters* xiv, 102–6; *Spectator* No. 187.

[12] *Smith* ii, 218–19; *Howarth* 180–1; *Rawl. MSS. A.* 189, ff. 25, 27; *D.* 23 Aug. 1665.

[13] *Smith* II, 219; *Rawl. MSS. A.* 171, ff. 148–53; *A.* 179, ff. 18, 20–1; *A.* 189, f. 35; *Howarth* 184–5.

[14] *Braybrooke* (1825 ed. Reprint) 634; *Rawl. MSS. A.* 189, ff. 327–8.

[15] *Howarth* 178; *Rawl. MSS. A.* 189, ff. 296–7; *Evelyn* 19 April 1687.

[16] *Rawl. MSS. A.* 179, f. 122; *A.* 189, ff. 78, 148; *Smith* II, 216–17, 228–9; *Howarth* 189–90.

[17] *Rawl. MSS. A.* 179, ff. 126–31; *Smith* II, 132–5; *H.M.C. Hodgkin* 181; *Luttrell* I, 424–5; *Pepys Club Occasional Papers* II, 71; *D.* 21 July 1664.

[18] *Pepysian MSS., Adm. Letters* XIV, 106; *Rawl. MSS. A.* 177, ff. 238–9; *A.* 179, ff. 26, 28; *A.* 189, ff. 133, 235; *Smith* II, 58–9, 60–3.

[19] *Rawl. MSS. A.* 177, ff. 235, 238–9; *Ranke* IV, 378–84.

[20] *Ranke* IV, 385; *Macaulay; Burnet; Luttrell* I, 385, 390, 428–9.

[21] *Rawl. MSS. A.* 189, ff. 288–92.

[22] *Rawl. MSS. A.* 170, ff. 171, 215–16; *A.* 171, ff. 34, 110, 114–15; *A.* 186 f. 171; *A.* 189, ff. 308–11; *Pepysian MSS.,* No. 1490, pp. 76, 90, 372; *Adm. Letters* XIII, 386–7; *Naval Minutes* 277–8; *Memoires* 85; *Ailesbury* I, 107.

[23] Letter in possession of the Dowager Countess of Gainsborough; *Wheatley and Tanner MSS.; Rawl. MSS. A.* 171, f. 76; *Pepysian MSS., Adm. Letters* XIV, 24, 114.

CHAPTER IV.
THE GATHERING STORM

[1] *Ranke* IV, 380–4, 401–5; *Rawl. MSS. A.* 186, f. 238; *Mackintosh* 372–3, 339, 402–4; *Luttrell* I, 428–9, 432–3, 434, 436; *Bramston* 305–6.

[2] *Pepysian MSS., Adm. Letters* XIV, 7–8, 44; *Rawl. MSS. A.* 186, ff. 194–5, 243; *Luttrell* I, 426, 429.

[3] *Luttrell* I, 426, 433; *Burnet; Dalrymple; H.M.C. Rep.* V, 378; *Clarendon, Diary* I, 15 January 1688; *Mackintosh* 202–6, 400, 408; *Bramston* 303.

[4] *H.M.C. Portland* III, 405; *Ranke* IV, 341–5; *Mackintosh* 240–1, 381–90; *Ailesbury* I, 169; *Evelyn* 15, 29 April 1688; *Clarendon, Diary* 6 Feb. 1688; *Luttrell* I, 438–9; *Bramston* 302, 307; *Reresby* 494–5.

⁵ *Luttrell* I, 434, 436–8; *Smith* II, 117–19; *Rawl. MSS. A.* 170, ff. 214–15; *A.* 171, ff. 141–6; *Evelyn* 8 May 1688; *Mackintosh* 422; *Pepysian MSS., Adm. Letters* XIV, 148–9.

⁶ *Pepysian MSS., Adm. Letters* XIV, 148–9, 158, 162, 166–7; *Smith* II, 120–3; *Rawl. MSS. A.* 171, ff. 141–6.

⁷ *Rawl. MSS. A.* 186, ff. 245–6; *Mackintosh* 422; *Smith* II, 120–3; *Ellis* I, 224.

⁸ *Pepysian MSS., Adm. Letters* XIV, 145, 156–7, 159; *Smith* II, 120–3.

⁹ *Pepysian MSS.*, No. 2879, Miscellanies XI, 913–25; *Adm. Letters* XIV, 156–7; *Powley* 15–16; *H.M.C. Rep.* V, 378; *Luttrell* I, 438–9; *Clarendon, Diary* 8–9 May 1688.

¹⁰ *Pepysian MS.* No. 2879, Miscellanies XI, 925–6.

¹¹ *Rawl. MSS. A.* 179, f. 12; *A.* 186, f. 6; *Pepysian MSS., Adm. Letters* XIV, 16 et passim, 326–7, 337, 344.

¹² *Rawl. MSS. A.* 179, f. 34; *A.* 186, f. 8; *Pepysian MSS., Adm. Letters* XIV, 12, 27, 37, 54, 69, 93, 121, 224.

¹³ *Rawl. MSS. A.* 179, ff. 8, 14, 32, 88, 117, 120; *A.* 189, f. 9; *Howarth* 183–4, 186–9; *Smith* II, 127–8; *Pepysian MSS., Adm. Letters* XIV, 214.

¹⁴ *Pepysian MSS., Adm. Letters* XIV, 35, 190–1, 277 et seq.

¹⁵ *Ranke; Burnet* III,193–5; *Luttrell* I, 429–33; *H.M.C. Portland* III,408; *Ailesbury* 162–3; *Bramston* 301–7.

¹⁶ *Pepysian MSS., Adm. Letters* XIV, 79–80; *C.P. MSS.* I, 219; *Rawl. MSS. A.* 171, f. 61; *Smith* II, 125–7

¹⁷ *Ranke* IV, 347–51; *Mackintosh* 247–51; *Evelyn* 18, 20 May 1688; *Dalrymple* I, 195; *Clarendon, Diary* 12, 16, 17, 18, 23 May 1688; T. *Lathbury, History of the Non-Jurors* (1845) 5–8; *H.M.C. Portland* III, 408; *Reresby* 498; *Bramston* 307–8; *Luttrell* I, 438–9; 440; *Verney Memoirs* II, 456–7; *Burnet* III, 226–32; *Bevill Higgons, Short View* 333.

¹⁸ *Luttrell* I, 434, 437, 442; *Clarendon, Diary* 18, 20, 28 May; 5, 7, 15 June 1668; *Evelyn* 16 March; 8 May; *Burnet* III, 228–32; 8 June 1688; *H.M.C. Rep.* VII (*Verney* 501–2); *Hatton* II, 81; *H.M.C. Portland* III, 410; *Shakerley MSS. Chester Castle papers; Verney Memoirs* II, 456; *Dalrymple* I, 197–8; *Mackintosh* 256–63; *Bramston* 309; *Ailesbury* I, 170.

¹⁹ W. *Cobbett and Howell, State Trials* XII, 349 et seq.; F. *Hargrave, State Trials* (1776) IV, 303–96; *Evelyn* 29 June 1688; *Mackintosh* 263–77; *Ellis* II, 2–3; *Dalrymple* I, 198–9; *H.M.C. Portland* III, 413; *Sir H. Ellis, Original Letters,* 2nd Series, IV, 105–6, 109; *Clarendon, Diary* 25, 27–30 June 1688; *Burnet* III, 233–6.

²⁰ *Ellis* II, 5; *Verney Memoirs* II, 458–9; *Ailesbury* I, 170–1;

Churchill, Marlborough I, 270; *Dalrymple* I, 199–200; *Reresby* 501, 503–4; *Burnet* III, 237, 240–1, 274; *Mackintosh* 408–13, 416–20.

[21] *Pepysian MSS., Adm. Letters* XIV, 220, 222; *Mackintosh* 400–1; *Clarke* II, 200; *Luttrell* I, 442; *Burnet* III, 246–57; *D'Orleans* 298; *Evelyn* 10 June 1688; *Dalrymple* I, 201; *Ailesbury* I, 172–4; *Hatton* II, 81; *Ellis* I, 352, 364; II, 52, 54–5; *Clarendon, Diary* 15 Jan.; 10, 11 Feb. 1688; *H.M.C. Portland* III, 311.

[22] *Pepysian MSS., Adm. Letters* XIV, 166–8, 176–7, 200–2, 204–5, 208, 210–11; *Admiralty Papers in P.R.O.,* cit. *Powley* 15; *Burnet* III, 237; *Ailesbury* I, 170–1.

[23] *London Gazette* 28/31 May; 14/18 June 1688; *Hatton* II,80; *Rawl. MSS. A.* 186, f. 206; *Dalrymple; Luttrell* I, 443; *H.M.C. Portland* III, 410–11; *Pepysian MSS., Adm. Letters* XIV, 210–12, 218, 220, 228, 232–3, 240; *E.H.R.* III (1893), *J. R. Tanner, Naval Preparations of James II in 1688* 272; *Burchett* 407–8; *Torrington* 18.

[24] *Rawl. MSS. A.* 170, ff. 214–16; *C.P. MSS.* I, 89; *Pepysian MS.* No. 1490, p. 372; *Verney Memoirs* II, 460; *Ailesbury* I, 107.

[25] *Ranke* IV, 382–404; *Dalrymple; D'Avaux; Prideaux* 147.

[26] *Ranke* 404 et seq.; *Luttrell* I, 441, 445, 450–1; *H.M.C. Portland* III, 411; *Dalrymple* III, App. I, 200–1; *Mackintosh* 422–5, 457–8; *Burnet* III, 240–1, 260–2, 276–85; *Reresby* 503; *Clarke* II, 176; *Torrington* 18–19, 27; *Ellis* II, 63; *Burchett* 408; *Pepysian MSS., Adm. Letters* XIV, 254, 260–1, 272, 276.

[27] *Luttrell* I, 450–1; *Howarth* 191–2; *Smith* II, 130–2; *Rawl. MSS. A.* 179, f. 70; *Ellis* II, 30, 52, 62, 67; *Pepysian MSS., Adm. Letters* XIV, 278.

[28] *Rawl. MSS. A.* 177, ff. 78, 82–104; *Ellis* II, 98; *Pepysian MSS., Adm. Letters* XIV, 282–3, 288, 290, 294; *Luttrell* I, 453.

[29] *Mackintosh* 427–9; *D'Orleans* 302–3; *Pepysian MSS., Adm. Letters* XIV, 304; *Dalrymple* III, App. I, 212–15; *Ellis* II, 14, 52, 101; *H.M.C. Rep.* V, 378–9.

[30] *London Gazette* 20 July/2 Aug. 1688; *Torrington* 19; *Luttrell* I, 451; *Rawl. MSS. A.* 186, f. 171; *Francis Edwards, Catalogue* No. 507 (1928), Item 339.

[31] *Luttrell* I, 457; *Rawl. MSS. A.* 179, f. 68; *A.* 186, f. 173; *A.* 189, ff. 100–1.

[32] *Ranke* IV, 384, 403–21; *Dalrymple* III, App. I, 200–4; *Mackintosh* 425, 428–9.

[33] *Prideaux Papers* 147; *Luttrell* I, 420–3, 432–3, 436–7, 439, 455, 457; *Churchill, Marlborough* I, 279–80; *Burnet* III, 19; *Macaulay; Dalrymple* III, App. I, 139–49.

[34] *Pepysian MSS., Adm. Letters* XIV, 296 et seq.; *Rawl. MSS.*

A. 179, ff. 42, 179, 253; *Evelyn* 23 Aug. 1688; *Smith* ii, 142.

[35] *Rawl. MSS. A.* 186, ff. 57–60, 84, 88; *Pepysian MSS., Adm. Letters* xiv, 345, 386–7; *Luttrell* i, 455; *Burchett* 408; *H.M.C. Hodgkin* 182; *Ellis* ii, 128, 130, 139; *Torrington* 19; *Smith* ii, 135–7.

CHAPTER V.
INVASION

[1] *Pepysian MSS., Adm. Letters* xiv, 349–52, 354–5, 357–60, 362–3, 366, 376; *Burchett* 408–10; *Torrington* 19–20; *Ellis* i, 125, 148; *E.H.R.* viii, 273–4; *Powley* 18; *Luttrell* i, 455–6; *Rawl. MSS. A.* 179, ff. 92–3; *A.* 186, f. 257.

[2] *Pepysian MSS., Adm. Letters* xiv, 362–76, 409; xv, 1–44, 55; *Rawl. MSS. A.* 179, ff. 92–3; *A.* 186, f. 257; *E.H.R.* viii, 274.

[3] *Hatton* ii, 90.

[4] *Mackintosh* 428–9, 431–2, 436–7; *Dalrymple* iii, App. I, 202–6; *Reresby* 506, 509; *Burchett* 408–11; *Torrington* 20–3; *Powley* 19–20.

[5] *Luttrell* i, 457–8, 460; *H.M.C. Rep.* v, 379; *Powley* 22–3; *Pepysian MSS., Adm. Letters* xiv, 363–70, 371–9, 381–4, 386–7, 389–407, 409–22; xv, 21, 35, 39–41, 49, 79, 90, 93, 100, 119–20, 141, 157, 160, 164–5, 222–3, 228, 241–2, 261, 292, 376; *Ellis* ii, 130–1, 139, 141–2, 147–8, 153–4, 158–9.

[6] *Pepysian MSS., Adm. Letters* xiv, 386, 392; xv, 8–10, 15, 35–8, 40, 42, 46–9, 53–4, 71 et seq.; *Rawl. MSS. A.* 186, f. 311; *Braybrooke* (1825) 645–6; *Ellis* ii, 154, 191.

[7] *Smith* ii, 146–9; *Rawl. MSS. A.* 179, f. 22; *A.* 186, f. 311; *Braybrooke* (1825) 645–6; *Howarth* 193; *H.M.C. Dartmouth* i, 139; *Pepysian MSS., Adm. Letters* xv, 12, 13, 44.

[8] *Ranke; Luttrell* i, 457; *Bramston* 312; *Reresby* 506; *Feiling* 227–8; *Evelyn* 7 Sept. 1688; *Smith* ii, 140–4; *Rawl. MSS. A.* 179, ff. 44, 184, 186; *Braybrooke* (1898) iv, 243; *Pepysian MSS., Adm. Letters* xv, 30–1; *Ellis* ii, 144, 187.

[9] *Mackintosh* 442; *Clarke* ii, 177; *Hatton* ii, 91–2; *Luttrell* i, 452, 458, 461; *Rawl. MSS. A.* 186, f. 311; *Braybrooke* (1825) 645–6; *Feiling* 227–8; *Torrington* 23; *Burchett* 411; *Clarendon, Diary* 23–24 Sept. 1688; *Pepysian MSS., Adm. Letters* xv, 1–2, 20, 45, 147–8; *Bramston* 316; *Ellis* ii, 141–2, 162, 203, 218, 230–4; *Evelyn* 18, 30 Sept. 1688.

[10] *Ranke* iv, 422–7; *Feiling* 228–9; *H.M.C. Fleming* 212; *Lut-*

trell I, 462; *Clarendon, Diary* 22 Sept. 1688; *Reresby* 516; *Ellis* II, 201–2, 207, 209–10, 231, 235; *Burnet* III, 316–17.

[11] *Ranke* IV, 425; *Luttrell* I, 464–71; *Mackintosh* 448–9; *H.M.C. Rep.* V, 379; *Clarendon*, Diary 28–30 Sept.; 1–14 Oct. 1688; *Letters from the Bodleian Library* (1813) I, 49–50; *Evelyn* 7 Oct. 1688; *Ellis* II, 211–12, 219, 224, 227, 245, 247–8; *Burnet* III, 336; *Bramston* 316–26; *H.M.C. Portland* III, 418; *H.M.C. Dartmouth* I, 139, 141–43, 167; *Reresby* 522; *H.M.C. Fleming* 213; *Hatton* II, 94–5; *Feiling* 228–9.

[12] *Mackintosh* 441; *Clarke* II, 186; *Burchett* 411–14; *Pepysian MSS., Adm. Letters* XV, 34–6; *Powley* 25; *H.M.C. Dartmouth* I, 255; *Burnett* III, 285; *Bramston* 319; *H.M.C. Fleming* 212; *H.M.C. Portland* III, 417; *Smith* II, 149–52.

[13] *Burchett* 410–14; *Pepysian MSS., Adm. Letters* XV, 51–2, 55–9, 63–5, 69–70, 73–4, 81–2, 84–6, 96–7, 102–3; *Torrington* 23–6; *E.H.R.* VIII, 275; *Mackintosh* 453; *Clarke* II, 186–91; *H.M.C. Dartmouth* I, 138, 255; *B.M. Sloane MSS.* 3650, ff. 7–11; *Fighting Instructions 1536–1826* (ed. J. S. Corbett, 1905) 170–2.

[14] *Pepysian MSS., Adm. Letters* XV, 45, 139–40; *H.M.C. Portland* III, 417; *Hatton* II, 93.

[15] *Rawl. MSS. A.* 186, f. 324; *Smith* II, 153–4; *H.M.C. Dartmouth* I, 141–3; *Hatton* II, 95; *Ellis* II, 241, 250; *Burnet* III, 315; *Burchett* 412; *Lediard* II, 615–16; *B.M. Sloane MSS.* 3650, ff. 7–11; *Fighting Instructions* (ed. J. S. Corbett, 1905) 170–2.

[16] *Pepysian MSS., Adm. Letters* XV, 78–80, 85, 89–92, 94–5, 103–10, 115–21, 123–7, 130–5, 147, 164–71, 180–7, 204–5, 219–23, 241–5, 253–7, 262–6, 283–6; *H.M.C. Dartmouth* I, 139–41 et seq.; *Hatton* II, 93; *Rawl. MSS. A.* 186, f. 332; *Smith* II, 159–62; *E.H.R.* VIII, 267.

[17] *Pepysian MSS., Adm. Letters* XV, 78–80, 82, 89–93, 114, 140–1, 155, 157, 172, 212–13; *H.M.C. Dartmouth* I, 139–43, 149–51; *Rawl. MSS. A.* 186, f. 323; *Smith* II, 155–8.

[18] *Rawl. MSS. A.* 186, f. 353; *Pepysian MSS., Adm. Letters* XV, 89–92.

[19] *H.M.C. Dartmouth* I, 149, 155–7; *Pepysian MSS., Adm. Letters* XV, 130–5.

[20] *Pepysian MSS., Adm. Letters* XV, 21, 49, 78–80, 123–7, 228; *Rawl. MSS. A.* 186, f. 332; *Smith* II, 159–62; *H.M.C. Dartmouth* I, 139–43, 1949–55.

[21] *Pepysian MSS., Adm. Letters* XV, 127; *H.M.C. Dartmouth* I, 153–5.

[22] *Rawl. MSS. A.* 186, ff. 225–9, 304; *Pepysian MSS., Adm. Letters* XV, 72; *Torrington* 18.

²³ *Pepysian MSS., Adm. Letters* xv, 137, 180–7, 193–5; *Powley* 54–5; *H.M.C. Dartmouth* I, 141–3, 149, 162–7.

²⁴ *Pepysian MSS., Adm. Letters* xv, 130–3, 145–7; *H.M.C. Dartmouth* I, 141–3, 149, 155–7.

²⁵ *Pepysian MSS.,* No. 1490, pp. 76, 369–81; *Adm. Letters* xv, 90–1, 148–9, 163–4; *C.P. MSS.* I, 89–91, 95–6; *Memoires* 69; *H.M.C. Dartmouth* I, 159.

²⁶ *Pepysian MSS., Adm. Letters* xv, 148; *C.P. MSS.* I, 90–1; *Ailesbury* I, 107; *Memoires* 69.

²⁷ *Pepysian MSS., Adm. Letters* xv, 64 et seq., 211–12; *Rawl. MSS. A.* 186, f. 323; *Smith* II, 155–8, 162–4; *H.M.C. Dartmouth* I, 141–4.

²⁸ *Rawl. MSS. A.* 186, ff. 323, 332; *Smith* II, 155–62; *H.M.C. Dartmouth* I, 256–8.

²⁹ *H.M.C. Dartmouth* I, 152, 158, 257–8; *Ailesbury* I, 186; *Powley* 39; *Burnet* 315.

³⁰ *H.M.C. Dartmouth* I, 158, 257–8.

³¹ *Evelyn* 14 Oct. 1688; *Powley* 61–3; *Rawl. MSS. A.* 186, ff. 352, 355; *H.M.C. Dartmouth* I, 162–4; *Pepysian MSS., Adm. Letters* xv, 186–7; *Clarendon, Diary* 16 Oct. 1688.

³² *Pepysian MSS., Adm. Letters* xv, 99–100, 135–8, 155–6, 159–60, 191, 193–5, 208, 212–16, 228, 261–2; *H.M.C. Dartmouth* I, 159–61, 164–7, 171–4; *H.M.C. Rep.* v, 372.

³³ *Ailesbury* I, 184–5; *H.M.C. Dartmouth* I, 259–61; *Burnet* III, 329; *Torrington; Mackintosh* 475; *Clarke* II, 208.

³⁴ *Hatton* II, 96; *Ellis* II, 233–5, 241, 246–7, 254; *Shakerley MSS.* Oct. 1688.

³⁵ *H.M.C. Dartmouth* I, 164–7; *Ellis* II, 253, 256; *Pepysian MSS., Adm. Letters* xv, 196–202.

³⁶ *H.M.C. Dartmouth* I, 168–70, 259–61; III, 59–60; *Rawl. MSS. A.* 186, f. 364; *Smith* II, 166–70.

³⁷ *Pepysian MSS., Adm. Letters* xv, 241–5; *Powley* 66; *H.M.C. Dartmouth* I, 168–9, 171–4.

³⁸ *Pepysian MSS., Adm. Letters* xv, 239–43, 262–7; *H.M.C. Dartmouth* I, 178–80, 267.

³⁹ *Ellis* II, 240, 257–9, 265, 267–9; *Mackintosh* 449–52; *Clarendon, Diary* 21–23 Oct. 1688; *Reresby* 522–3; *Ailesbury* I, 183; *H.M.C. Dartmouth* I, 167, 169–70; *Pepysian MSS., Adm. Letters* xv, 218, 228; *Burnet* III, 318–23; *H.M.C. Portland* III, 419–20; *Bramston* 327; *Feiling* 230; *Evelyn* 28 Oct. 1688; *H.M.C. Rep.* v, 379; *H.M.C. Fleming* 216.

⁴⁰ *H.M.C. Dartmouth* III, 59.

⁴¹ *H.M.C. Dartmouth* I, 158; *Powley* 62–6.

⁴² *Pepysian MSS., Adm. Letters* xv, 252–5; *H.M.C. Dart-*

mouth i, 170, 175; *Mackintosh* 462–4; *Bramston* 327; *Torrington* 28; *H.M.C. Portland* iii, 420; *Clarendon, Diary* 27 Oct. 1688; *Burnet* iii, 310–13.

[43] *Pepysian MSS., Adm. Letters* xv, 253–5; *H.M.C Dartmouth* i, 175–8.

[44] *H.M.C. Dartmouth* i, 262; iii, 60–1; *Rawl. MSS. A.* 186, f. 368; *Burchett* 414; *Powley* 71–4; *Torrington* 26–8; *Dalrymple* ii, App. I, 241.

[45] *Rawl. MSS. A.* 186, f. 90; *Smith* ii, 328–9; *Pepysian MSS., Adm. Letters* xv, 266–8; *Burnet* iii, 307–8, 324–5.

[46] *H.M.C. Dartmouth* i, 262.

[47] *Ellis* ii, 262, 268–9, 273–4; *H.M.C. Dartmouth* i, 183, 262–3; iii, 61; *Rawl. MSS. A.* 186, f. 372; *Pepysian MSS., Adm. Letters* xv, 288; *Powley* 78–81; *Dalrymple* iii, App. I, 243; *Burnet* iii, 325.

[48] *Pepysian MSS., Adm. Letters* xv, 293, 297–8; *H.M.C. Rep.* vii (*Graham* 412); *H.M.C. Dartmouth* i, 181–4; *Powley* 79–81; *Ellis* ii, 274; *Bramston* 329; *Torrington* 29; *Clarendon, Diary* 3 Nov. 1688.

[49] *Pepysian MSS., Adm. Letters* xv, 297–8; *Powley* 91–4; *H.M.C. Dartmouth* i, 183–4; *Naval Minutes* 273–4, 292.

[50] *Pepysian MSS., Adm. Letters* xv, 303–9, 311; *H.M.C. Rep.* vii (*Graham* 412–13); *H.M.C. Dartmouth* i, 184–5; *Evelyn* 4, 5 Nov. 1688; *H.M.C. Fleming* 218; *Hatton* ii, 98–9; *Burnet* iii, 327; *Bramston* 330; *Ellis* ii, 280–4; *Clarendon, Diary* 6 Nov. 1688; *J. R. Tanner, Mr Pepys* 267 n.

[51] *H.M.C. Dartmouth* i, 263–5; *Powley* 78–81; *Rawl. MSS. A.* 186, f. 374; *Pepysian MSS., Adm. Letters* xv, 311–12; *Smith* ii, 332–5.

[52] *Pepysian MSS., Adm. Letters* xv, 304, 308–9; *Powley* 83–5, 88, 94; *Bramston* 329; *Torrington* 29; *H.M.C. Dartmouth* i, 263–5; iii, 61–2; *Rawl. MSS. A.* 186, f. 374.

CHAPTER VI.
THE GLORIOUS REVOLUTION

[1] *Macaulay; Rapin; Ranke* iv, 434, 443–5; *Mackintosh* 431–2, 480–2; *G. N. Clark, The Later Stuarts* 132–3; *H.M.C. Dartmouth* i, 187–90; *Ellis* ii, 288–9; *Bramston* i, 333; *Burnet* iii, 329–30.

[2] *Pepysian MSS., Adm. Letters* xv, 303–54; *Smith* ii, 173–6;

Howarth 195–6; *H.M.C. Dartmouth* I, 187–94, 265–7; III, 62; *Ellis* II, 289.

³ *H.M.C. Dartmouth* I, 187–9, 268–9; *Howarth* 197–8; *Smith* II, 176–8.

⁴ *H.M.C. Rep.* V, 379; *Bramston* 331; *Ellis* II, 287; *Burnet* III, 330–1, 337–8; *Ranke* IV, 441–3; *Macaulay*; *H.M.C. Dartmouth* I, 192–4; *Clarke* II, 209; *Macpherson* II, 160; *Mackintosh* 479, 482.

⁵ *Ranke* IV, 441–3; *Ellis* II, 291; *Macaulay*; *Mackintosh* 460, 692–701; *H.M.C. Dartmouth* I, 266–7; *Bramston* 332; *H.M.C. Fleming* 221; *Verney Memoirs* II, 467–8.

⁶ *Pepysian MSS., Adm. Letters* XV, 353; *H.M.C. Dartmouth* I, 192–4, 268–9; III, 260–1; *Howarth* 197–8; *Smith* II, 176–8.

⁷ *Pepysian MSS., Adm. Letters* XV, 336–84; *H.M.C. Dartmouth* I, 194–201, 267; *Powley* 99–100; *Ellis* II, 292; *Smith* II, 337–8; *Rawl. MSS. A.* 179, f. 86; *A.* 186, f. 400.

⁸ *H.M.C. Dartmouth* I, 194–8; *Smith* II, 337–8; *Ellis* 292; *Pepysian MSS., Adm. Letters* XV, 347, 364, 399–400.

⁹ *H.M.C. Dartmouth* I, 194–8; *Powley* 102–4; *Smith* II, 337–8.

¹⁰ *H.M.C. Rep.* VII (*Graham* 416); *Ellis* II, 289–94; *Macaulay*.

¹¹ *Ellis* II, 289–300, 319–24; *Hatton* II, 99–100.

¹² *Feiling* 232–3; *London Gazette*; *Macaulay*; *H.M.C. Fleming* 220; *Macpherson* II, 160–1; *Burnet* III, 331–3; *Bramston* 333–4; *Mackintosh* 485–6.

¹³ *Ellis* II, 289–94, 319–24; *Burnet*; *Evelyn* 15, 18 Nov. 1688; *Macaulay*; *Hatton* II, 102; G. N. Clark, *The Later Stuarts* 134; *Ranke* IV, 444–5; *Verney Memoirs* II, 468.

¹⁴ *Macaulay*; *Mackintosh* 489–90; *Macpherson* II, 161; *D'Orleans* 311; *Stuart Papers at Windsor Castle, MSS.*, Vol. I, 17 Nov. 1688 (communicated by O. F. Morshead).

¹⁵ *Ranke* IV, 445–6; *Feiling, Tory Party* 232; *Bramston* 334–6; *Ellis* II, 301, 307–8; *Macpherson* II, 161–2.

¹⁶ *H.M.C. Fleming* 220; *H.M.C. Rep.* VII (*Graham* 348); *Ellis* II, 301; *H.M.C. Dartmouth* I, 204; *Tanner and Wheatley MSS.*, letter communicated to the late Dr J. R. Tanner by the late Lt.-Col. Frederick Pepys Cockerell.

¹⁷ *Pepysian MSS., Adm. Letters* XV, 384–5, 387, 399–400; *Powley* 108; *H.M.C. Dartmouth* I, 205–10, 267–8, 270–2; III, 66–8; *Torrington* 29–30; *Ellis* II, 301, 305–13; *Evelyn* 18 Nov. 1688; *Smith* II, 336; *Rawl. MSS. A.* 186, f. 18; *Burnet* III, 329.

¹⁸ *Ellis* II, 305–13; *H.M.C. Rep.* VII (*Graham* 349); *H.M.C. Dartmouth* I, 205–10; *Hatton* II, 106.

¹⁹ *Ellis* II, 309–13, 324–31; *Rawl. MSS. A.* 186, ff. 18–19.

²⁰ *Rawl. MSS. A.* 186, ff. 18–26; *Pepysian MSS., Adm.*

Letters xv, 406–7, 410–11.

21 *Pepysian MSS., Adm. Letters* xv, 413–16, 421–2; *H.M.C. Dartmouth* I, 211–13; III, 66–8; *Ellis* II, 330–6; *Hatton* II, 111–12; *Rawl. MSS. A.* 186, ff. 106, 108.

22 *H.M.C. Dartmouth* I, 211–13, 271–2; III, 66–8.

23 *Ailesbury* I, 188–90; *Ranke* IV, 448; *Macaulay; Sir Patrick Hume, Diary* 20 Nov. 1688; *Ellis* II, 329; *Burnet* III, 333, 337; *D'Orleans* 311–12; *Macpherson* II, 162; *Churchill, Marlborough* I, 291–4; *Bramston* 336; *Mackintosh* 492–4; *H.M.C. Rep.* VII (*Graham* 417).

24 *Ranke* IV, 449–50; *H.M.C. Fleming* 220; *Macaulay; H.M.C. Rep.* VII (*Graham* 417, 420); *Ellis* II, 314–19, 324–31; *Feiling* 235; *H.M.C. Leeds* 26; *Reresby* 528–32; *Hatton* 111–12.

25 *Ranke* IV, 448–9; *H.M.C. Rep.* VII (*Graham* 418, 424); *Ellis* II, 331; *Macaulay; Mackintosh* 495–8; *Dalrymple; Burnet; Macpherson* II, 162–3; *Burnet* III, 336; *Churchill, Marlborough* I, 298–303; *Hatton* II, 111–12; *Ailesbury* I, 190–1; *Bramston* 336–7.

26 *H.M.C. Dartmouth* III, 133–4.

27 *Dalrymple* III, App. I, 255; *Ellis* II, 336, 340; *Macaulay*.

28 *Pepysian MSS., Adm. Letters* xv, 427–31; *H.M.C. Dartmouth* I, 214–15; *Smith* II, 179.

29 *Ranke* IV, 452–3; *Macauley; H.M.C. Dartmouth* I, 216–17; *Reresby* 535; *G. N. Clark, The Later Stuarts* 135–6; *Burnet* III, 339–40; *Clarendon, Diary* 27, 29 Nov. 1688; *Ailesbury* I, 192–3; *Bramston* 337–8.

30 *Rawl. MSS. A.* 179, ff. 264–6; *Smith* II, 170–2, 180–1.

31 *Macaulay; H.M.C. Dartmouth* I, 216; *Ellis* II, 313.

32 *Ranke* IV, 452–3; *Macaulay*.

33 *Ranke* IV, 450–4; *Clarendon, Diary* 3, 4 Dec. 1688; *Burnet* III, 336, 339–40; *H.M.C. Rep.* VII (*Graham* 419, 421); *D'Orleans* 313; *Mackintosh* 514.

34 *Pepysian MSS., Adm. Letters* xv, 435–6; *H.M.C. Dartmouth* I, 214–15, 220; *Macpherson* II, 164–5.

35 *Ranke* IV, 459; *Pepysian MSS., Adm. Letters* xv, 444–8; *H.M.C. Dartmouth* I, 217–19; III, 68; *Rawl. MSS. A.* 186, f. 214.

36 *Mazure* III, 218–19; *Macaulay; Mackintosh* 509, 520–3, 526; *H.M.C. Dartmouth* I, 216, 220; *Dalrymple* III, App. I, 256; *Rawl. MSS. A.* 186, f. 218; *Braybrooke* IV, 243; *Pepysian MSS., Adm. Letters* xv, 448.

37 *Pepysian MSS., Adm. Letters* xv, 449–50; *H.M.C. Dartmouth* I, 216, 220.

38 *H.M.C. Dartmouth* I, 217, 220–3, 272–4, 275–7; *Powley* 120, 136; *Macaulay; Macpherson* II, 165; *Mackintosh* 517; *Hatton*

II, 101; *Nash, History of Worcestershire* I, 501.

³⁹ *H.M.C. Dartmouth* I, 216, 275–7; *Powley* 134–6; *Dalrymple* III, App. I, 257–60.

⁴⁰ *H.M.C. Dartmouth* I, 223–5, 277–8; *Powley* 136–41; *Dalrymple* III, App. I, 245–7; *Torrington* 33; *H.M.C. Fleming* 225; *Pepysian MSS., Adm. Letters* XV, 457; *Reresby* 536.

⁴¹ *H.M.C. Fleming* 226; *Hatton* II, 120; *Mackintosh* 515; *H.M.C. Dartmouth* I, 277–8; *Macaulay; Clarendon, Diary* 11 Dec. 1688; *Ailesbury* I, 213; *Feiling* 235; *Reresby* 535–6; *Wood* III, 286–7.

⁴² *Macaulay; Feiling* 237–9; *Burnet* III, 340–2; *H.M.C. Lindsey* 452; *Ellis* II, 342–4; *Foxcroft, Halifax; Ranke* IV, 455–7; *Clarendon, Diary* 8–9 Dec. 1688.

⁴³ *Macpherson* II, 165; *Ranke* 459–64; *Burnet* III, 342; *Mazure; Bramston* 341–2; *Ailesbury* I, 194–7.

⁴⁴ *Macaulay; Ailesbury* I, 193; *Marquise de Campana de Cavelli, Les Derniers Stuarts à St Germain en Laye* II, 397–413; *J. S. Clarke, Life of James II* 246; *Rapin; Mackintosh* 523–4; *H.M.C. Dartmouth* I, 225–6; *Rawl. MSS. A.* 186, f. 222.

⁴⁵ *Ranke* IV, 459–64; *Ailesbury* 194–7; *D'Orleans* 315–16; *Mackintosh* 526–9; *Macaulay; H.M.C. Dartmouth* I, 226; *Reresby* 536–7.

⁴⁶ *H.M.C. Dartmouth* I, 226–9; *Pepysian MSS., Adm. Letters* XV, 457–61.

⁴⁷ *Rawl. MSS. A.* 186, f. 222; *Braybrooke* IV, 243; *H.M.C. Dartmouth* I, 225–6; *Smith* II, 191–8.

CHAPTER VII.
THE INTERREGNUM

¹ *Ranke* IV, 459–64, 478; *Macaulay; H.M.C. Rep.* VII (*Verney* 502); *G. N. Clark, The Later Stuarts* 136–7; *Feiling* 239; *Reresby* 538–9; *H.M.C. Dartmouth* I, 228–9; *Stuart Papers* I, 77; *London Gazette* 13 Dec. 1688; *Clarke* II, 251; *Ailesbury* I, 197–9; *Mackintosh* 532–4.

² *Rawl. MSS. A.* 186, f. 216; *Smith* II, 190; *H.M.C. Dartmouth* I, 228–9; *Pepysian MSS., Adm. Letters* XV, 464–5.

³ *H.M.C. Dartmouth* I, 229–30, 232–3; *Ellis* II, 346–8, 350–2; *Reresby* 537; *G. N. Clark, The Later Stuarts* 137; *Rapin; H.M.C. Rep.* V, 379; *H.M.C. Portland* III, 420–1; *Hatton* II, 124; *Macaulay; Bramston* 339–40; *Mackintosh* 529–30; *Feiling* 239;

Howarth 198; *Rawl. MSS. A.* 179, f. 84; *Verney Memoirs* II, 469–71; *Pepysian MSS., Adm. Letters* XV, 467–8.

⁴ *Oldmixon; Macaulay; Bramston* 339; *Burnet* III, 348–9; *Reresby* 537–8; *H.M.C. Dartmouth* I, 232–3; *H.M.C. Portland* III, 421; *Hatton* II, 125–6; *Verney Memoirs* II, 469–70.

⁵ *Howarth* 198; *Rawl. MSS. A.* 179, f. 84.

⁶ *Ellis* II, 356–7; *Ranke* IV, 479; *Mackintosh* 531–2; *Macaulay; Hatton* II, 124–6; *Ailesbury* I, 200; *H.M.C. Portland* III, 420–1; *H.M.C. Dartmouth* I, 232–3.

⁷ *H.M.C. Dartmouth* I, 219, 228–9, 231–2, 235, 279; III, 69–70, 135; *Dalrymple* III, App. I, 245; *Powley* 143–7; *Torrington* 30–5.

⁸ *Macaulay; Wood* III, 288–91; *H.M.C. Dartmouth* I, 213–30; *Hatton* II, 123, 125–6; *Reresby* 539; *Mackintosh* 536–41; *H.M.C. Fleming* 228; *Ellis* II, 362–4; *Diary and Correspondence of John Evelyn* (ed. Wheatley, 1906) III, 427; *Macpherson* I, 165/6; *Ailesbury* I, 201–13; *Verney Memoirs* II, 472.

⁹ *H.M.C. Fleming* 229–30; *Shakerley MSS., Chester Castle Letters* Dec. 1888; *Letters from the Bodleian Library* (1813) I, 51–2; *Barillon* 17/27 Dec. 1688; *Wood* III, 291.

¹⁰ *H.M.C. Dartmouth* I, 226, 279–80, 282; *Hatton* II, 126; *Rawl. MSS. A.* 186, f. 222.

¹¹ *Wood* III, 289; *Ellis* II, 262–3, 369; *Mackintosh* 542–3; *Ranke* IV, 465; *Macpherson* I, 166–7; *H.M.C. Dartmouth* I, 236, 238; *Reresby* 540; *London Gazette* 16 Dec. 1688; *D'Orleans* 316–17; *Ailesbury* I, 214–15; *Evelyn* 11 Dec. 1688; *J. S. Clarke, Life of James II* II, 262.

¹² *Diary and Correspondence of John Evelyn* (ed. Wheatley) III, 427–8; *Wood* III, 289; *H.M.C. Dartmouth* I, 240; *Burnet* III, 353; *Dalrymple* III, App. I, 268–9; *Macaulay; Mackintosh* 543–4; *Bramston* 340.

¹³ *Wood* III, 289; *Ailesbury* I, 216–18; *Macaulay; Ranke* IV, 465; *G. N. Clark, The Later Stuarts* 137; *Diary and Correspondence of John Evelyn* (ed. Wheatley) III, 428–9; *Diary* 18 Dec. 1688; *Ellis* II, 372–3; *Burnet* III, 352–8; *Bramston* 340–1;) *Tanner, Corr.* I, 24–7; *H.M.C. Dartmouth* I, 236; *Macpherson* I, 167–8; *Reresby* 540; *Clarendon, Diary* 15–18 Dec. 1688; *John Sheffield, Duke of Buckingham, Works* (1753) II, 85; *J. S. Clarke, Life of James II* II, 265; *Mackintosh* 546–51.

¹⁴ *Macaulay; Ellis* II, 369; *Ranke* IV, 482–3; *Reresby* 541; *Clarendon, Diary* 19 Dec. 1686; *Burnet* III, 359; *H.M.C. Dartmouth* I, 236, 238; III, 135; *Ailesbury* I, 218–20.

¹⁵ *Clarendon, Diary* 20 Dec. 1688; *Ellis* II, 373; *Burnet* III, 360–1; *Evelyn* 18 Dec. 1688; *Verney Memoirs* II, 472; *Rawl.*

MSS. A. 181, f. 154, *Smith* II, 198–9; *H.M.C. Dartmouth* I, 240.

¹⁶ *Wood* III, 291; *Reresby* 541; *Pepysian MSS., Adm. Letters* xv, 465 et seq.; *Rawl. MSS. A.* 179, ff. 59–60; *Howarth* 198.

¹⁷ *H.M.C. Fleming* 231.

¹⁸ *Macaulay; Ranke* IV, 484; *Clarendon, Diary* 21 Dec. 1688.

¹⁹ *Rawl. MSS. A.* 175, f. 279; *A.* 179, ff. 140–1, 150; *A.* 194, ff. 257–8; *Pepysian MSS., Mornamont* I, 1209, 1223–5; *Tangier Papers* 321–2; *H.M.C. Dartmouth* I, 242; III, 142–3; *Smith* II, 199–200.

²⁰ *Wood* III, *Clarendon, Diary* 22–23 Dec. 1688; *Ailesbury* I, 222–5; *Macaulay; Clarke* II, 275; *Ranke* IV, 484–5.

²¹ *Feiling* 246; *Macaulay; H.M.C. Dartmouth* III, 139–41; *Clarendon, Diary* 24, 29 Dec. 1688.

²² *Ranke* IV, 466, 487–9; *Feiling* 246; *Reresby* 542; *Clarendon, Diary* 24, 26 Dec. 1688; *Macaulay; H.M.C. Dartmouth* I, 242; III, 140–1; *Bramston* 343–5.

²³ *H.M.C. Dartmouth* I, 239–40; III, 70; *Pepysian MSS., Adm. Letters* xv, 470 et seq.; *Smith* II, 350–1.

²⁴ *H.M.C. Dartmouth* I, 241, 245, 247; III, 140, 142–2; *Smith* II, 350–1; *Rawl. MSS. A.* 186, f. 173.

²⁵ *Royal Society MSS., Ne III* 129, 28 Dec. 1688.

²⁶ *Pepysian MSS., Adm. Letters* xv, 490–500, 504, 507–9, 534; *H.M.C. Dartmouth* I, 242–4; *Powley* 157; *Rawl. MSS. A.* 186, ff. 113–17, 119; *Luttrell* I, 493–4; *Evelyn* 7 Jan. 1689; *Clarendon, Diary* I, 3 Jan. 1689.

²⁷ *Smith* II, 200–1.

²⁸ *H.M.C. Dartmouth* I, 247; *Smith* II, 210–12.

²⁹ *Pepysian MSS., Adm. Letters* xv, 490, 496–8; *Luttrell* I, 494; *H.M.C. Dartmouth* I, 177–8, 240–1; *Rawl. MSS. A.* 186, f. 119; *H.M.C. Fleming* 232; *Reresby* 545; *Mackintosh* 580–1.

³⁰ *Rawl. MSS. A.* 170, f. 201; *Smith* II, 211–12; *Pepysian MSS., Adm. Letters* xv, 500–2, 504, 507–9, 518–19; *H.M.C. Dartmouth* I, 249; *Wood* III, 291; *Howarth* 199–200.

CHAPTER VIII.
DEFEAT

¹ *Wood* III, 297; *Luttrell* I, 494, 497; *Bramston* 345; *Clarendon, Diary* 9, 11 Jan. 1689; *Cambridge Historical Journal* 1937 (J. H. Plumb, *The Elections to the Convention Parliament of* 1689) *Diary and Correspondence of John Evelyn* (ed. Wheatley) III, 429–30.

² *Rawl. MSS. A.* 179, ff. 140, 147, 149, 151, 153, 156, 159,

161, 163, 165–7, 173, 225; *Braybrooke* (Chandos Library reprint of 1825 ed.) 647–8.

[3] *H.M.C. Dartmouth* I, 242–4; *Pepysian MSS., Adm. Letters* xv, 525–6, 532, 547–8, 554.

[4] *Pepysian MSS., Adm. Letters* xv, 513–14, 520, 536.

[5] *Pepysian MSS., Adm. Letters* xv, 520, 527, 532; *Rawl. MSS. A.* 186, ff. 121v–6; *Mackintosh* 581–2.

[6] *Evelyn* 15 Jan. 1689; *H.M.C. Portland* III, 421; *H.M.C. Fleming* 232; *Clarendon, Diary* 14, 15, 16, 17 Jan. 1689; *Burnet* III, 373–5; *Mackintosh* 587–90.

[7] *Rawl. MSS. A.* 179, ff. 169, 171, 173, 218, 223, 225; *A.* 186, f. 126v; *Pepysian MSS., Adm. Letters* xv, 542–3; *Howarth* 200; *Braybrooke* IV, (1898), 245–6.

[8] *Rawl. MSS. A.* 179 ff. 177, 210, 221; *D.* 4 Dec. 1668.

[9] *Luttrell* I, 497–8; *Grey* IX; *H.M.C. Portland* III, 422, 424; *Bramston* 346; *Mackintosh* 591.

[10] *Grey* IX, *Ranke* IV, 493–511; *Mackintosh* 599–603; *Macaulay; Roger North, Lives of the Norths* (1890) III, 136; *Evelyn* 29 Jan. 1689; *Burnet* III, 375–88; *Reresby* 545–6, 548–9; *C.J.; L.J.; Clarendon, Diary* 29–31 Jan.; 1–6 Feb. 1689; *Mackintosh* 593–614; *Ailesbury* I, 230–7; *H.M.C. Rep.* XII (*House of Lords,* 1689–90, 15); *H.M.C. Portland* III, 424–5, 427; *Luttrell* I, 497–9; *Feiling* 252–3; *Wood* III, 297.

[11] *Grey* IX; *L.J.; C.J.; Mackintosh* 620–8; *Macaulay; Reresby* 551, 554; *Burnet* III, 390–408; *Foxcroft, Halifax* II, 203–4; *Clarendon, Diary* 6, 12–13 Feb. 1689; *C.S.P.D.* 1689–90: I; *Luttrell* I, 500–2; *H.M.C. Portland* III, 428; *Mackintosh* 615–28; *Wood* III, 298; *Evelyn* 6, 21 Feb. 1689; *Feiling* 246, 253–5; *H.M.C. Rep.* V, 376; *Ranke* IV, 509–11, 516–18; *Rawl. MSS. A.* 179, f. 216.

[12] *Rawl. MSS. A.* 186, ff. 112, 138–40; *Pepysian MSS., Adm. Letters* xv, 586; *Evelyn* 26 May 1703; *Ailesbury* I, 227, 236–7; *Clarendon, Diary* 1 March 1689.

[13] *Evelyn* 26 May 1703; *Luttrell* I, 501–2; *H.M.C. Fleming* 235–6; *Rawl. MSS. A.* 170, f. 79; *A.* 179, f. 262; *A.* 186, ff. 112, 134–5, 138–40; *Pepysian MSS., Adm. Letters* xv, 524–5, 575–98; *D.* 20 Feb. 1665.

[14] *Pepysian MSS., Adm. Letters* xv, 586, 590; *H.M.C. Stuart Papers* I, 35.

[15] *Rawl. MSS. A.* 170, ff. 176, 178–82, 186; *A.* 186, ff. 138–40; *H.M.C. House of Lords,* 1689–90, 185; *Pepysian MSS., Adm. Letters* xv, 589–92

[16] *Pepysian MSS., Adm. Letters* xv, 589–92.

[17] *Pepysian MSS., Adm. Letters* xv, 596–8.

[18] *Luttrell* I, 504, 507; *Pepysian MSS., Adm. Letters* xv, 598;

D. 5 July 1660; *Rawl. MSS. A.* 170, f. 71; *A.* 189, f. 27.

[19] *Mariner's Mirror* XXIII, No. 4 (Oct. 1937); *G. F. James, Josiah Burchett* 477–8; *Torrington* 17; *Wheatley and Tanner MSS.* (from a letter of S. P. to Dr Charles Davenant of 6 Aug. 1697 given to Red Cross Sale by Sir Hercules Reed).

Index